THE FRANCISCAN REVIVAL
IN THE ANGLICAN COMMUNION

Brother Douglas feeding chickens on the roof of
Westminster Hospital towards the end of the
Second World War. Westminster Abbey is seen
in the background.

THE FRANCISCAN REVIVAL IN THE ANGLICAN COMMUNION

Barrie Williams

Foreword by Bishop John Moorman

Darton, Longman and Todd
London

First published in 1982 by
Darton, Longman and Todd Ltd
89 Lillie Road, London SW6 1UD

© 1982 Barrie Williams

ISBN 0 232 51549 2

British Library Cataloguing in Publication Data

Williams, Barrie
   The Franciscan revival in the Anglican communion.
   1. Anglican Communion   2. Francis, *of Assisi,*
Saint
   I. Title
   255'.8   BX5005

   ISBN 0–232–51549–2

Phototypeset by Input Typesetting Ltd, London SW19 8DR.
Printed in Great Britain by the Anchor Press Ltd,
and bound by Wm Brendon and Son Ltd,
both of Tiptree, Essex

Contents

III
Communities of American origin

IV
The Society of St. Francis

Foreword

It is interesting to know that, until 1870, there was no life of St. Francis published in English. He was known through articles like Sir James Stephen's brilliant study in *Essays in Ecclesiastical Biography* (1849) and was admired by Matthew Arnold in his lecture on 'Pagan and Medieval Religious Sentiment' (1864) with its delightful translation of the Canticle of the Sun. But, apart from these, there was not much interest among English-speaking people in the saint who is now so greatly loved. Mrs. Oliphant published her life of the saint in 1870, and translations of some of the early sources came out; but it was the French Calvinist, Paul Sabatier, who, in 1893, published his monumental Life of St. Francis, which was translated into English in the following year by an American lady. People then became interested in St. Francis in a big way, especially as the one who literally followed Christ and who adopted complete poverty as his ideal.

It was St. Francis' poverty which appealed to people in England in the 1890's. This was a time when there was considerable concern for the desperately poor people of England, of whom there were vast crowds in the greater cities. People were taking an interest in them, not just *de haut en bas*, visiting them occasionally, 'going slumming' as it was called, but wanting to live among them and share their poverty. So in 1894 J. A. Adderley founded the Society of the Divine Compassion which was followed shortly after by the Community of St. Francis, for women, who settled at Dalston in 1908.

From then onwards various individuals took up this call – Luigi Josa, Arthur S. Cripps, Brother Edward. But the first attempts to found a religious order came with Brother Douglas at what was called Flowers Farm at Cerne Abbas in Dorset in 1922. I remember very well visiting the place in 1927 when there were only four friars there. I even went on the roads with one of them and slept in a common lodging house. But the little community failed to attract more members, until Father Algy joined them, since when the Society has grown, and is still growing, rapidly with off-shoots in many parts of the world. The old work of tramping the roads and bringing Christ to those whom they called 'wayfarers' is now over; but the Society still helps ex-prisoners, alcoholics, drug-addicts and many others in need of spiritual and mental health.

This book tells us the story of 'Franciscanism' in the Anglican Communion, especially in England and in the United States of America. It introduces many individuals and many attempts to found something permanent in its early days. This is a thrilling story. When most religious communities are losing numbers, the Society of St. Francis flourishes in all parts of the world. Poverty is still the keynote which binds them together – not the absolute poverty of St. Francis with his begging-bowl and his sleeping in old churches and barns, but great simplicity of life which is the modern equivalent of Franciscan poverty.

I read this book with great interest, and warmly commend it to all who are interested.

John R. H. Moorman

Acknowledgements

I owe a debt of gratitude to many more than I can name. I must however thank Brother John Charles who prepared much of the original source material I have used and Brother Bill Lash for his ready help when using the Hillfield archives. Bill Lash, too, has been one of the many whose reminiscences of events, people and places has been one of the most illuminating parts of the work, and whose addition or correction of points of detail has proved invaluable.

Anyone working on Anglican religious communities must be aware of the debt he owes Peter Anson for *The Call of the Cloister*, and the number of references to that work makes clear the extent of my own indebtedness to him and to all who have worked in this field before me. I must thank Methuen & Co. Ltd. for their permission to publish the lengthy quotation from Edward Hutton's *Cities of Umbria*. I wish to thank the Society of St. Francis for permission to reproduce the frontispiece.

I wish to thank all the Franciscan communities in Britain and the U.S.A. whose hospitality I have shared and who have welcomed me into their fellowship while writing this book, and I must thank the Brethren of the Society of the Atonement for their help. I greatly appreciate the time and trouble of all those who have read some part of the draft, not one of whom has failed to make helpful comments and suggestions; above all Brother Alban who read the entire draft.

Not least I must thank the Society of St. Francis for their conception of the book, for entrusting the task to a humble tertiary priest, and for their unfailing moral and spiritual support throughout.

Barrie Williams

*Trinity Hall
Cambridge*

June 1982

Abbreviations

Bibliographical

AFG	Fr. Joseph O.S.F., *Adventure for God*.
CC	Peter Anson, *The Call of the Cloister*.
CSS	Jack Winslow, *Christa Seva Sangha*.
ED	Jack Winslow, *Eyelids of the Dawn*.
FR	A. Clifton Kelway. ed., *A Franciscan Revival*.
Gt. Chap.	Great Chapter Minute Book (S.D.C.)
ITD	Mother Elizabeth O.S.E.H., *Into the Deep*.
LDN	Mother Elizabeth O.S.E.H., *Letting Down the Nets*.
ROC	Peter Anson, *The Religious Orders and Congregations of Great Britain and Ireland*.

Religious Societies

B.H.C.	Brotherhood of the Holy Cross.
B.L.C.	Brotherhood of the Love of Christ.
B.S.F.A.	Brotherhood of St. Francis of Assisi.
C.R.	Community of the Resurrection.
C.S.F.	Community of St. Francis.
F.S.J.M.	Franciscan Servants of Jesus and Mary.
G.S.A.	Guild of St. Alban.
M.S.C.S.F.	Mission Sisters of the Charity of St. Francis.
O.G.S.	Oratory of the Good Shepherd.
O.S.E.H.	Order of St. Elizabeth of Hungary.
O.S.F.	Order of St. Francis.
S.A.	Society of the Atonement.
S.D.C.	Society of the Divine Compassion.
S.I.E.S.	Society of the Incarnation of the Eternal Son.
S.S.F.	Society of St. Francis.

NOTES

Unless otherwise indicated, postal districts without place name e.g. Cable St, (E1) refer to London.

Full bibliographical details of works referred to in the notes are given on pp. 208–9.

INTRODUCTORY

1

Before the Anglican Revival

1. The Structure of the Roman Catholic Franciscan Order

Religious communities have existed in the Church of England since the mid-nineteenth century. One of the earliest sisterhoods followed a rule based on the Franciscan way of life, and since the turn of the century, there has been more than one community at any time following a Franciscan rule. But in the history of Western Christendom, these communities are relatively small and recent. Comparison needs to be made with the much larger and older Franciscan Order in the Roman Catholic Church on which the Anglican communities have been to some extent modelled.

The structure of the Franciscan Order is complex, and 750 years of experience have gone into making it. The division into three orders – of men, of women, and tertiaries – is only a beginning. One basic principle of the Franciscan life is that the Rule is above the Order; the Order exists only to observe the Rule.[1] The complexity has come very largely from different attempts to observe the Rule more faithfully. The first Rule of St. Francis dates from 1210. It is no longer extant, though its contents may be conjectured.[2] Friars follow the Rule drawn up in 1223 towards the end of St. Francis' life. His women disciples, the Poor Clares, were granted a Rule on the lines of the Benedictine Order in 1218. This was revised by the Pope in 1247, and by St. Clare herself in 1253. The Third Order was founded by St. Francis in 1221 and their Rule revised in 1289. All Franciscans therefore follow a way of life which was inspired by St. Francis and which originated in his lifetime. Anglican Franciscans have likewise sought to abide by the letter and spirit of the early Rule.[3]

The Friars Minor – the Lesser Brothers – as the First Order is correctly called, has three subdivisions. The Friars Minor of the Regu-

1. Peter Anson, *The religious orders and congregations of Great Britain and Ireland* (ROC) (Stanbrook Abbey, Worcs., 1949), p. 95.
2. See J. R. H. Moorman, *Sources for the life of St. Francis*, (Manchester, 1940) pp. 38–54.
3. See *Source Documents* (privately printed for the Society of St. Francis 1978).

lar Observance testify to the life by observing the Rule, as their name implies. The Observants began in 1415 and first came to Scotland in 1447. Their first house in England was at Greenwich (1480) where proximity to the royal palace made them well known. Pope Leo XIII brought together four groups of Observants in 1897. The brown habit is a distinguishing mark of the Observants.

Until the Observants arrived, all Friars Minor in the British Isles were Conventuals – those who from the lifetime of St. Francis were willing to live in houses placed at their disposal. Their habit caused them to be known as the Grey Friars, though nowadays the Conventuals wear black. In medieval England they were in effect *the* Franciscan friars. In modern times, Conventuals are markedly fewer.[4]

The third subdivision, the Capuchins,[5] began like the Observants as a reform movement. They stressed prayer and contemplation but many of them became great missionaries. The movement began in 1528, too late to reach England before the Reformation. The first arrived here with Queen Henrietta Maria in 1625. Between the Restoration (1660) and Roman Catholic Emancipation (1829) some of them worked quietly among the English Roman Catholics.

The Second Order, which began with St. Clare and her companions, are usually called 'Poor Clares' but more correctly 'Poor Ladies'. St. Clare practised absolute poverty, but the rigour of their life was modified by the great Franciscan reformer, St. Bonaventura. A movement to restore primitive strictness was led by St. Collette, born in 1381. Most of the houses following St. Collette's reform are in France, and they were an important influence on Dr. Pusey. The Capuchins have their counterpart in the Second Order, the Capuchinesses. The whole Second Order is contemplative and enclosed. They found few recruits in medieval England, and there were only three houses of Poor Clares at the Reformation. Nevertheless, the Second Order was important in keeping English Franciscanism alive through the penal times.

The Third Order, or tertiaries, was founded by St. Francis in 1221 for men and women who sought to follow his way but whose responsibilities, such as family ties, kept them from joining the Friars and Clares. In time, some of the unmarried tertiaries wished to withdraw from the world and live in community, often engaged in charitable work, though some became enclosed – there was a house of enclosed tertiaries at Foligno in 1397. In 1521 they were granted a new constitution and allowed to take solemn vows. In the Roman Catholic Church, there is a clear distinction between Tertiaries Secular, who more closely resemble the original men and women of the Third Order,

4. Peter Anson (ROC) lists only four Conventual houses in England and none in Ireland.
5. So named from their *capuche* or pointed cowl.

and Tertiaries Regular, men or women bound by vows and following the religious life. Communities of women engaged in active work are Tertiaries Regular, not members of the Second Order.

The Anglican Franciscan communities have not kept all these distinctions. The trend with most communities has been to regard men religious as the First Order, women religious as the Second, and men and women not under vows as tertiaries. The Community of St. Francis (q.v.), made up of women religious engaged in active work, was at first regarded as a kind of Second Order but is now part of the First Order. In the Roman Catholic Church they could only be Tertiaries Regular. Tertiaries Regular are not unknown in the Anglican Communion, though they are few in number. From time to time, however, Anglican tertiaries have shared a common purpose and a common life, so becoming nascent communities in the way some of St. Francis' disciples did in the thirteenth century.

2. *Franciscans in the British Isles before the Reformation*

The Friars Minor reached England in 1224, two years before St. Francis' death, and Ireland in 1229. In the three centuries to the Reformation, well over a hundred houses of Friars were founded in the British Isles, many of them in centres of trade and learning. British Franciscans such as Roger Bacon, Duns Scotus and William of Occam were great names in European culture. Most English Franciscans of this period were Conventuals or Grey Friars who accepted the dispensations from absolute poverty granted by the Church. The Observants only came to Britain within a century of the Reformation, at which they had six houses in England and nine in Scotland.

Women seeking the religious life more often became Benedictine nuns. As well as the three houses of Poor Clares in England, there were Grey Sisters (Tertiaries Regular) at Aberdour (1486) and Dundee (1502) in Scotland, but none in England. In the thirteenth century, groups of English women Franciscans tried to live the mendicant life and styled themselves 'Sisters Minor'. They were discouraged by the Church authorities, particularly by Pope Innocent IV in 1250.[6] There were certainly Franciscan Tertiaries Secular, though little is known about them. Queen Katharine of Aragon is thought to have been one, likewise some of the hermits and anchoresses of late medieval England.[7]

In the late Middle Ages and at the Renaissance, the Franciscans

6. J. R. H. Moorman, *The Franciscans in England* (London & Oxford, 1974), pp. 42–3.
7. ibid., p. 48.

became the butt for satire and abuse. Chaucer's Friar, who preferred the company of inn-keepers and tapsters to that of sick lepers, is well known.[8] Welsh bards, like Italian scholars, poked fun at the Friars.[9] Sometimes the satirists made an exception of St. Francis himself while accusing his followers of the worst excesses of the Church. Much of this criticism was well founded, but as J. R. H. Moorman has observed, ordinary folk still had sufficient respect for the Friars to make numerous gifts and legacies, right up to the Reformation. But by the sixteenth century, the Friars, like other religious, were short of recruits. At the Reformation, all the religious houses were closed. Among the few re-opened by Mary Tudor was the Friary of the Observants at Greenwich. But the Franciscans produced men ready to die for the 'Old Faith', among them Friar Forrest and the Welsh martyr John Jones. Titus Oates' 'Popish Plot' (1678) led to the last martyrdoms in Britain, which included the executions of two English Franciscans and one Irish.[10] Despite the abuses of the Middle Ages and the official proscription of the religious orders by Henry VIII and Elizabeth I, the Franciscan Order showed its capacity to survive among the British nation.

3. *British Franciscans in the penal times (1559–1829)*

In 1596, a group of English ladies from recusant families were professed as Poor Clares at St. Omer in Artois. They were joined by some Irish Sisters and formed their own house at Gravelines in 1607. The Community flourished sufficiently for them to found daughter houses at Dunkirk, Aire and Rouen. They supported themselves by teaching.[11] They maintained these houses until the French Revolution, when they were expelled. The climate of opinion in England had by this time changed, and the Community from Rouen were able to move to Haggerstone Castle, Northumberland. In 1807, they moved to Scorton Hall near Catterick where in 1836 they were joined by survivors of the Aire community. The Gravelines and Dunkirk communities, however, died out. In 1857, the Community moved from Scorton Hall to Darlington where, at St. Clare's Abbey, they still remain.

In 1629, six Irish Clares from Dunkirk settled in Dublin. They had a chequered career, moving first to Lough Rea near Athlone. Their convent was pillaged during the rising of 1641, but fourteen of the

---

8. *Canterbury Tales*: Prologue, ll.245–50.
9. William Hughes, *The Church of the Cymry* (London 1916), p. 199.
10. Moorman gives an account of the Franciscan martyrs in Chapter 9 of *The Franciscans in England*.
11. ROC, p. 367.

sisters moved to found a convent at Galway. From time to time, they were forced to abandon their enclosure and their habit, but the Community survived. In 1825, they moved to Nun's Island, Galway Bay, where they remain.[12] The convents at Darlington and Galway represent a succession of English and Irish ladies leading the Franciscan life for nearly four centuries – the longest in English and Irish history.

The Franciscan life for men was restored in 1629 when Fr. John Jennings opened a new English Province with its headquarters at Douai. Here Friars were trained to work among English recusants. The Franciscans were able to open a school at Osmotherley, Yorks., in 1665 – a remarkable achievement in penal times. Removed later to Edgbaston and then Baddesley, Warwicks., the school closed in 1829 – ironically at the very time of Roman Catholic Emancipation. At its height in the eighteenth century, there were about 100 friars in the English Province. In 1799, a novitiate was opened at Osmotherley. But the French Revolution closed their base at Douai, and after 1800 there was a serious fall in recruits. An unsuccessful attempt was made to open a novitiate at Aston in 1818. The few English novices at that time were trained at Palestrina, near Rome, but a Chapter at Clifton in 1838 was attended by only nine friars.[13] The English Province ground to a halt in 1840. The Friars, therefore, failed to sustain the continuity achieved by the Clares, and their history falls into three periods – the Middle Ages; the penal times during which they flourished under persecution only to perish under tolerant scepticism; and the modern revival.

4. The revival of Roman Catholic Franciscan communities c. 1829–1900

Roman Catholic Emancipation (1829), Irish immigration (particularly after the famine of 1845) and hostility on the Continent to the religious life (the legacy of the French Revolution) encouraged the revival of Roman Catholic religious orders in England, including the Franciscans. In 1858, Recollect Fathers[14] from Belgium settled at Sclerder, Cornwall. They soon spread to Gorton (Manchester, 1862), Stratford-at-Bow (East London, 1863) and Glasgow (1868). In 1858, other Recollect Fathers settled at Gorey, County Wexford, moving in 1861 to Killarney. In the years 1885–93, Killarney became the novitiate for a revived English Province. These Belgian friars were therefore the fountain-head of a revived English Franciscanism.

12. ibid., p. 369.
13. Moorman, *The Franciscans in England*, pp. 104–05.
14. Observant Friars from France, Flanders and Germany, founded 1595.

The Irish friars survived the penal times better than their English brethren. The Observants were conspicuous in keeping the Roman Catholic faith alive in Ireland after the Reformation. In the seventeenth century, Irish friars at Rome and Louvain included men of learning and culture.[15] In the nineteenth century, Irish Observants pioneered work in Australia and Newfoundland and served as missionaries in China. The Franciscan mission in Australia became a separate province in 1939.[16]

The English Friars received an injection of new blood when the Observants were expelled from France in 1880. One group settled at Taunton, moving to Clevedon in 1882. Capuchins came from Italy to Peckham (South London) in 1850, and from Belgium to Pantasaph (North Wales) in 1852. Like the Observants, Capuchins in Ireland were active in the penal times, and established eight houses between 1624 and 1644. When persecution increased, they went into hiding, but continued their ministrations. By 1800, their numbers were falling, but revived later in the century.[17]

Franciscan communities of the Roman Catholic Church are now too many to list in detail; a comprehensive survey is to be found in Peter Anson's *Religious Orders and Congregations* (1949). A few of special interest should be noticed. The Convent of Our Lady of Dolours is by far the oldest British community of Tertiaries Regular. Founded at Brussels in 1621, its first Superior was Sister Margaret Paul of the Poor Clares at Gravelines. In 1637 the Sisters moved to Nieuport and in 1663 to Bruges. They were expelled from Bruges by the revolutionaries in 1794. They moved to Winchester and then in 1808 to Taunton, where they remain. An early foundation in Scotland (1847) was that of the Franciscan Sisters of the Immaculate Conception. They began at Glasgow under Mother Adelaide Vaast of Comines. One distinctive group in these islands is the Congregation of Newry, so named after their present mother house in Northern Ireland. They originated with six Clares from Galway who established a house at Dublin in 1712. Because of dire poverty, they were allowed by Pope Pius VII to undertake active work, taking charge of an orphanage in 1807. Their houses are mainly in Ireland, but there are a few in England and Wales and one in Australia. Two Franciscan communities which began with Anglican converts will be mentioned in Chapter 2.

15. ROC, p. 107.
16. ibid., p. 100.
17. ibid., p. 107.

5. Roman Catholic Franciscans in North America

It has been observed[18] that the Franciscans were the first missionaries, not only in those parts of North America once under Spanish rule, but in much of what at one time was British and French territory as well; that a Franciscan, Fr. Hennepin, first explored the Great Lakes and called Niagara Falls after St. Anthony of Padua; that the City of the Golden Gate commemorates by its name the Franciscan missionaries on the Pacific Coast. In the age of the old colonial empires which lasted until the eighteenth century, French Franciscans found a firm base in both Canada and Louisiana, and worked along the Mississippi Valley and into Michigan, linking up the scattered French settlements. Spanish Friars similarly worked in from Mexico and the Caribbean islands into parts of what is now the United States – Florida, Georgia, New Mexico, Arizona, Texas and California.[19] These missionaries endured great hardships, and some, particularly in the early days, suffered martyrdom.

The old order in North America was shattered in the eighteenth century. Canada passed from French to British rule in 1763, but the statesmanship of Lord North left Quebec for a time the part of the British Empire where the Roman Catholic faith was most freely practised. The thirteen British colonies gained their independence in 1783 and rapidly began to expand westwards into territory where Roman Catholic missionaries had worked among the Red Indians. The Spanish Empire began to disintegrate, and many former Spanish territories passed into British or American hands. Many Roman Catholic missionaries, including Franciscans, were expelled and their missions closed. The only mission in the U.S.A. with a continuous history from Spanish colonial times is at Santa Barbara (California).[20] The climate of opinion in the U.S.A. after independence was not favourable to the Roman Catholic missions, but English and Irish Franciscans continued their work and one, Michael Egan, became the first Bishop of Philadelphia in 1810.[21]

As in England, the expansion of the Franciscans in the U.S.A. from 1850 owed much to immigration from Europe. Franciscan friars came to minister to people of their own nationality. Tyrolese came to Ohio in 1844, Italians to Buffalo in 1855, Westphalians to Illinois in 1858. German Franciscans, refugees from the *Kulturkampf*[22] came to New

18. Cardinal Spellman in his introduction to David Gannon, *Father Paul of Graymoor* (New York, 1959).
19. *Catholic Encyclopaedia*: Friars Minor.
20. ibid.
21. ibid.
22. The struggle between the Papacy and the new German Imperial state in the 1870s.

York in 1876. Close behind the Friars came Tertiary Sisters Regular – French to Milwaukee in 1856, Italians to New York in 1865, Polish to Wisconsin in 1874 and Pennsylvania in 1894, Germans to New York in 1875. But not all the early American communities were of immigrants. There were American sisterhoods at Glen Riddle (1855), Syracuse (1860), Manitowoe (1869) and Milwaukee (1874). Poor Clares in the U.S.A. began with a settlement of Italians at Cleveland (Ohio) under Mother Maria Maddalena and Mother Maria Costanza.[23] In 1877, German Collettines under Mother Veronika von Elmendorff also came to Cleveland. In 1878, the Italian Clares moved on to Omaha (Nebraska) and ceded their convent to the German Collettines. From these two houses (Cleveland and Omaha), all subsequent American convents of Poor Clares take their origin.[24] An early American foundation of Tertiaries Regular was that of the Franciscan Brothers of Brooklyn (1858).

Whether of European or American origin, these Franciscan communities have struck root in American soil. They have expanded not only through the United States and North America, but some of their members have returned to Europe or gone further afield to South America and Asia.

23. These ladies were by birth sisters of the aristocratic House of Bentivoglio.
24. *Catholic Encyclopaedia.*

2

The Revival of Devotion to St. Francis in the Anglican Communion

1. The Reputation of the Franciscans after the Reformation

With the Dissolution of the Religious Orders, Englishmen for the most part lost contact with the Franciscans, though diplomats, merchants and tourists going to the Roman Catholic parts of Europe did not have to travel far before they encountered the Friars. The Englishman's idea of the Franciscans was likely to be influenced by writers who for the most part carried on the bitterly critical attitude of the late Middle Ages and Renaissance. Dr. Faustus in Marlowe's play (1588) bids Mephistopheles

> Go and return an old Franciscan friar;
> That holy shape becomes a devil best.

Greene in *Friar Bacon and Friar Bungay* (1592) and Shakespeare in *Romeo and Juliet* (1594) presented more attractive stage Friars. But even when he appears in plays on the side of virtue, the Tudor Friar has an air of mystery – he is usually skilled in subtle plots, knows about secret potions, may even practise magic. Milton was more scathing and placed 'embryos and idiots, eremites and friars' together in his 'limbo of vanities'.[1] Edward Gibbon in Rome heard 'barefoot friars . . . singing vespers in the Temple of Jupiter'[2] and felt moved to write his monumental indictment of the Christian Church, *The Decline and Fall of the Roman Empire*. The Friar was likely in popular imagination to be not only crafty and superstitious but lecherous as well:

> If you become a nun, dear,
> A friar I will be.
> In any cell you run, dear,
> Pray look behind for me.[3]

Hallam described St. Francis as a 'harmless enthusiast, pious and

1. *Paradise Lost*, Book III.
2. *Autobiography* (1970), p. 85.
3. Leigh Hunt, *The Nun* (1821), after the Song *Se Monaca ti fai*.

10

sincere, but hardly of sane mind, who was much more accessory to the intellectual than to the moral degradation of mankind.'[4] Anglican clergy often shared the attitude of the men of letters. G. S. Faber dismissed St. Francis as 'this impostor'[5] and even the great Dean Hook as a 'fanatic'.[6] The Victorian Age witnessed many revolutions, but not the least remarkable was the rescue of St. Francis from the 'limbo of vanities' to enjoy first respectability and then apotheosis.

2. The Oxford Movement and the Revival of the Religious Life

The religious houses of medieval England disappeared in the general dissolution under Henry VIII. The few foundations revived under Mary Tudor did not survive the reforms of Elizabeth I. In the three centuries which followed, a number of attempts were made in the Church of England to establish new communities dedicated to a life of prayer, simplicity and good works. Divines such as Francis White,[7] John Bramhall[8] and William Sancroft[9] appreciated that the Church had suffered a real loss through the total abolition of the religious houses. By far the most famous experiment between Elizabeth I and Victoria was the extended family community at Little Gidding in the reign of Charles I. The story of the Ferrar family and their life at Little Gidding has been the subject of several books, notably that of A. L. Maycock;[10] it reached fiction with J. H. Shorthouse's *John Inglesant* (1882) and poetry with the last of T. S. Eliot's *Four Quartets*. But Little Gidding was no isolated experiment. Men who felt called to a celibate life sometimes found fulfilment in the colleges of Oxford and Cambridge which until the mid-nineteenth century were mostly communities of unmarried clergy. Other ordained men found fulfilment in combining a dedicated ministry with a disciplined life of prayer.[11]

4. Quoted in Okey's introduction to the Everyman edition of the *Little Flowers of St. Francis*.
5. *The Ancient Vallenses and Albigenses*, (1838), p. 397n. In fairness, Faber was discussing an early tradition concerning the stigmata that not only did the marks of Christ's wounds appear in the Saint's hands and feet but that four nail-heads were visible in the wounds. As Faber says, this conveniently refuted a current opinion condemned as a 'heresy' that Christ had been crucified with three nails (one through both feet) as is usually shown on crucifixes. Mrs. Oliphant discusses this tradition regarding the stigmata on which she keeps an open mind; later writers disregard it.
6. Luigi Josa, *St. Francis of Assisi and the Third Order in the Anglo-Catholic Church* (1903), p. 28.
7. Francis White, Bishop of Ely 1631–38.
8. John Bramhall, Archbishop of Armagh 1661–63.
9. William Sancroft, Archbishop of Canterbury 1678–91.
10. *Nicholas Ferrar of Little Gidding* (first published 1938).
11. e.g. among bishops, Godfrey Goodman of Gloucester (1625–56); among parish priests, George Herbert, Rector of Fugglestone with Bemerton, Wilts. (1630–33).

For women, the opportunities were fewer. Margaret Blagge (later Mrs. Godolphin) followed a rule of life from the age of 11 and kept it with increasing strictness when she became a lady at the court of Charles II. Bishop Thomas Ken in his retirement became spiritual director to Mary and Anne Kemys; William Law the non-juror was likewise director to Mrs. Hutchinson and Hester Gibbon. William Sancroft when Dean of St. Paul's was director to twelve ladies who wished to establish a 'Protestant nunnery', but the leading lady, after going to Flanders to study the Benedictine life, turned Roman Catholic, and the project was abandoned.

Communities of English religious, both men and women, existed in the Roman Catholic Church during these centuries, either on the Continent, or under cover in England. They undoubtedly helped to foster the 'call of the cloister' in the Church of England and the desire to fulfil it without leaving that Church. Even before Roman Catholic Emancipation (1829) and the Oxford Movement (1833) the atmosphere in England became more favourable to the revival of the religious life. Monks and nuns fleeing from the French Revolution were allowed to settle. The secularism of the Revolution produced a reaction in favour of Catholicism. The Romantic Movement, powerfully expressed in Sir Walter Scott's novels, found a new charm in the Middle Ages, including its monasteries. Another Romantic, the Poet Laureate Robert Southey, pleaded eloquently for a revival of religious communities.[12] Romanticism was blended with a realistic appreciation of the need for organized works of charity among the poor, as expressed by Rev. A. R. C. Dallas in his *Protestant Sisters of Charity* (1826).[13]

The Oxford Movement produced John Henry Newman, who made the first new experiment, and Edward Bouverie Pusey who guided the formation of the first new sisterhoods. When 'Tract 90' was condemned in 1841, Newman went into semi-retirement at Littlemore.[14] He and a group of young men who joined him lived in a set of cottages converted from a granary and stables. One room was fitted up as an oratory.[15] Furniture throughout was sparse. The five men who joined Newman – William Lockhart, Ambrose St. John, J. D. Dalgairns, Richard Stanton and E. S. Bowles – were Oxford graduates whose Tractarian beliefs jeopardized their prospects in the Church of England but who to begin with had no wish to turn Roman Catholic.[16] These

12. In *Sir Thomas More* (1829).
13. Peter Anson gives a comprehensive coverage of the whole period 1540–1833 in the Introduction to *The Call of the Cloister* (CC).
14. At the far end of his parish, St. Mary the Virgin, Oxford.
15. Holy Communion was not celebrated in the oratory, but it was used for the Daily Office and private prayer.
16. CC p. 37.

men led a life of 'retirement, prayer and study', reciting the hours from the Breviary, keeping strict fasts and working on the *Lives of the Saints*. The community was soon referred to by outsiders as a 'monastery' though Newman denied that it was 'in anything approaching to the Romanist sense of the term'.[17] Anson observes that 'This foundation was something more in the nature of a post-Tridentine society of men without vows.'[18] However it is described, Littlemore was the most significant experiment in the Religious Life in the Church of England since Little Gidding. It did not survive Newman's conversion to Rome in 1845. Lockhart, whose departure inspired Newman to preach *The Parting of Friends* (1843), and Dalgairns had already gone over before him.

At the same time, Rev. Frederick Faber had gathered a group of his male penitents into a community at his Rectory of Elton, Hunts.[19] After only two years, Faber was received into the Roman Catholic Church (November 1845) and seven members of his Brotherhood followed him. Like Newman, they became Oratorians, and so contributed to the revival of Roman Catholic monasticism in England. W. F. Hook, when Vicar of Leeds (1837–59) wrote a letter to Gladstone in which he described 'a society of persons' in Leeds, a clergyman, another priest and three or four laymen who called themselves an Order of Mercy and worked among the poor of the city. It was a thing 'not to be talked about', probably because of the odium and ridicule Newman had incurred. Little, therefore, is known about them, but Anson is probably right that they 'lacked the knowledge and experience of community-life to establish the "Order" on firm foundations.[20]

The first attempts to establish Anglican Sisterhoods were also made in the 1840s. In 1846 William Butler became Vicar of Wantage, Berks., a parish which was extensive and suffering from spiritual neglect. Butler, a contemporary of John Mason Neale at Trinity College, Cambridge, conceived the idea of founding a Sisterhood to help his ministry, particularly with teaching children. He consulted Henry Manning, then Archdeacon of Chichester, who recommended to him Elizabeth Lockhart, sister of Newman's disciple. Like William, their mother had turned Roman Catholic (1846) but for the time being Manning and Butler persuaded Elizabeth to remain in the Church of England. After Easter 1848, she began life as a religious at Wantage. She was joined by Mary Reid, formerly a schoolmistress at Chichester, also recommended by Manning. With two servant girls who they hoped would

17. Quoted in CC p. 36.
18. CC p. 36.
19. Elton is only some ten miles from Little Gidding, but Fr. Faber seems to have been inspired by post-Tridentine Roman Catholicism rather than Caroline Anglicanism.
20. CC p. 46.

find a vocation, Misses Lockhart and Reid lived simply in two cottages. They had a small oratory where they recited the Day Hours from the Sarum Breviary, but also attended daily Mattins and Evensong in Wantage parish church.

Their work began by teaching the children of the parish. Elizabeth Lockhart, however, felt drawn to penitential work with women and girls, and in February 1850 she opened a House of Penitents at Wantage. Only a month later, her faith in the Church of England was shattered by the Gorham Judgment.[21] She and Miss Reid went over to Rome, followed in April 1851 by Archdeacon Manning. The Community at Wantage nevertheless survived. Harriet Day, who had come as a postulant in 1849, took over as Superior, and as the Community of St. Mary the Virgin Fr. Butler's foundation grew into one of the most famous Anglican Sisterhoods.

From 1852, Elizabeth Lockhart and other lady converts from Anglicanism worked in Greenwich. In 1857, Manning became Provost of Westminster Cathedral Chapter. He guided Miss Lockhart into founding a Sisterhood of Franciscan tertiaries who worked among the poor in Bayswater and later in Kensington. She and her companions served a novitiate with the Franciscan Sisters of the Immaculate Conception in Glasgow.[22] Mother Elizabeth (as she became) and her Community continued to work in West London until 1896 when they moved to two houses in Essex, at Braintree and Clacton-on-Sea.

Elizabeth Lockhart had thus helped to establish two communities, one Anglican, the other Roman Catholic. The latter was explicitly a Franciscan community, but before her conversion to Rome neither Miss Lockhart nor her directors seem to have had specifically Franciscan ideals.

Her career is paralleled by that of Mother Francis Basil and the five ladies who with her founded the Congregation of the Five Wounds. They too were converts from Anglicanism. After their conversion, they served a novitiate with French Franciscan sisters in Calais. They returned to England in 1868 and worked first in Hackney, then established themselves at St. Mary's Abbey, Mill Hill. They later set up two daughter houses in England and one in Ireland.[23]

Henry Phillpotts, the unsuccessful prosecutor of Gorham, became Bishop of Exeter in 1831, but it was not until seventeen years later in January 1848 that he appealed publicly for volunteers to work in the

21. The Rev. C. C. Gorham was deemed by Bishop Phillpotts of Exeter to be unsound on the doctrine of baptismal regeneration. On appeal to the Privy Council, the Judicial Committee ruled that his views were compatible with the doctrine of the Church of England.
22. Founded in 1847 (ROC) pp. 268–69.
23. ROC p. 269.

poor districts of Plymouth and Devonport. His appeal was answered by Priscilla Lydia Sellon, a naval officer's daughter. Miss Sellon already felt called to the religious life, and had considered joining the Park Village Sisterhood founded in London under Pusey's guidance. By temperament, she was better suited to lead her own community. Joined by four other ladies, the new Community began at Devonport in October 1848.

They undertook works of mercy on an extensive scale. Within two years, they had opened nearly twenty charitable institutions,[24] including schools and homes, especially for seafarers and sailor-boys. The work spread from Devonport and Plymouth to Bristol, Alverstoke (Hants.) and London. The Sisters showed exceptional devotion in nursing victims of the cholera epidemics of 1849 and 1853. They requested and were allowed the privilege of daily Communion during the outbreak – so far as is known, the first time that the Eucharist had been celebrated daily in the Church of England since the Reformation. So quickly did their numbers grow that eight Sisters were sent out to assist Florence Nightingale in the Crimean War.

Miss Sellon, or Mother Lydia as she became in religion, had a genius for consolidation and organisation equal to her enterprise in works of mercy. The Park Village Sisterhood of the Holy Cross amalgamated with the Devonport Sisters of Mercy (as they were first known) in 1856. Both Sisterhoods were under the spiritual guidance of Pusey. New statutes were drawn up when they amalgamated which were revised in 1861. Pusey hoped that Mother Lydia might become Superior-General of the Sisterhoods in the Church of England, with the Abbey at Plymouth as the Mother House,[25] but this remained only a dream. But such was the strength of the Devonport Sisterhood that in 1864, Mother Lydia was able to send three Sisters to superintend a school for native girls in Honolulu, and three more Sisters went to join them in 1867. This was the first time than an Anglican Community had sent out religious to the mission field.

The amalgamated Sisterhood took the name the Society of the Most Holy Trinity. From 1856, it had three orders resembling those of the Franciscan Order, though the Society as a whole was not Franciscan. The first order kept the name the Sisters of Mercy. They lived at St. Dunstan's Abbey, Plymouth. They were actively engaged in works of mercy and charity, though an important part in their life was taken up with the Daily Office, private prayer and meditation. It was a 'mixed' community in having this balance of prayer and active work. The first order continued the original work of the Sisters in Devonport

24. CC p. 263.
25. ibid., p. 265.

and Plymouth, and that of the Park Village Sisterhood. In drafting the Rule for these Sisterhoods, Pusey drew chiefly on the Rule of St. Augustine and the Constitutions of St. Francis de Sales.[26]

Dr. Pusey was a great believer in the 'mixed' life in Religion, and although the second order placed greater emphasis on contemplation, they too were engaged in active work. The Sisters were never to leave their house, except to attend church, save by the direct order of the Superior.[27] Their first object was to offer, day and night, mourning for sin, intercession for grace, and adoration of the Divine Trinity and the Love of Jesus. Prayer for the conversion of sinners and for the work of the other two orders was their especial concern, also for the Dying and for the Unity of Christendom. But when a permanent home was found for the second order at Ascot Priory, it included a convalescent ward with thirty-three beds – one for each of the years of Our Lord's earthly life. Sick children were also cared for, and in 1894 an orphanage was dedicated and in 1910 a permanent wing for convalescent children. All these active works had to be carried on within the precincts of the Convent. In recent years, the orphanage and the convalescent ward have been leased out and made into a residential home for the elderly. The Sisters still run St. Gabriel's Home for old ladies and a small retreat house and conference centre. Pusey based the statutes of the second order on those of the Poor Clares as revised by St. Collette. Originally, the Sisters wore a white habit. In 1861, they adopted the brown habit of the Clares, but this was soon changed for purple. Since 1861, they have worn in choir a white cloak with a red leather pierced heart, similar to that worn by the Carmelites. Their day of prayer began at 3.0 a.m. with Mattins and Lauds. Even recreation was kept in silence except on Sundays and Wednesdays. The Sisters kept in turn an hour's vigil through the night until Mattins. Their regimen was mitigated in 1889. As well as prayer and household duties, the Sisters undertook embroidery, illumination and writing.

The third order resembled Franciscan tertiaries in that some of them continued to live in their own homes. Others lived a semi-conventual life at St. Saviour's, Osnaburgh Street (London NW1) or in the Society's mission house at Bethnal Green. All members of the third order were engaged in works of charity among the sick and poor.

Fr. Edward Stuart of St. Mary Magdalen's, Munster Square, in whose parish St. Saviour's was situated, obtained for the second order use of a house at Bradford-on-Avon, Wilts. Then a legacy from Pusey's mother, Lady Lucy, made possible the purchase of a forty-acre site at Ascot. New buildings were designed by Butterfield, and the second

26. T. J. Williams, *Priscilla Lydia Sellon* (1950), pp. 16–17.
27. CC p. 269–70.

order moved there in 1863. Ascot Priory became the novitiate for the first and second orders; its seclusion provided the ideal atmosphere in which to train new sisters.

The early rapid growth of the Society was not sustained. Mother Bertha, who was Superior 1874–90, received no new postulants to the first and third orders, but concentrated wholly on the second order. More recruits came under her successor, Mother Georgiana, but the Society gradually cut back on some of its work. St. George's College for Sailor Boys at Plymouth was abandoned as early as 1861, and other charitable works were wound up. The sisters withdrew from St. Dunstan's Abbey in 1906. The continuing work of the Society became more and more concentrated at Ascot Priory.

Mother Lydia suffered a paralytic stroke in 1861, and retired to Ascot for her last years. After 1864, Dr. Pusey usually spent the Long Vacation from Oxford in a house in the grounds known as the 'Hermitage'. In his last years he was Warden of the community, and he died at Ascot in 1882. From 1855 to 1877, one of the second order Sisters lived as an anchoress, keeping perpetual silence – probably the first to take up the solitary life following the Oxford Movement. Pusey acted as her spiritual director.[28]

Although Pusey took the constitutions of the Collettines as a model rather than a blue-print, there was an 'unmistakable dominance of the Franciscan spirit' at Ascot.[29] Mother Lydia imparted the spirit of poverty, obedience and love of silence characteristic of the Poor Clares and Collettines.[30] The Sisters of Ascot Priory have a three-fold significance in the revival of Franciscanism. They are by far the earliest community in the Church of England to have a rule based on a part of the medieval Franciscan order; the only Franciscan community to have been founded under the influence of Dr. Pusey; and until the founding of the Community of St. Clare, the only Sisterhood following the contemplative way of the Franciscan second order. 'Both by natural endowment and early training in the spiritual life these women were fitted for high adventure along the paths of contemplative prayer and self-oblation. No less did that endowment and that training fit them for humble and generous service of the poor, the sick and the suffering.'[31]

Under the influence of the Oxford Movement, attempts were made earlier to revive communities of men, as at Littlemore and Elton, but the sisterhoods were the first to achieve stability. It was not until the 1860s that two more successful attempts were made to revive the

28. ibid., p. 270.
29. ibid., p. 274.
30. Williams, op. cit., pp. 210–11.
31. ibid., p. 211.

religious life for men. The first was the revival by Joseph Leycester Lyne, Fr. Ignatius, of the Benedictine life in the community which eventually settled at Llanthony, Monmouthshire. The community survived its founder by only a year or two, but it had a life of nearly half a century.[32] The second community was started in 1865 by Richard Meux Benson and a companion, and became the Society of St. John the Evangelist, the 'Cowley Fathers'. This continues to the present day after more than a century. Its work has extended to the U.S.A., Canada, India, Japan and South Africa.

A quarter of a century later, there was a great expansion of communities for men. The Order of St. Paul was founded in 1889, the Community of the Resurrection (Mirfield Fathers) in 1892. In 1894 came the Society of the Sacred Mission and the earliest Franciscan community for men, the Society of the Divine Compassion. All four of these communities were active rather than contemplative, engaged in evangelistic or missionary work; all were to some extent inspired by the Christian Socialism which became fashionable at that time. In the 1920s, the popularity of St. Francis inspired the foundation of three new communities for men. From these, and from the Franciscan sisterhoods, the Society of St. Francis was to grow.[33]

In the U.S.A., attempts were made to revive religious communities almost as early as in England. The first men's community to endure was the American house of the Society of St. John the Evangelist at Boston (1872). The first men's community of American origin dates from 1884, the Order of the Holy Cross at West Park, New York. The Community of St. Mary at Peekshill, New York (1865) is the oldest surviving women's community, though there was the earlier Sisterhood of the Holy Communion (1852), now defunct, which was 'not influenced in any way by the Tractarian movement'.[34] Franciscan communities began only a little later than in England, and quite independently. The Society of the Atonement began in 1898, the Poor Brethren of St. Francis in 1919. Both began with the idea of parallel communities of Brothers and Sisters. The English communities, by contrast, began as separate houses, either for men or for women, which were later drawn together into a single Society.

32. The Community began life at Claydon, Suffolk, in 1863. Fr. Ignatius died in 1908. The surviving members of his Community joined the Benedictines at Caldey Island eighteen months later.
33. The Society of the Incarnation of the Eternal Son (1894) began almost as a sister community to the Society of the Divine Compassion. The Community of St. Francis (1905) and the order of St. Elizabeth of Hungary (1912) were founded between these two and the Brotherhood of St. Francis of Assisi (1921). The Community of St. Francis is the oldest community to form part of the present Society of St. Francis.
34. CC p. 554.

3. *The Christian Socialist Movement*

The Industrial Revolution brought poverty and squalor to London and many English manufacturing cities. From early in the nineteenth century, Church leaders were aware of these conditions, the need to alleviate them, and the hindrance they made to preaching the Gospel. More churches were provided for industrial cities;[35] the voluntary societies provided schools for working class children; godly laymen like Lord Shaftesbury pioneered Acts of Parliament to improve working conditions, particularly for women and children. Mr. Stooks, an Anglican clergyman in London asserted that 'the first thing towards the spiritual and moral improvement of the people would be to improve their physical and social conditions.'[36] The concern of the churches took two forms, Christian philanthropy and Christian Socialism.[37]

Robert Owen, who is often regarded as the Father of British Socialism, was a Freethinker.[38] Among his many ideas was one for villages run on co-operative lines. Although this attracted the support of Edward Stanley, Bishop of Norwich (1837–49), and the Tory M.P. Lord John Manners, the experiment was never tried out in Britain. His achievements included managing a factory at New Lanark with vastly improved conditions for his workers (and still making a profit), helping to promote the early Factory Acts, and launching the Co-operative Movement. Socialists had done little except to disseminate their ideas by 1848 when the Chartist Movement came to a head. This was a genuine working class movement in favour of further reform of parliamentary representation. The Chartists were sometimes anti-clerical, but were certainly not anti-Christian, and at the height of their agitation visited churches and chapels, believing 'that they could make their voices heard through the churches'.[39] The same year 1848, revolutions broke out in Palermo, Paris, Vienna and most of the capital cities of Germany and Italy. On the Continent, the revolutionary leaders were often hostile to the Church (particularly the Roman Catholic Church) as well as to the old regime. These violent upheavals seemed to achieve little. The great Chartist demonstration in London ended in fiasco. And although Marx and Engels had published their Manifesto in 1848 urging the workers of the world to unite, by 1850

35. Edward Norman, *Church and Society in England 1770–1970* (Oxford 1976), pp. 47 ff.
36. Quoted in O. Chadwick, *The Victorian Church* (1966) p. 346. Stooks was probably Thomas Fraser Stooks, Curate of St. Martin-in-the-Fields 1845–48. He served in the Diocese of London until 1874.
37. There were non-Christian philanthropists and non-Christian Socialists of distinction, though they lie outside the scope of this book. Christian attitudes were shared by members of most of the main churches.
38. Norman, op. cit., p. 33.
39. Chadwick, op. cit., p. 336.

the dynasties were firmly back in control in all the countries of Europe except France. The world of ideas did not so quickly regain its stability.

John Malcolm Forbes Ludlow was descended from Cromwell's officer, Edmund Ludlow. He had been brought up in France, and understood events there better than most Englishmen. The revolution in Paris and the Chartist Movement in England convinced him of the need to Christianise Socialism and make Christianity socially conscious. He practised as a barrister at Lincoln's Inn, whose Chaplain since 1846 had been Frederick Denison Maurice, author of *The Kingdom of Christ* (1838). Ludlow and Maurice allied with two writers of fiction, Charles Kingsley of *The Water Babies* and Tom Hughes of *Tom Brown's Schooldays* to lead a movement which in 1850 called itself *Christian Socialist* and began to publish a periodical with that title. 'The church must be taken out of the sanctuary and into the world' said Ludlow, its editor. The movement did not aim at political Socialism, though Ludlow and Hughes helped to promote an Act in 1852 to protect Co-operative Societies. Maurice had opposed the Chartist Movement.[40] He believed that the State neither could nor should be communist – its duty was to protect property. But the Church was 'communist in principle'.[41] The original Christian Socialist Movement broke up in 1855. Kingsley 'recanted' some of his earlier views and became a supporter of Disraeli's social reforms. Maurice put his energies into educating the working classes. Ludlow felt himself deserted, but he lived long enough (till 1911) to see his ideas make some headway.

With the collapse of Chartism, the constructive energies of the industrial workers went into forming trade unions. The Amalgamated Society of Engineers (1852) is often regarded as the first modern trade union. Many working men, particularly in the towns, received the vote in 1867, but a working class party, or even working class Members of Parliament, came only later.[42] Some of the worst social conditions, particularly in public health and housing, were improved under Disraeli's legislation (1874–80) but poverty still existed on a scale difficult to imagine today. A prolonged slump began in the mid-1870s and brought hardship to many workers. The newly formed unions first really flexed their muscles during this slump, and a number of strikes took place in 1888–89, notably the London Dock Strike. Industrial strife was sometimes bitter. This climate revived interest in the ideas of Ludlow and Maurice, particularly in Church and University circles. Their movement was reborn when Henry Scott Holland founded the

40. Norman, op. cit., p. 170.
41. Chadwick, op. cit., p. 335.
42. The Independent Labour Party was formed in 1893. Few Labour members were elected until the General Election of 1906 when 53 were returned.

Christian Social Union in 1889. Brook Foss Westcott, Regius Professor of Divinity at Cambridge and from 1890 Bishop of Durham, became its first President. By 1897, it had recruited 2,600 members.[43]

Between the two phases of the Christian Socialist Movement, philanthropists and evangelists had been busy in the slums. William Booth began his work in 1865, and in 1878 his movement took the name the Salvation Army. Dr. Barnardo opened his first home in Stepney (E1) in 1867 and began sending poor boys to a new start in life in Canada.[44] In 1882, Wilson Carlile founded the Church Army to work in the slum quarters of Westminster. Samuel Barnett, Vicar of St. Jude's, Whitechapel (E2) began in 1875 to encourage undergraduates from Oxford to spend time in the East End, to learn at first hand what conditions were like, and to encourage working people by practical help. Walsham How, titular Bishop of Bedford and in fact Suffragan of East London 'brought Eton to Hackney Wick and Christchurch to Poplar' in 1881.[45] Oxford House was founded in 1883 as a centre for Oxford men to work in East London.

4. The Rediscovery of St. Francis

It was in such a world that, towards 1900, Victorian England rediscovered St. Francis of Assisi. He had brought the light of the Gospel and care for the poor to the misery of industrial cities in medieval Italy. His life became an inspiration and a challenge to the modern world.

Edward Hutton has wisely questioned whether in Roman Catholic Europe St. Francis ever needed to be 'rediscovered' or had ever been forgotten.[46] But his rediscovery in the countries of Reformed Europe is something of a mystery. Hutton regarded Karl Hase's <i>Franz von Assisi</i> (1856) as the first modern study of the Saint. More influential, probably, was F. Prudenzano's <i>Francesco d'Assisi</i> (1857). It went through fourteen editions before 1914 and was translated into French and German. Under the impact of this book, the first to make St. Francis a patron of Christian Socialism, 'Franciscan fathers had their hands full trying to steer the laypeople in their "Third Order" away from socialism, and to keep their attention focused on the kindhearted, peaceable Francis.'[47] There is little direct evidence that English Social-

43. Chadwick, op. cit., p. 279.
44. S. C. Carpenter, <i>Winnington-Ingram</i> (1949), p. 30.
45. ibid., p. 27. Walsham How was Suffragan Bishop of Bedford 1879–88 when he became Bishop of Wakefield.
46. In the introduction to his translation of Abbé Englebert's life of St. Francis (1950).
47. Adolf Holl, <i>The Last Christian</i> (New York 1980).

ists were influenced from Italy, but indirect influence through French writers such as Renan and Sabatier (see below) is at least possible.

There had already been some revival of interest in St. Francis through tourism. The Grand Tour was part of an English gentleman's education in the seventeenth and eighteenth centuries. Interest was primarily in the great cities of the Renaissance and their art treasures – Milan, Florence, Venice, Rome and Naples – but slow coach travel between these cities helped to focus attention on the medieval cities, often the home of earlier schools of painting – Siena and Assisi. The part played by Giotto's frescoes in the Upper Basilica at Assisi in keeping alive the legend of St. Francis should not be underestimated. One English tourist, visiting Assisi about 1820, described it thus:

> Assisi with its magnificent cloisters and churches on the hill-side; the church of Madonna degli Angli; the Porziuncola of St. Francis, like the house of Loretto, its shrine lighted up and full of kneeling figures under its low roof, like an ark within a magnificent temple. Two Franciscans kneeling on the out-side and a woman of middle age with an expressive countenance.[48]

A great Frenchman in Italy was the novelist Stendhal (Henri Marie Beyle). Although he described friars and feudalism as 'those twin cankers that eat out the heart of the body politic' both, he acknowledged, were 'excellent institutions in their time' and he added, 'Personally I regard St. Francis of Assisi as a very great man.'[49]

The first important biography of St. Francis to be written in English in modern times was that by Mrs. Oliphant in 1870. This aroused interest in St. Francis long before the influence of the Christian Social Union was felt. Mrs. Oliphant saw her hero as a religious revivalist in the true sense – one of those sent from time to time 'who came full of the primitive spirit of the Gospel to renew the religious life,[50] and bring a fresh flood of genuine spiritual influence upon the world.'[51] Mrs. Oliphant's interest in him was primarily religious. She handled the subject of his visions and the stigmata with tact and judgment – an important consideration when he was still likely to be dismissed as a fraud and a deceiver.

But something happened in the next generation which made the real 'breakthrough' in the reputation of St. Francis. Professor Owen Chadwick has written:

> The repute of St. Francis . . . fitted another trend of Victorian

48. *The Italian Journal of Samuel Rogers*, ed. J. R. Hale (1956), p. 204.
49. Stendhal, *Rome, Naples and Florence* (1959), p. 346.
50. i.e. the Christian Faith, not the monastic life.
51. op. cit., Introduction p. xi.

devotion, which intellectually touched the quest for the historical Jesus. They were more conscious of Jesus the man. They therefore realised the possibility of a literal, i.e. a human imitation of him in his humanity. *The Imitation of Christ* was a book which sold in increasing numbers, and the idea of imitation became prominent in sermons.[52]

An important influence was the French philosopher Ernest Renan whose *Vie de Jesus* (1863) sought to remove the supernatural from his account of the 'historical Jesus'.[53] Renan regarded St. Francis as, after Jesus Himself, 'the only perfect Christian'.[54] Renan's pupil was the Calvinist pastor, Paul Sabatier, whose life of St. Francis (1893; English translation 1894) was not only a great work of scholarship but one of the most widely read books on the Poor Man of Assisi ever written. Sabatier saw St. Francis as a great spiritual Reformer in the tradition of Isaiah, St. Paul and St. Augustine.[55]

As the patron saint of the poor and outcast, St. Francis had a rival for most of the nineteenth century in St. Vincent de Paul. Southey in his *Sir Thomas More* (see above) asked why no Vincent de Paul had been heard in Anglican pulpits, not Francis of Assisi.[56] In 1902, James Adderley, founder of the Society of the Divine Compassion, hailed St. Vincent as 'a Christian Social Reformer.'[57] St. Vincent de Paul's eclipse was as remarkable as St. Francis' rise.

St. Francis had an appeal on quite different grounds, carefully cultivated, according to Adolf Holl, by the Franciscans, the 'kind-hearted, peaceable Francis,' lover of the created world, tamer of Brother Wolf and preacher to the birds. This side of St. Francis was portrayed in another best seller, again by a Protestant, Johannes Jörgensen's life (1907) which 'signalled the transition to the sentimental Francis of our time.' Jörgensen became a convert to Rome and had a street named after him in Assisi. Two years earlier Edward Hutton in *Cities of Umbria* (1905) was already castigating the sentimentalised cult of St. Francis. But he had harder strictures for Sabatier and his school, for whose scholarship, nevertheless, he always had the highest praise.

> M. Sabatier has gradually made clear for us those things which were hidden and obscure, throwing a new light on that life of peculiar perfection, so that he seems to suggest that under all the beauty and

52. op. cit., p. 468.
53. *Oxford Dictionary of the Christian Church*: Ernest Renan.
54. Hutton, op. cit., p. 13.
55. op. cit., xxii.
56. CC p. 26.
57. *Monsieur Vincent* (1902), p. 2.

sweetness that have led men to think of St. Francis as an imitation of Christ there lies the revolutionary, the progressive reformer, intent on his own freedom of spirit and the liberty of the hearts of men. And whatever we may think of so new a reading of the parable of St. Francis' life, we are from the first surprised to find one whom we had always considered as the most humble of saints suddenly converted into a kind of divine schismatic, an amiable Martin Luther at least in his intentions, accusing the Church, rather by his conduct, it would seem, than by his teaching, of the betrayal of mankind into a kind of slavery from which he, the little poor man, would set it free.[58]

He goes on to state the real reason why the inspiration of St. Francis will never fail:

He was not concerned with the tremendous politics of the Catholic Church, but in the dust and dirt he found the lilies of her love. For the real revolution for which St. Francis worked, was a resurrection of love among men.[59]

In the 1890s, therefore, the three elements were present which fused to produce the Anglican Franciscan communities. The religious life had already been revived, and the Society of St. John the Evangelist, stable for a generation, time and again was to enter the Franciscan story offering inspiration, guidance and sometimes refuge to those trying to form new communities. Concern for the poor and their evangelisation had already led men to leave the universities to work and preach in East and South London. And men and women were already discovering in St. Francis both an imitation of Christ and an example to follow.

But the Franciscan revival might never have taken place but for the leadership of one man and the creative skill of another. Charles Gore, later to achieve fame as Bishop of Birmingham and Oxford, took over the leadership of the Oxford Movement after Pusey's death in 1882. Pusey House was established as his memorial to be a place of prayer and study, and in 1884 Gore, then aged 29, was appointed its first Principal Librarian. Gore had some hesitation in accepting the post. He was the nephew of the Earl of Arran, and his family was always Whig; Pusey had been a High Tory. But more important than political differences, Gore had absorbed the German methods of Biblical criticism which Pusey and his disciple Liddon had so long opposed. This was not fully apparent to the academic world until *Lux Mundi* was published in 1889. As editor and author of one of the most controversial

58. op. cit., p. 243.
59. ibid., p. 244.

essays, much of the storm broke around Gore's head. It was all the more remarkable that he was able to assert an ascendancy over the Catholic Movement at Oxford such as no one had exercised since Newman went over to Rome in 1845 – Pusey's influence had been quieter, though perhaps more lasting and more deeply spiritual. It was a three-fold influence.

First, he formulated and expounded a school of 'Liberal Catholicism', combining the new Biblical criticism with Catholic ceremonial in worship. Secondly, he awakened the Anglo-Catholic 'social conscience'. He was a close friend of Scott Holland, and with him became a joint Vice-President of the Christian Social Union when it was formed in 1889. In politics, he was a Radical, a disciple of T. H. Green of Balliol, rather than a Socialist.[60] But he had much sympathy for the Socialist movement. Ben Tillett the labour leader was his guest at Pusey House, and he invited Stewart Headlam of the Guild of St. Matthew to speak in Oxford.[61] Thirdly, he helped to foster the new religious communities for men. He is particularly remembered for his work in founding the Community of the Resurrection. He attempted, with less success, to guide the Benedictine Community on Caldey Island.[62] But he also inspired and guided a number of men aspiring to the religious life, many of whom felt drawn to the Franciscan Way. One of these was James Adderley, the man without whose creative ability the first men's Franciscan community might never have come into being. Both the Community of the Resurrection and the Society of the Divine Compassion aimed to explore the experience of sharing material possessions as a lesson they could teach to others in the industrial slums. Their religious life was a practical expression of their Christian Socialism.

But before Adderley launched his community, another, a stranger by birth and a missionary by calling, had already begun to pioneer the Franciscan life.

60. G. L. Prestige, *The Life of Charles Gore* (1935), p. 91.
61. ibid., pp. 68, 91.
62. CC pp. 177 ff.

PART I

THE AGE OF JAMES ADDERLEY

3

Luigi Josa

In the period down to the Great War, the influence of James Adderley stands out above that of any other in the Franciscan story. He founded a Franciscan-style community for men, the Society of the Divine Compassion, and with Gertrude Bromby, one for women, the Society of the Incarnation of the Eternal Son. Those inspired by the Society of the Divine Compassion founded three further communities – the Community of St. Giles, the Brotherhood of St. Francis of Assisi and the Franciscan Servants of Jesus and Mary, while William Sirr and Edward Bulstrode tried without success to found others. Adderley's disciple John Hawes helped to found the Community of St. Francis, and had two attempts at establishing a community for men. But it is still possible to exaggerate his influence. The earliest known attempts at introducing the Franciscan life in the Anglican Communion, at Durham in 1891 and Guiana in 1895, were too early to have been influenced by Adderley. Both of these involved tertiaries, not men or women under solemn vows. Josa, who worked in Guiana, was an Italian, born and bred in Rome, where the influence of Roman Catholic Franciscanism upon him needs no explanation. That Adderley influenced him later is clear, since he quotes his writings. The influences upon Canon Body of Durham are not clear – since he was associated with Josa in writing a book, Josa may have influenced him as he certainly influenced Josa. The uncertainty surrounding Body and Josa makes it clear that although the creative skill and personal inspiration of Adderley were probably decisive factors, there was something of a 'climate' of Franciscanism already before he got to work.

Luigi Josa was an Italian by birth who took British nationality. Brought up a Roman Catholic, he became a priest in the Church of England. He was born in Rome in 1851 and baptized in St. Peter's Basilica. His family were impoverished, but his father and great-grandfather both held the office of Papal Chamberlain. He received the equivalent of a grammar school education as an acolyte of St. Peter's. It was his very proximity to papal power that made him restless. He grew up during the 1860s when the Papal States were under increasing pressure from the new Kingdom of Italy.

The Ultramontanes were keen at that time on making the temporal power into a dogma, and when they saw that this dogma could never become an article of faith, then the dogma of 'the Infallibility' was worked for all it was worth.[1]

It is possible that he was influenced by Prudenzano; like him, a reaction against Ultramontanism and temporal power led him to a form of Christian Socialism inspired by St. Francis of Assisi. He came into contact with English clergy visiting Rome, and through Dr. Finch, Curate of St. Stephen's, Garlickhythe, he was invited to England and received into the Anglican Church. He had thoughts at one time of becoming a sculptor, but he chose instead to become a missionary, and trained at the Mission College, Warminster, and then at St. Augustine's, Canterbury. He was ordained deacon in 1874 and priest in 1875. Most of his ministry was spent in the diocese of Guiana. He held the important positions of Vicar of Christ Church, Georgetown; Canon of St. George's Cathedral; Rural Dean of Demarara; Archdeacon and Vicar General of Guiana. He had an exceptional gift for languages. He had intended to go out to India, and was first sent to Guiana to work among the Indian labourers. He mastered Hindi and published a Hindi grammar in 1907. He returned to England during the Great War. Like many missionaries returning home, he did not find a new post easily. However, he became Curate of St. Teath in Cornwall and then Rector of St. Endellion. It was here in 1920 that he wrote *The Tale of a Roaming Catholic*. As an autobiography, it is an invaluable source for his life, though his career in the Church of England can be reconstructed from *Crockford*. He also used it to express his views on theology and Church History. He makes many perceptive comments on people close to him. Of Fr. Congreve of Cowley he said, 'He reminded me more than anything else of St. Francis of Assisi.'[2] Josa was for a time a missionary on the estates of Quentin Hogg, later first Viscount Hailsham, whose care for his workers greatly impressed Josa. 'He was a modern St. Vincent de Paul.'[3] St. Francis of Assisi; St. Vincent de Paul: the same two saints inspired Josa as his younger contemporary James Adderley. Josa knew Adderley's writings, to which he refers, including the novel *Stephen Remarx*. It seems unlikely that they should have met, at least before Josa's return to England, or that Josa in Guiana should have influenced Adderley, at least directly. While in Guiana, Josa wrote *St. Francis of Assisi and the Third Order in the Anglo-Catholic Church*, first published in 1898, and reprinted in 1903.

1. Luigi Josa, *The Tale of a Roaming Catholic* (1920), p. 3.
2. ibid., p. 70. George Congreve was Curate of Warminster 1859–61, Vicar of Frankby, Cheshire, 1861–73 and Cowley St. John 1874–87.
3. ibid., p. 74.

It is an extremely rare book, but it remains a source of information on some early Franciscan experiments which would otherwise have passed without record.

Apart from Adderley's writings, Josa mentions Mrs. Oliphant's life of St. Francis, a Salvation Army life of 'Brother Francis' and a 'Third Order Book' of Mrs. Skeffington. Paul Sabatier's great life seems to have appeared too late to influence him. 'If Christianity does not teach socialism,' he wrote in *St. Francis of Assisi*, 'we don't know what it teaches.' But he dissociated himself from 'subverters of governments, the uprooters of society, the dynamiters.'[4] His Christian Socialism seems to have been at least as broad as that of Adderley or Mother Elizabeth (q.v.).

The preface to *St. Francis of Assisi* was written by George Body, Canon of Durham.[5] On 28 October 1891, Canon Body admitted six men and women as Franciscan tertiaries,[6] probably the first in the Church of England since the Reformation. Josa wrote his book to make the Franciscan ideal better known, and particularly the Third Order. At the time of writing, Canon Josa (as he had become) was working single-handed in a parish of 2,000 communicants whose labours and talents he hoped to organise, but he aimed too to convert the English working classes. Canon Josa began a Third Order in the Diocese of Guiana in 1895 with himself as Chaplain-General.[7] Unfortunately, he makes no reference to this Third Order in *The Tale of a Roaming Catholic*. It seems likely that both it, and Canon Body's tertiary group, were short-lived.

Josa followed St. Francis in no spirit of uncritical admiration. The first Franciscan martyrs in Morocco were 'unable to understand the spirit of Christ that we should not court persecution.'[8] He accepted Ranke's stricture that at the Reformation the Franciscans were 'the most profoundly corrupt' of all the religious orders.[9] Like many before him, Josa believed that the rot had set in with Brother Elias who aimed 'at making the Franciscan Order a power in the world.'[10] He was optimistic that 'the Church of England will not . . . ever assimilate into her system the vagaries of the Franciscans, nor the errors of the Church of Rome, while her sound common sense will work wonders.'[11]

Luigi Josa is still remembered for his Franciscan joy – indeed, sense

4. op. cit., pp. 49–50.
5. George Body was Rector of Kirkby-Misperton, Yorks., 1870–84; Canon Missioner for the Diocese of Durham, 1883. In 1890 he was living at The College, Durham.
6. *St. Francis of Assisi*, p. 126.
7. ibid., p. 136.
8. ibid., p. 59.
9. ibid., p. 62.
10. ibid., p. 63.
11. ibid., p. 127.

of fun – as well as his great warmth and openness of heart. His own life-story shows how great an influence St. Francis had upon him. How many others he influenced and for how long is uncertain, but he was clearly one of the first torch-bearers of the Franciscan movement in the Church of his adoption.

4

James Adderley

James Granville Adderley was the fifth son of Sir Charles Bowyer
Adderley, Conservative M.P. for North Staffordshire 1841–78, Presi-
dent of the Board of Trade in Disraeli's government 1874–78 and first
Baron Norton. The father has been described as a 'kindly Christian
gentleman and a high-minded statesman' and his housing estate at
Saltley 'the best of its kind'.[1] In religion, he was a devout Evangelical.
His son James inherited neither his politics nor his churchmanship,
but may have acquired from his father a concern for social welfare. Sir
Charles headed Disraeli's Royal Commission on the Sanitary Laws in
1868.[2]

James Adderley's outlook matured slowly. He remembered hearing
a sermon at Eton by Henry Scott Holland which was clearly above
the run of school chapel sermons, but it was their later contact that
led him to write

> I would especially thank God, as Kingsley thanked God for Maurice,
> so would I for Holland. But for him I should never have gone to
> Oxford House or the Christ Church Mission, and without them I
> might have been an atheist or a 'moderate' Anglican parson.[3]

From Eton, Adderley went up to Christ Church, Oxford, where he
took a degree in History. His biographer says, 'Little is known of
Adderley's religious life at Oxford', adding that he was probably
influenced by Scott Holland.[4] Adderley himself says that Charles Gore
was

> very near and dear to me since Oxford days. He taught me practi-
> cally all the theology I know . . . Few people outside Oxford know
> the extraordinary patience and care with which Dr. Gore, when
> Principal of the Pusey House, dealt with individuals like myself.[5]

1. T. P. Stevens, *Father Adderley* (1943), p. 9.
2. Robert Blake, *Disraeli* (1974), p. 495.
3. J. G. Adderley, *In Slums and Society* (1916), pp. 34, 36.
4. Stevens, op. cit., p. 13.
5. op. cit., p. 118.

They were later to be in close contact again when Gore was Bishop of Birmingham and Adderley Vicar of Saltley from 1904 to 1911. Gore's work in the Christian Social Union and Community of the Resurrection cannot have been other than a major influence on Adderley. The retreat which led to the formation of the Society of the Divine Compassion took place at Pusey House, though Gore had then recently moved to be Vicar of Radley.

After Oxford, Adderley moved to London to read for a career in law, but became thoroughly involved in church work in his spare time. He wrote that it was the sermons of Robert Eyton at St. Mary's, Graham Street, which 'first converted [him] to a practical Christianity', Eyton himself being a disciple of F. D. Maurice and Scott Holland.[6] He became directly concerned with church life in the East End at Oxford House, Bethnal Green, first under the Rev. W. E. Jackson, succeeding him as head of the house in 1884–85. Here he and other young Oxford men learned at first hand the conditions in which the working classes of London lived. In those early days, Oxford House was a converted schoolroom, with cubicles partitioned off on the upper floor and a stove in the sitting room over which the occupants shivered in winter.[7] It was while living in these spartan conditions that Adderley became familiar with the great labour leader, Ben Tillett, with whom he used to wander about Whitechapel on Sunday mornings. 'Then', he says, 'I made up my mind to be ordained'.[8]

Two of James Adderley's elder brothers were already in the sacred ministry, and perhaps it was only a matter of time before he followed them. In 1887, he left Oxford House and was ordained deacon to serve as curate at St. John's, Bethnal Green. He stayed only five months, succeeding his brother Reginald, whom he greatly admired, as head of the Christ Church Mission, Poplar. He was curate of All Hallows, Barking, from 1893 to 1894 before going to St. Philip's Mission church in Plaistow. As such, he was a member of the community of priests or Mission College founded in 1884 by the Vicar, Arthur James Mason. How far Mason and his community influenced Adderley's work is uncertain. Writing *In Slums and Society*, he says that Mason 'wanted to be a preaching friar, but the authorities of the Church dissuaded him, and perhaps they were right', but curiously enough, he does not mention his own membership of the All Hallows College.

Adderley's heart and soul were in Christian Socialism. But his outlook was neither narrow nor partisan. He was present at the coronation of King Edward VII and wrote of it,

6. op. cit., pp. 10 ff. Eyton was Rector of Upper Chelsea (1884).
7. Adderley, op. cit., p. 18.
8. ibid., p. 196. James Adderley's entry in *Crockford* cites him as Curate of St. John's, Bethnal Green, 1888 and St. Frideswide's, Bromley-by-Bow, 1888–93.

I felt inclined to say, 'This is Socialism at last.' Why? Because at a coronation we experience, if only for a short time, the power and glow of a united nation, all agreed about a great national act. That is the root principle of Socialism.[9]

Of the Great War, he declared 'with all its horrors, [it] has its great compensation for us Socialists . . . it shows us . . . the splendid enthusiasm possible in a united (that is, a socialist) nation'.[10] Adderley, however, supported the formation of the Independent Labour Party in 1893, which Stewart Headlam and most of the Christian Social Union opposed.[11] Lord Rosebery once declared, 'Socialism is the end of all faith'. Adderley replied, 'It was the beginning of mine'.[12] Looking back to the Dock Strike of 1889, he wrote, 'The message of Christ was only half given if it did not touch the social problem'.[13]

An unusual turn to Adderley's career came through the publication of his novel Stephen Remarx. It was refused by twenty publishers, but became a best seller. It was hardly a good, let alone a great novel, but the author was right in claiming that 'it caught the mood of the times' when 'slumming was the fashion among religious people of the upper classes, and Socialism of a very mild type was beginning to be indulged in, even by duchesses'.[14] It ran to twelve editions. It was readable, like all Adderley's books, and not the least of his gifts was a talent for publicity.

The hero was partly based on Adderley himself.[15] Stephen Remarx is described as a 'beastly sap' at Eton who nevertheless acquires there a 'peculiar charm of real gentility' and a 'high sense of honour'. At Oxford, he acquires from his tutor a questioning 'Whether God really meant great crowds of men to live in poverty and overwork, while many live in luxury and idleness upon the labours of the rest.'[16] He becomes a curate in the East End, and then Rector of St. Mark's, Chelsea, where he shocks his uncle the Marquis of St. Alphege by his Socialist sermons but attracts a docker, John Oxenham, a character probably based on Ben Tillett. Remarx and Oxenham found a religious community, which, in addition to its six members has 250 'irregulars' who form a kind of Third Order. Stephen Remarx dies in an odour of sanctity after being snowballed and run over by a cart.

9. ibid., p. 216 f.
10. ibid.
11. Edward Norman, Church and Society in England 1770–1970 (1976), p. 185.
12. op. cit., p. 235.
13. ibid., p. 199.
14. ibid., p. 170.
15. Norman, op. cit., p. 164, describes the book as 'nearly autobiographical', though much of it is anticipated autobiography.
16. Stephen Remarx (1893), p. 6.

Despite its shortcomings, this novel was an event of church history. It attracted to him the men with whom he formed a community concerned with 'the social problem', a phrase much used in the novel. These were the Rev. Henry Chappel, a graduate of Exeter College, Oxford, who was working at the Cheltenham College Mission in Nunhead, and Henry Ernest Hardy, better known as Father Andrew, who was then an ordinand at Ely Theological College. Adderley had originally met them at Oxford House. Father Waggett of Cowley drew up a rule and conducted the retreat for them. At Pusey House on 20 January 1894, Adderley, Chappel and Hardy bound themselves to the rule and to the three religious vows for one year.[17] Adderley and Chappel then went to St. Philip's Mission in Plaistow. Hardy joined them in March when he had completed his training at Ely. When he was ordained priest at Trinity 1895 by Bishop Festing of St. Alban's, Hardy was the first Anglican to be ordained in a religious habit since the Reformation.[18] Four lay brothers completed the numbers of the community.

There is no specific reference to St. Francis of Assisi in *Stephen Remarx*, nor was the Society of the Divine Compassion, as the new community was called, specifically Franciscan. Peter Anson states correctly that it

> came into being so far as its founder was concerned, not so much from any positive urge to be Franciscans, as from the conviction that the Co-operative Movement, Trade Unionism, and Socialism had failed largely because working men were unwilling to accept leadership; hence the hope that the example of a small group of men living under vows of poverty, chastity and obedience might achieve more in the long run than further schemes for social reform.[19]

At this time, Adderley's inspiration seems to have come mainly from St. Vincent de Paul. In the biography he wrote in 1902, he says.

> S. Vincent was a Christian Social Reformer, and 'Christian Socialism' is in the air . . . our most 'modern' and 'original' methods, both in philanthropy and church work, were known and in full swing 250 years ago, and emanated from the brain of one man, and that man a poor peasant priest of the French Church.[20]

Adderley, however, soon became a disciple of the cult of St. Francis which grew up in the 1890s. His motives help to explain his short-lived association with his community. The story of that community will be

17. Peter Anson, *The Call of the Cloister*, p. 153.
18. ibid., p. 155.
19. ibid., p. 152.
20. J. G. Adderley, *Monsieur Vincent* (1902), p. 2.

traced in the next two chapters. Adderley's own work moved away from the centre of the community in Plaistow to the Berkeley Chapel, Mayfair, where he conducted a mission to the wealthy and aristocratic very reminiscent of that of the fictitious Stephen Remarx in Chelsea. In 1897 he resigned as Superior and left the Society, continuing his work at Berkeley Chapel until 1900. Peter Anson comments,

> while Hardy and Chappel shared Adderley's social conscience, it seems probable that they were more concerned than he was with the Religious Life as an end in itself.[21]

The tension which grew up in the small community led to Adderley's departure. 'The view handed down in the Community was that it was his vocation to be founder but not to remain in holy religion'.[22]

Adderley says little about the community in his *In Slums and Society*. When he wrote it in 1916, the Society was flourishing. To have said much could easily have implied criticism of those with whom he parted. He treated the matter with true gentlemanly reserve.

He continued to serve the Christian Socialist Movement. He took pride in being the first member of the Labour Party to become a canon of an English cathedral (Birmingham, 1913) and took a prominent part in the Conference on Christian Politics, Economics and Citizenship ('Copec') in 1924.[23] Nor had his contribution to the Franciscan movement come to an end. *Francis, The Little Poor Man of Assisi* was not a very original work, being mainly a digest of Sabatier's life with references to Brother Leo's *Mirror of Perfection* and the *Fioretti*. It was part of the growing literature on St. Francis, but it helped to establish a friendship between Adderley and Sabatier.

The book which he published with C. L. Marson in 1902, *Third Orders*, was more original and important. Marson translated and introduced an early version of the rule of the Third Order discovered by Sabatier. Adderley followed with a chapter on Third Orders in which he wrote,

> It is becoming increasingly clear to all students of S. Francis that, even in the case of his First Order, the 'Brothers Minor', the object of the Saint was much more to evangelize all men than to found a community.[24]

He went on to write of the possibility of capturing a truly Franciscan spirit in the Church of England as a whole, pointing to the tradition of godly layfolk forming associations – the Society for the Reformation

21. op. cit., p. 152.
22. ibid., p. 156.
23. Norman, op. cit., Chapter 7.
24. *Third Orders* (1902), p. 23.

of Manners, William Law, the early Methodists, the Clapham Sect and the societies which supported the Anglican Sisterhoods. His approval of the Methodists and Evangelicals accords with his claim that he had

> learned to combine the best in Evangelical religion with the best in Catholicism, or rather to know that they are not two religions, but one, if rightly understood.[25]

Other disciples of St. Francis similarly sought the formula of Evangelical Catholicism. Adderley also believed that the Third Order more truly represented the spirit of St. Francis, the First and Second Orders being the work of the Papacy.[26] He had little time for 'spikes' as he termed the Romanisers in the Church of England, praising Percy Dearmer, with whom he worked at the Berkeley Chapel, for establishing a genuine English Catholicism.[27] There was more to his outlook than disillusionment with religious communities and suspicion of Rome. He believed that the spirit of St. Francis had been lost when the Franciscan movement, under the influence of the Papacy, became institutionalised. If he were right, modern disciples of St. Francis have need to heed his wisdom.

Immediately after leaving the Society of the Divine Compassion, Adderley attempted to form a new community, the Community of the Holy Spirit of Truth. Father John Mark left the Society of the Divine Compassion to join him, but the venture only lasted until 1900. Father John Mark returned to Plaistow, but was never professed, though he remained with the Community until 1912.[28] When he was Vicar of St. Saviour's, Saltley, Adderley encouraged his curate, John Hawes, to form a simple, Franciscan community, but the experiment was short-lived. He also suggested, without success, that Hawes should try to form a community with George Martin. The Community of the Holy Spirit of Truth seems to have been the last time Adderley himself tried to live in community. He was 'not the kind of man to do a life's work anywhere';[29] Scott Holland simply called him a rolling stone. He became incumbent of six successive parishes in London and Birmingham between 1900 and his retirement in 1937[30] as well as working in France during the Great War for the Y.M.C.A. and Church Army.

25. *In Slums and Society*, p. 15.
26. *Third Orders*, p. 57.
27. *In Slums and Society*, p. 81.
28. SDC Great Chapter Minute Book 30/5/12.
29. Stevens, op. cit., p. 24.
30. Adderley was at the Berkeley Chapel 1897–1900; St. Mark's, Marylebone, 1901–04; St. Saviour's, Saltley, 1904–11; St. Gabriel's, Birmingham, 1911–18; St. Paul's, Covent Garden, 1918–23; St. Anne's, Highgate, 1923–29; St. Edmund King and Martyr with St. Nicholas Acons, 1929–37.

He might have exercised greater influence in the Anglo-Catholic Movement if, about 1900, his theology had not moved towards Liberalism. About the same time, he ceased to be a great draw as a preacher.[31] By the world's standards, his work in the Franciscan movement was a failure, and even the community which he founded, and left, no longer remains as his monument. But his life was a sincere attempt to live out the ideals of St. Francis. He could laugh at himself enough to quote Frederick Temple's remark, 'Shall I tell you why [Adderley] can never be really poor? Because he washes'.[32] But his biographer wrote of him, 'His rank, culture or dignity never separated him from any except the base'.[33] As a parish priest, he continued to live simply in a vicarage without carpets attended only by a manservant, offering hospitality to young men whom he encouraged towards the sacred ministry.[34] In the 1890s, he made vows privately to Bishop Mandell Creighton by which he lived even though he ceased to be a member of a religious community.[35] This must have been after Mandell Creighton became Bishop of London in 1897. Bishop Creighton, from his study of the Middle Ages, was a great admirer of St. Francis, and helped to foster Adderley's own devotion. According to the Bishop, 'Francis and Napoleon had a greater effect on European history than any other men', and 'No revolution has ever been so great as that made by St. Francis.' The prebend of St. Paul's and the City parish which concluded his ministry were marks of earthly recognition, but the description of him as a 'lovable (but often tiresome) Christian gentleman'[36] says more about the heart of the man, and his wish that his ashes should be scattered in the East London cemetery, where some of his most caring work had been done, was fully in character. He wrote of St. Francis,

> His is a light that no man can ever extinguish, for it is a light that derives its brightness from the glory of Him who lighteth every man that cometh into the world. May it shine with renewed brilliancy in the midst of the dimness of our own dark days, when the mockers mock and the love of many has waxed cold![37]

Few would deny that some part of that same light shone in the life of James Adderley.

---

31. Stevens, op. cit., p. 70.
32. *In Slums and Society*, p. 66.
33. Stevens, op. cit., p. 79.
34. ibid., pp. 52, 79.
35. ibid., p. 22.
36. ibid., p. 58.
37. J. G. Adderley, *Francis, The Little Poor Man of Assisi* (1908), p. 150. These are the concluding words of the book.

5

The Society of the Divine Compassion
1894–1914

In *A Franciscan Revival: The Story of the Society of the Divine Compassion*[1], J. R. Moore Smith, Mayor of West Ham, wrote an article on 'A forerunner of the Society of the Divine Compassion'. Many then living in West Ham would have been able to remember an experiment in the religious life which, but for this article, is now virtually unknown. It developed from the Guild of St. Alban, one of the many Anglo-Catholic fraternities, and its moving spirit was George Malim, or 'Brother George'. With himself as Master, three or four 'regular' brethren and a few 'externs' formed the Community of St. Alban living at first in Paddington, from which in February 1876 they moved to Ivy House, Balaam Street, Plaistow, which they renamed St. Dunstan's, with a chapel decorated by the Rev. E. Geldart.[2] The community was one of laymen. Curates of the local parish church, St. Andrew's, Plaistow, joined them from time to time, and with the consent of the clergy, they engaged in parochial work. Their real achievement, however, was with the young men and lads who were attracted to the house, thirty or forty of whom were admitted as 'associates'. They were pledged to attend the Eucharist weekly, communicate corporately at fixed intervals, join the Brethren in the house on Good Friday, engage in definite church work and report to the monthly chapter. In return, they were allowed to attend chapel in the house, take tea with the Brethren on Sundays and introduce friends on high days and holidays. Moore Smith wrote:

> Looking back I cannot speak too highly of the good work done, in spite of the seeming failure. Go where you will about the borough today you find old associates of 'St. Dunstan's' (now mostly married men with families), not only 'churchgoers', but consistent Churchmen, and many of them still engaged in active Church work.[3]

1. Edited by A. Clifton Kelway and published by Whitwell Press, Plaistow (1908). (FR)
2. Vicar of St. Andrew's, Plaistow. See *Crockford*.
3. FR p. 16.

Two things seem to have blighted this promising beginning. In 1879, a large hall was erected in the garden as a club-house. But 'as a means of adding to the number of Associates, or even (with few exceptions) bringing those who joined it under the Church's influence, it absolutely failed.'[4] Worse seems to have been 'the introduction of politics at the time of the 1880 General Election.'[5] That election was one of the most bitter of the last century, remembered chiefly for Gladstone's 'Midlothian Campaign' denouncing Lord Beaconsfield's forward imperial policy. The Conservatives, on the other hand, had the best record of social reform in the century. It must have been difficult to vote according to conscience, and 'The presence of the Brethren on political platforms and at committee rooms, in the chapels and public houses, estranged their political opponents and many of their friends, including most of the clergy of St. Andrew's. After the election, the Brotherhood had no official connection with St. Andrew's, and many Associates withdrew.'[6] The Community rapidly lost ground. The lease of St. Dunstan's was surrendered in 1882. An unsuccessful attempt was made to carry on at St. Gabriel's, Canning Town, and other churches, and for a time mission work was done in St. Philip's parish, Plaistow, when it was without a priest. Brother George's health began to decline, and his Community of St. Alban in effect terminated with his death in 1895.

The Community has interest as being composed entirely of laymen, with the associates forming a kind of tertiary group. It prepared the ground in Plaistow for the Society of the Divine Compassion, and the latter avoided the earlier Community's mistakes. 'Those in charge of the mission at St. Philip's' wrote Reginald Tribe, S.D.C. 'are not very fond of clubs and football teams, organisations which are now so popular as items of church work; the mission makes very few appeals that are not directly religious, and clubs scarcely come under this category.'[7] The writer added that at St. Philip's starving men and women were 'made almost to forget their troubles in the knowledge that it scarcely matters what our bodies suffer if we keep our souls from harm.'[8]

It has already been related how Fr. Adderley, as priest-in-charge of St. Philip's mission church, Plaistow, attracted Henry Chappel and Henry Ernest Hardy to form the Society of the Divine Compassion in 1894. It is appropriate to speak briefly of his two associates on whom so much of the future of the community was to depend.

4. ibid.
5. ibid.
6. ibid.
7. ibid., p. 27.
8. ibid., p. 28.

Henry Chappel was born in 1867, the son of Canon Chappel, Rector of Camborne in Cornwall. He was educated at Marlborough and Exeter College, Oxford. He played rugger at Oxford, and retained an interest in rugger and cricket to the end of his life. He was also a keen walker. His 'muscular Christianity' was not out of place at Plaistow. If ever trouble broke on the streets, the appearance of Fr. Chappel was usually sufficient to restore order. He was ordained in 1891 by Randall Davidson, then Bishop of Rochester, and began his ministry at the Cheltenham College Mission in Nunhead. Three years later he joined Adderely at Plaistow. They had already met at Oxford House.

Henry Ernest Hardy is better known under the name he took in religion, Fr. Andrew. It was Fr. Chappel, his senior, who was known as Fr. Henry. Hardy was born on 7 January 1869 at Kasauli, India, his father being a colonel in the Indian army. Through his mother, Fr. Andrew was descended from a sister of Nicholas Ferrar of Little Gidding.[9] His home background was Evangelical, and like Adderley he sought to blend the best in the Evangelical and Anglo-Catholic traditions. For a short time he was at school at Clifton College before studying art – painting always remained one of his interests. In 1888, he went up to Keble College, Oxford, where he took a fourth in Theology, his studies hampered by hay-fever. It was through A. F. Winnington-Ingram and Oxford House that he met Adderley and Chappel. He went to Ely Theological College at Easter 1893. He had not finished reading for ordination when he joined the retreat at Pusey House in January 1894, but was already committed to the Community which was then formed. He joined his colleagues at Plaistow two months later on 26 March 1894. He was more closely identified with the Society of the Divine Compassion than any other man. He was twice to hold office as Superior (1912–16 and 1924–35) and was to serve the Community in Rhodesia as well as in England. It survived him by only six years. The full story of his life is recounted in Kathleen Burne's biography, and his personality still lives in the letters which she edited.

The history of the Society may conveniently be divided at 1914. Until the First World War, the leading figures in the Community were James Adderley, Henry Chappel and William Sirr, who between them held the office of Superior from 1894 to 1912. By 1914, however, Adderley had left the Community, Chappel was dead and Sirr was already turning towards the contemplative life. In the period after the First World War, the leading figures in the Community were Fr. Andrew and Arthur Carus-Wilson, better known as Fr. Barnabas.

After only three and a half years, a rift developed between the

9. Kathleen E. Burne, *The Life and Letters of Father Andrew, S.D.C.* (1948).

founder and his two original colleagues. Peter Anson's comment on Adderley's departure has already been quoted,[10] but this rift can be looked at in several ways. Soon after he left the Community, Adderley wrote to them (September 1897): 'Immediately that it became evident to me that I could not satisfactorily develop the Community life if it was to be in direct connection with the parish I communicated my feelings to my brothers in Chapter.'[11] In other words, the conflict was not between social conscience and the religious life, but between the religious life and the work of the parish. This is confirmed by his adding: 'I believe the Church of England has no need of more parochial developments, but has very great need of broader activity on non-parochial lines. The Oxford House is the greatest proof of this.' Even before this, in 1895–96, Adderley had made three attempts to move and resettle the Community: to the rural parish of Ufford, where he was offered the rectory, to Walthamstow, and – the most interesting possibility – to join Fr. Kelly of Kelham as the Home Mission of the Society of the Sacred Mission. None of these proposals had the support of his Chapter, and Fr. Adderley decided to withdraw from the community he had founded. The Society of the Divine Compassion and later the Brotherhood of the Holy Cross were to discover the difficulty of training novices and nurturing the religious life in a busy slum parish. Under Fr. Chappel and Fr. Andrew, the Society was destined to have over fifty years' close link with St. Philip's, Plaistow, and much of its special character came from its parochial work, but it is possible that the connection in the long run inhibited the growth and survival of the Community. Though Fr. Adderley was to spend nearly his entire career as a parish priest, he was not alone in seeing the Church of England's need for something beyond the parochial ministry.[12]

The work of the Society in Plaistow had been accompanied by that of a Sisterhood under Gertrude Bromby (Sister Gertrude) who greatly admired Fr. Adderley. When he left, the Sisters also withdrew, and Sister Gertrude wrote to Fr. Chappel in no uncertain manner:

> The Superior's Office is a most sacred one, and . . . God directs him, though mistakes may be made, into paths He knows best for the community . . . I started my life among you all trusting in you *all* equally and believing fully in Fr. Adderley's powers to guide us as a society and in his gt. holiness of life . . . a Superior of a new order especially, is indeed handicapped when his novices' want of

10. See Chapter 4.
11. S.D.C. Chapter Minute Book 20/9/1897 (SDC). In this chapter, references to the first minute book except where otherwise stated.
12. Similar views have been expressed to the author by an Anglican Benedictine and a suffragan bishop.

faith and trust, prevent his carrying out a conceived plan for his order, which he believes God has set before him. I am sure we can trust ourselves to God and that He will give to Father Adderley sometime in the future those He knows will support and help him . . . My sisters unanimously agree with what I have written.[13]

Sister Gertrude's subsequent career is traced in the chapter on the Sisterhood of the Incarnation of the Eternal Son, a Community which settled in Fr. Adderley's parish of Saltley.

In fact, the future lay with the surviving members of the Society of the Divine Compassion, not with any future experiments of Fr. Adderley. The survival of the Community after the withdrawal of both the founder and the Sisterhood was the achievement of Fr. Chappel more than anyone. He had already taken over charge of St. Philip's from Adderley, and combined this with the duties of Superior of the Community from 1897 to 1906. He continued to take care of the church until his death in 1913. The *In Memoriam* published in October 1913 gives the picture of a hard-working but unimaginative parish priest. He was described as 'extremely serious'. He was absolutely faithful in his daily attendance at the Eucharist and the Divine Office.

He was a man of blameless and absolutely virgin life. His life had no dark chapter in it, one might say, no soiled pages. A teetotaller from boyhood, he had never known the taste of tobacco, he had never indulged the smallest bet, no profane or questionable word ever passed his lips. His interests were always wholesome, usually serious, latterly entirely religious, he had no hobbies, and despised holidays.[14]

One may wonder whether the contempt for relaxation did not hasten his death at the comparatively early age of 46. It was also noted that 'Colour and form had no meaning for him.' This lack of an artistic gift was in strong contrast with Fr. Andrew, and in a different way, James Adderley. The *In Memoriam* in the *Church Times* described him as 'First a Religious, secondly a mission priest'.[15] It should probably be the other way round. Not only did the poor of the parish throng St. Philip's church (described in the press as 'an ugly building') for the funeral, but the streets themselves were crowded, the shops put up black shutters and the Dockers' Union laid flowers.[16] This was a tribute to Fr. Chappel's gift of conveying great truth in simple and clear language

13. SDC 17/9/1897.
14. *In Memoriam Henry Rivington Chappel*, published by Whitwell Press (1913).
15. *Church Times* 24/10/13.
16. Letter of Fr. Andrew to *Stratford Express* 25/10/13.

and his pastoral care in especial for working class men and boys. He was surely in the great tradition of Anglo-Catholic slum priests.

The years down to 1914 were ones of consolidation and expansion for the Society. It became fully established as a religious community when Father Chappel and Father Andrew, who had hitherto been in temporary vows, were professed in 1899. The Chapter Minute Book records a steady stream of young men, both priests and laymen, who came to test their vocation with the Community. Many left, but enough became fully professed for the Society to take on extra duties. It took on the East London cemetery as a 'corporal act of mercy'. In the smallpox epidemic of 1901–02, ten members of the Society at various times ministered at the Dagenham Isolation Hospital, and in fact undertook most of the Anglican chaplaincy work there.

The first venture overseas came in 1904 when Brother John Mark, a certificated teacher, was sent to St. Mary's College, Thlotse Heights in South Africa. He was ordained by the Bishop of Bloemfontein (A. Chandler), and attempted to gather a community of the Society from local recruits. This was not a success, and one of the first duties of Fr. William Sirr as Superior in 1906 was to visit South Africa and withdraw Fr. John Mark. 'The Society sincerely hopes that it has only retired to leap again,'[17] was their comment in 1908.

In 1905, the Society purchased Potter's Farm at Stanford-le-Hope, Essex. This was a better site than the mother house at Plaistow for training novices, set as it was in peaceful countryside. It also served as a place of refreshment and retirement for the community, and it was here that Fr. Chappel died in 1913. The minimum expense was undertaken in converting the buildings; the calving sheds became cells, the stable a chapel.[18]

The parochial ministry in Plaistow itself was carried out in the widest possible way. From early days, there was a tradition of Monday night meetings in the 'Iron Rooms' as they were called, at which anything from 40 to 150 men might be present. The aim was to stimulate thought and discussion.[19] Fr. Andrew's particular genius was in the production of the 'Bethlehem Tableaux'. 'Simple people very often learn through their eyes better than through their ears.'[20] The tableaux were shown for three nights at Canning Town Public Hall, and also in Putney, Dulwich, Romford and Ilford, and at the Union workhouse at Leytonstone. About 4,000 people might see a particular production. Fr. Andrew also wrote a nativity play, *The Hope of the World*, which was produced at the Old Vic in 1919–20. If he had not

17. FR p. 9. For William Sirr see Chapter 7.
18. FR p. 12.
19. FR p. 4.
20. ibid. p. 7.

been a religious, Fr. Andrew might well have had a distinguished career in the theatre. He was for a time Chaplain to the Theatre Girls' Club.[21]

Despite the inherent difficulties, a balance was struck between parochial duties and the religious life. Fr. Chappel had for a time combined his parochial duties with those of Superior, but in 1908, Fr. Sirr laid it down that both Plaistow and Stanford should have a resident Superior who did not have duties outside. The first ones to be elected were Br. Raphael (Plaistow) and Br. Edwyn (Stanford).[22] This was one opportunity for the lay members to assume greater responsibility. The whole work of the Society was an attempt to live out an ideal. Part of the vision was the interrelation of prayer and work. 'The sacrificial aspect must come first. It is no good to distribute unconsecrated bread to the people; the life must be lifted up before it is given out.'[23] Another part of the vision was to link St. Francis to the twentieth century:

> St. Francis embraced poverty literally. The need of this age is to emphasise the dignity of labour – not to beg with the beggar, but to work with the worker. Moreover, to do what can be done to ensure that all have the opportunity to work, and to work under righteous conditions. Love for the poor – or rather the oppressed and starving – is best expressed in helping them into work, and by example, influencing them to do the work conscientiously, as for God.[24]

Practical examples of their ideal were the Whitwell Press run by the Brothers and a shop where Br. Philip opened a watchmaking business with an apprentice.[25] Ordained members of the Society preached in other parishes and helped out their fellow clergy in Plaistow and around Stanford-le-Hope.[26] For taking services, they expected the usual fees, though these were returned where clergy were poor.[27]

One truly Franciscan work undertaken by the Society was charge of the Homes of St. Giles at East Hanningfield, Essex, assisting the Sisterhood of St. Giles in the care of leprosy patients.[28] But already before 1914, the Society was finding its resources strained. In 1903, Fr. Chappel declined becoming Chaplain to the Sisters of the Holy

21. Burne, op. cit., p. 52.
22. SDC 19/8/08, 2/9/08, 6/10/09, 20/4/10.
23. FR p. 7.
24. ibid., p. 10.
25. SDC 11/9/01 et passim.
26. FR p. 12.
27. SDC 28/3/06.
28. Anson, op. cit., p. 160. For the Community of St. Giles see below, Chapter 9.

45

Childhood because of the pressure of his existing duties,[29] and the venture at Thlotse failed partly because no Brothers could be spared to support Fr. John Mark.[30] Nevertheless, in 1914 the Society undertook to provide Chaplains for the Community of the Holy Name and for the House of Prayer at Pleshey.[31] In 1913, a house was offered to the Society in St. Jude's parish, Bristol, and Fr. Sirr was sent there. In April 1915, however, he withdrew, and the Society did not replace him.[32] Early in 1914, an American priest approached the Society wishing it to train novices for a Franciscan community he wished to found in the U.S.A., but the Chapter felt unable to undertake this.[33]

An important part in the Community was played between 1902 and 1912 by Fr. William Sirr. He ran a club in the Community House for confirmation boys, and weekly meetings called 'Thoughts for Thinking Men'.[34] In the years 1906–12, he was Superior. He became something of a national figure in May 1906 when he joined the procession of the unemployed, mostly dockers, in their march from the Embankment to Hyde Park.[35] Fr. Sirr's political views were strongly left-wing, something which was not true of all members of the Society. Although he was a distinguished member of the Society for ten years, it is possible that Fr. Sirr never felt completely fulfilled in this community. He had at one time the wish to join Fr. John Mark at Thlotse, but about 1911 he began strongly to feel the call to a life of prayer, and in the following year began the course which was to lead him to Glasshampton. (See Chapter 7.)

In 1914, there were fourteen professed members of the Society. The experience of twenty years had stabilised the life of the Community, and was important for the whole religious life in the Church of England, for apart from the Cowley Fathers, the other communities of men were as recent as the Society of the Divine Compassion. A number of men had tested their vocation who were quite unsuited to be religious; abrupt departure, secession to Rome and actual dishonesty occurred, and caused the Society to consider its discipline very carefully. In 1907, Br. Paul asked in chapter whether novices should be allowed to take vows; 'He thought the constant breaking or dispensation tended to lessen the solemnity of all vows.'[36] Fr. Chappel, however, took the view that vows were a great help to novices and

29. SDC 4/6/14.
30. ibid. 27/2/06.
31. ibid. 4/6/14. For the part played by CHN in forming the Second Order see Chapter 26. The house at Pleshey is now a retreat house.
32. SDC 30/4/15, 4/2/16.
33. ibid. 12/2/14. Possibly Fr. Joseph, who visited S.D.C. in 1914.
34. Anson, op. cit., p. 157.
35. ibid.
36. SDC 8/5/07.

gave them stability. The matter continued to raise discussion and Fr. Chappel was asked to present a paper to the chapter on 5 August 1908. He made three points of great importance: the founders of the Society had specified five years as a time of testing; candidates should be at least thirty years of age; and the Bishop of St. Alban's should have power to dispense from vows – a power which subsequently passed to the Bishop of Colchester (Henry Frank Johnson) when he became Warden. The Bishop (Edgar Jacob) exercised his power with discretion and sometimes with reluctance. Three of those dispensed had taken vows under thirty. Fr. Chappel was asked to draw up a solemn declaration on the indissolubility of vows which the professed members were to sign, which Fr. Andrew redrafted before it was accepted by the Chapter.[37] Many communities in recent years have had to re-examine the same questions.

The procedure for electing the Superior had already been decided – Fr. Andrew drew up a scheme which was accepted in 1905. The Superior was to be elected by all professed members of the Society, those overseas being allowed a postal vote. If there was no clear majority on the first vote, there was to be a second vote to decide between the two top candidates. The election for Superior took place annually at the meeting before St. Francistide – 4 October. Though, as has been noted, the Society did not begin by being specifically Franciscan, the significance of this feast shows that it had become so by 1905. Under this procedure, Superiors were re-elected to make a reasonable but not permanent tenure of office. The Superiors of the Society of the Divine Compassion were as follows:

1894–97: Fr. James Adderley
1897–1906: Fr. Henry Chappel
1906–12: Fr. William Sirr
1912–16: Fr. Andrew
1916–18: Fr. George
1918–24: Fr. Barnabas
1924–35: Fr. Andrew
1935–46: Fr. Barnabas
1946–52: Fr. Edward

It was also laid down in 1905 that before being made novice, Brothers should hand over a statement of all their worldly possessions, and should have no part in administering them during the noviciate.[38] Difficulties could arise over the personal possessions of Brothers who left the Society.[39]

37. ibid. 19/8/08, 2/9/08.
38. ibid. 1/2/05.
39. As happened with Fr. Adderley himself.

The Society had begun life in Meredith Street, Plaistow, but in 1896 they moved to a larger house at 42 Balaam Street near where the Community of St. Alban had once lived. In 1907, they were able to purchase this house for £1,100 – a considerable sum in those days – and raised the money through an appeal launched in the *Church Times*.[40] The property was to be held in trust for the Community, the usual practice with religious orders. On 8 September 1908, the house was blessed. The Community were against building a 'permanent house',[41] preferring, as at Stanford-le-Hope, to adapt existing buildings. Repairs totalling £235–18–5d. were carried out in 1911,[42] but practical simplicity was the key-note, as is suggested by the installation of a gas radiator in 1917 'to warm the house in very cold or damp weather'.[43] A doctor or dietician was to be consulted on a scheme for healthy feeding.[44] Novices wore a Sarum cassock, with black cord and one knot with no linen collar. They wore cloaks with collar. Hats were not normally to be worn except with the Superior's permission, and then were to be of clerical cut, of felt and without laces.[45]

The Society was fortunate in having, during its formative years, a number of judicious friends. Among these were Dr. Festing, Bishop of St. Alban's who 'ever since the inception of the Society had taken a fatherly interest in its affairs'[46] and his successor Bishop Jacob. Mention must be made of the Bishop of Colchester, their first Warden, and his successors Canon Randolph and Fr. Frere of Mirfield. Not least, the Cowley Fathers were always available with advice on many subjects, not only specifically religious ones, but practical matters such as whether members should vote in a General Election.[47] With the guidance of such counsellors, the Society came of age, and was able to survive the strains imposed upon it by the First World War.

40. SDC 16/10/07, 20/11/07.
41. ibid. 30/9/08.
42. ibid. 13/12/11.
43. ibid. II f. 6 24/10/17.
44. ibid. (I) 2/7/13.
45. Ibid. 8/1/14.
46. Anson, op. cit., p. 156.
47. The question was raised by Fr. John Mark at the time of the General Election of January 1910 when Lloyd George's budget and reform of the House of Lords were hotly discussed. The Cowley Fathers' answer is not recorded.

6

The Society of the Divine Compassion
1914–52

The Great War of 1914–18 subjected the whole social life of Europe
to unprecedented stress. For a religious community of men in the
Church of England, the stresses were particularly severe, as the way
of life was still relatively new and uncertain. Nevertheless, the Society
of the Divine Compassion, like the contemporary communities at Mirfield and Kelham and the older society at Cowley, adjusted and survived. The first challenge of the war was in the spirit of the Society –
to accommodate eleven Belgian refugees, five at Plaistow and six at
Stanford-le-Hope.[1] The general expectation that the War, though severe, would not be protracted, comes over in the fact that the Bishop
of Chelmsford gave permission late in 1914 for a permanent church to
be built for St. Philip's parish.[2] But the strain on personal loyalty soon
began to be apparent. One Brother, who had already been restless
before the war, enlisted in the R.A.M.C. without the consent of the
Superior.[3] After the war, he wished to return, and was allowed to do
so, but as a postulant.[4]

In May 1915, the Chapter 'considered what might be the duty of
the Community to the Country in the case of a demand for national
service or conscription.'[5] The matter was discussed at several Chapter
meetings that year and advice was sought from other religious communities. On 27 October

> the Brethren were not able to come to any further decision [regard-
> ing the effect of the European crisis] than that attitude of submission
> to the discipline of perplexity which was the point of arrival in the
> last Chapter.[6]

1. SDC (I) 11/11/14.
2. ibid. 16/12/14. John Watts-Ditchfield became first Bishop of Chelmsford in 1914.
   Previously, Plaistow had been in the diocese of St. Alban's.
3. ibid. 2/2/15.
4. ibid. (II) 29/11/18, 26/6/19.
5. ibid. (I) 31/5/15.
6. ibid. 27/10/15.

The honest doubt which these words convey are more deeply impressive than any decision either way could have been. When conscription was introduced, it posed particular problems for the unordained religious. Brother Paul claimed to be considered as a 'minister of religion', and the Community supported his claim to the Registration Authorities on the grounds that he was bound by life vows long before the war to a service that was strictly ministerial – 'to serve God in the poor and suffering.'[7] The tribunal which heard his case granted exemption on condition that he did work of national importance.[8] He seems to have become unsettled, because early in 1919 he was released from his vows.[9] The war, however, did not disrupt the life of the Community, and in October 1917, four novices, two priests and two laymen, were admitted to vows.[10] In the air-raid of 19–20 May 1918, the Community House was badly damaged, and the furniture had to be stored.[11] Nevertheless, repair work was soon put in hand. The peace soon brought light relief. Peace celebrations at Stanford-le-Hope cost twice the sum raised, and the Community were soon complaining, not of the disruption by German raiders, but by children ringing the door-bell and running away.[12] In 1920, two homeless Australian boys were taken on at Stanford at the request of the Fellowship of Reconciliation[13] – a reminder of the continuing unsettlement caused by the war. During the post-war fuel shortage, the Community gave away some of its limited stock of coal to the sick.[14] Before turning from the Great War and its consequences, some words spoken by Fr. George (elected Superior in 1916) may be recalled: 'The Christianity of Nations is on its trial and in consequence that of each professing Christian. What shall be for any nation "after the war" we dare not attempt to predict. But we can and must ask ourselves, What am I now?'[15]

Several points, minor in themselves, reflect the concern to stabilise community life after the war. In 1920, the Superior (Fr. Barnabas) consulted the Bishop over the Lenten fast, proposing that Wednesdays and Fridays should be 'non-meat days' and that porridge and no bacon should be served for breakfast. The Bishop approved this dispensation from the full fast.[16] But fasting was regarded as an important part of the rule, and the Warden, Bishop Frere, at a later date stressed

7. ibid. (II) 10/1/18.
8. ibid. 16/9/18.
9. ibid. 8/1/19.
10. ibid. 13/9/17.
11. ibid. 27/5/18.
12. ibid. 24/9/19.
13. ibid. 15/12/20.
14. ibid.
15. Great Chapter Minute Book (Gt. Chap.) 4/10/17.
16. SDC (II) 9/2/20, 21/3/27.

that the customs of the Community ought to be observed.[17] But the Community kept a balanced outlook. In 1920, a doctor had advised 'that the Community is not fed properly', and the Superior took consultation over the diet.[18] The same year, night watches were introduced at Stanford-le-Hope. The Brethren at East Hanningfield assisted in keeping the watch by day.[19]

Since the turn of the century, the Whitwell Press had been an important part of the Community's work. From time to time, however, doubts arose as to whether to print for profit was in accordance with the principles of the Society. In 1912, the question was raised as to whether it constituted 'spiritual work', but it was dismissed.[20] Four years later, Hewlett Johnson (later to be well known as the 'Red Dean' of Canterbury) was consulted, and suggested that 'when the time was ripe' the press should be handed over to an association 'to be run on ideal lines.'[21] After the war, Brother Edward declared:

> If all this profit has been made by the workers, the Community has no right to its disposal . . . We should be more morally right in first seeing that a proportion, and that a liberal one, of the profits should be distributed amongst those who have earned them, as theirs by right.[22]

A resolution was passed to close the press.

The controversy suggests that since its origins, the Community as a whole had become steadily more socialistic in outlook. Fr. Barnabas (elected Superior in 1918) underlined this attitude when he said:

> Industrial unrest calls our attention to what the Rule says on Chastity about behaving "as strict followers of Christ in every detail of our ordinary life". However unqualified we feel to speak on labour questions our Community should be doing pioneer work in that direction.

He went on to express thankfulness for the growing bond of friendship between the Community and the dockers.[23] He added that the Society stood for three things:

1. The Gospel of applied Christianity;
2. A call to a limited area (i.e. St. Philip's);
3. The Religious Life in itself,

17. Gt. Chap. 6/10/37.
18. ibid. 7/1/20.
19. SDC (II) 11/5/20.
20. Gt. Chap. 24/4/12.
21. ibid. 3/5/16.
22. ibid. 12/2/19.
23. ibid. 8/10/19.

and these three should be strands in a strong cord. He concluded: 'Only by aggressive work in the direction of social righteousness would the growth of the Community be possible.' The order of priorities given by Fr. Barnabas marked out the course the Society was to follow under his leadership. Concern for the needs of the world prompted discussion in 1922 as to whether one of the brethren should be released to work among the starving in Russia, the victims of the Revolution and Civil War. The idea was not deemed practical, but one Brother suggested that the Community should move to a smaller house to release someone for this work. On one occasion, the Chapter voted £10 to help the Russian nuns in Palestine who were, of course, of the émigrée tradition.[24]

Some attention too was given to revising the Constitution. Even before the war, some concern had been felt about the government of the Society. By decisions reached in 1911, the Great Chapter had the final say in all matters not affecting the rule. With regard to the latter, a two-thirds majority was sufficient, subject to the approval of the Warden. If there were a clash between the Chapter (Executive) and the Great Chapter, the matter was to be suspended for six months and then decided by the Warden. In electing a Superior, a clear majority of one vote over all other candidates was deemed sufficient, but no candidate could vote for himself. The Chapter's powers were defined as electing the Warden, appointing the Bursar and altering the rule.[25] At least one of the Brethren felt that the two-tier arrangement of Chapters led to government by an oligarchy, and it was decided that the Chapter should never have less than seven members – half the number of the Brethren then professed.[26] In 1919, the names were changed: the Great Chapter, consisting of all the professed Brethren, became the Chapter, while the former Chapter was renamed the Superior's Council, with four members elected by the Community and two nominated by the Superior.[27] It is not clear, however, whether the Superior's Council had a constitutional function apart from advising the Superior. The position of non-ordained Brethren in the Community came under discussion, and in 1923 the idea was suggested, but not followed, of having two distinct but equal congregations, of priests and lay brethren.[28] Numbers in the Community declined in the 1920s, and in 1926 all the brethren remaining in England became members of the

24. SDC (II) 5/4/22, Gt. Chap. 7/1/42.
25. Gt. Chap. 22/5/11, 26/6/12.
26. ibid. 26/6/12.
27. ibid. 9/4/19.
28. ibid. 4/4/23.

Superior's Council.[29] Meetings of the Chapter ceased to be minuted after 1927.

Fr. George, Superior for two years 1916–18 died in April 1922, and his passing was keenly felt by the Community. Among his many gifts were his knowledge of the Classics and his musicianship. Fr. Andrew was Novice Master at Stanford-le-Hope in 1906–07, but apart from this and his time in Rhodesia, his life in the Community was centred entirely on Plaistow. His two terms as Superior (1912–16, 1924–35) have already been noted. His first term ended when he became Priest-in-charge of St. Philip's in October 1916, and he remained in charge of the parish until his death thirty years later. This remarkable period of service was combined with his second term as Superior and the sixteen months he spent in Rhodesia in 1932–33. He also saw the parish through the whole of the Second World War. Like Fr. Chappel, he was a great East End parish priest, the greatness of the two men coming across in their diversity. As his letters show, he was a great spiritual counsellor, and it is hardly surprising that he was much in demand to conduct retreats. His gift for painting, as well as for poetry and drama, made him an especially lovable person. The combination of Anglo-Catholic and Evangelical elements in his spirituality is borne out by a letter he wrote in 1900:

> The very illogical position of holding extreme Catholic views about the Sacraments and very broad Evangelical views about the love of God and loving to live the life of a Friar, is the only position in which I have ever found rest. Whenever I have tried . . . to be less 'high' or . . . less 'low', I have always lost the content of soul which is, I believe, a real symptom that one is abiding in Christ.[30]

Fr. Barnabas was five years younger than Fr. Andrew. After graduating at the St. Catharine's Society in Oxford, he served curacies in Lincolnshire, Kent and Southwark before joining the Society of the Divine Compassion in 1909;[31] he remained with the Society for the rest of his life. He was probably more of a religious and less of a parish priest than Fr. Chappel and Fr. Andrew. As well as twice serving the Community as Superior, much of his most important work was done as Novice Master and Prior at Stanford-le-Hope. This tribute was paid to him on his death:

> He himself could never have had the slightest idea of the degree of personal dedication he had reached. But others knew: in the chapel silence, on saint's–day picnics, weeding the drive, bathing in the

29. ibid. 5/10/26.
30. Quoted in Burne, p. 90.
31. *Crockford*, under Carus-Wilson, Arthur

Thames, counselling in the confessional, one was aware that there was within him no division in his allegiance to Christ.[32]

Mention should be made of Vernon Johnson, who was one of the most colourful members of the Community during the Great War and the 1920s. Vernon Cecil Johnson was a graduate of Trinity College, Oxford, and after training at Ely Theological College, he was ordained to a curacy at St. Martin's, Brighton, in 1910. After three years, he joined the Society of the Divine Compassion in 1913 and in 1924 became Chaplain at Stanford-le-Hope. He wrote several spiritual books at that time – *Confession and Absolution* (1924), *Happiness* (1926), *The Heart of Religion* (1927) and *Self-Expression* (on prayer, 1928). In 1924, he read the autobiography of St. Thérèse of Lisieux, and this moved him so deeply that he made a private pilgrimage to Lisieux in 1925. He returned in 1926, and his reflections led him to see behind her quiet and saintly acceptance of suffering the assurance of an infallible Church and Papacy. As he related in *One Lord, One Faith* (1930) it was this which led him to go over to Rome. He was conscious that his decision would cause pain to many of his friends, and his defence of the Papal claims provoked Eric Milner-White and Wilfred Knox of the Oratory of the Good Shepherd to reply with *One God and Father of All* which was answered in turn by G. J. Macgillivray in *Father Vernon and his Critics*. Fr. Vernon believed that he had been led into the Roman obedience through the prayers of St. Thérèse (having first set foot in Lisieux on the day of her canonisation) and his devotion to her led to his writing several books about her, the most important being *Spiritual Childhood* (1953).

The stature of Fr. Barnabas is enhanced by the fact that his time as Superior, particularly his second term, was a period when the Community was already entering difficult days, and it was his responsibility in the end to hand over its work to others. Fr. Andrew had misgivings over the novitiate, as to whether it repressed or really developed the character of the novice.[33] In 1930, the situation was reported on 'happily', but in 1934 the novitiate was down to one – and he was showing signs of feeling unsettled – in 1937 there were no novices and young men were showing each year less inclination to come forward.[34] The lack of new recruits had an unsettling effect on existing members of the Community. One sought to withdraw from work at St. Philip's; another, a lay brother, sought permission to proceed to Holy Orders lest the Community should collapse and leave him 'hanging in the

32. Obituary, *Church Times* 14/2/58.
33. Gt. Chap. 5/1/27.
34. ibid. 16/8/30, 4/4/34, 9/8/37.

air'.[35] The Community did not encourage his aspirations. It was with this element of uncertainty that the Community entered the Second World War, which was bound not to be a good time for recruitment. After the war, men did offer themselves again, and it was proposed at one stage to reduce the novitiate from five years to two.[36] But numbers never picked up again, and by the late 1940s the Society had become an aging, even a dying community.

Jack Putterill in his autobiography recalls how he might at one time have joined the Community. During the First World War, when he was still uncertain about his life's work, he says:

> I thought I would seek out the Society of the Divine Compassion and possibly enter this community, which I had heard had socialist principles. So I went down to Plaistow and found their little church in Balaam Street and after High Mass I stayed behind and tried to discuss the matter with one of the brothers. This came to nothing.[37]

Jack Putterill might have made a colourful recruit to the Community, but the Church would then have lost his remarkable ministry at Thaxted. He became a near neighbour of the Community in 1937 as Vicar of St. Andrew's, Plaistow. In 1942 he returned to Thaxted to assist his ailing father-in-law, Conrad Noel, and asked the Community to take temporary charge of St. Andrew's, but this they felt unable to do.[38]

Despite the demands on their limited manpower, the Society did for a time maintain a presence in the mission field in Africa. The brief period at Thlotse Heights, Basutoland, has already been referred to. After the 1914–18 War, Brother Chad went out to work alongside the Mirfield Fathers at Penhalonga, Rhodesia. In 1923, it was decided to send out Brother Stephen also. In 1927, there was a community of Fr. Lawrence, Brother Chad and Brother James (who had replaced Brother Stephen).[39] There was hope that a community could really establish itself which would recruit locally and ultimately become one of African Franciscans. In 1927, they sought permission from the Mother House to receive aspirants, admit to a special novitiate, and receive the annual vows of such as were elected there. Permission was only granted to receive aspirants, and in 1928 it was ruled that the brethren in Africa did not constitute a Chapter.[40] Fr. Lawrence was for a time their only priest. Brother Chad hoped to be ordained, and

35. ibid. 5/10/38, 8/10/41, 7/1/42.
36. ibid. 1/1/47.
37. Jack Putterill, *Thaxted Quest for Social Justice* (Marlow 1977), p. 13.
38. Gt. Chap. 21/5/42.
39. ibid. 20/8/21, 25/8/23, 5/1/27.
40. ibid. 4/1/28.

had had aspirations towards the priesthood since the war, but the Community did not feel able to recommend him.[41] Fr. Andrew took a great interest in the work, and expressed a wish to go out in 1925, though at that time there was no immediate need for him to go.[42] Fr. Edward visited the brethren in 1931, and Fr. Andrew was there for sixteen months in 1932–33. By that time, the position 'needed very faithful and persevering prayer'.[43] In Rhodesia, Fr. Andrew learned the local language and for the first time drove a car. 'However good any mission work may be,' he said, 'if its maintainance drains the vitality of the Community as a religious Community, the exterior life must be sacrificed for interior values.'[44] This was a theme very dear to his heart. He urged the Brethren 'even if living in Africa and spending their lives on trek to keep as corporate a life' as they could.[45] About a year later he wrote from Rhodesia:

> Whether I can keep some of the S.D.C. out here or not, I cannot yet tell, but I have honestly done my best; if I go home with a broken heart and an empty purse and a chastened soul, that soul is nevertheless a soul at peace, and I have behind me the experience of a year of prayer such as I never expected would be granted me and in which I have found the essential things of my religious life to be more precious than I knew they were.[46]

Fr. Andrew had to return to England for a major operation in 1933, but he said later that his greatest temptation was to remain in Africa and found a new community. His experience in Africa brought about a great change in him; 'one was aware of a great withdrawal.'[47] Although the work of the Society in Africa had to be wound up, it is of note that Brother Stephen later returned to the mission field under the auspices of the Universities Mission to Central Africa.[48]

The 1930s saw a drawing together among the various Franciscan communities. The Society of the Divine Compassion only became involved in its last days, but it had helped to father the younger community at Hilfield. Edward Kelly Evans, better known as Brother Giles, 'sprang from the ranks of S.D.C. in 1913.'[49] It was he who first began to share the life of tramps and who became Warden of the Wayfarers' Home at Hilfield in 1919. He became acquainted with

41. Gt. Chap. 20/4/27.
42. ibid. 15/8/25.
43. ibid. 7/10/31.
44. Quoted in Burne, p. 59.
45. Gt. Chap. 4/1/32.
46. Quoted in Burne, p. 190.
47. ibid. pp. 68, 72.
48. Gt. Chap. 4/10/43.
49. Letter by Herbert Pentin in *Church Times* 28/2/58.

Douglas Downes, and when Brother Giles suffered his breakdown after two years at Hilfield, it was to Brother Douglas that Lord Sandwich turned to carry on the work; and so began the Brotherhood of St. Francis of Assisi. This Community and the Brotherhood of the Holy Cross at Peckham grew up in the 1920s, and in the 1930s came into an informal association called the Fellowship of the Way. Fr. Barnabas represented the Society of the Divine Compassion on this body. But he had reservations about the other communities, saying on one occasion, 'Men want Franciscan work but not a Franciscan life'.[50] Nevertheless, the Society was invited to be represented at meetings of the Franciscan communities.[51] After the Second World War, the house at Stanford-le-Hope was sold to the Brotherhood of the Holy Cross, and the funds in hand were given to St. Philip's Restoration Fund.[52]

Although the 1939–45 War saw the Society declining in numbers and the Brethren advancing in years, it saw some of their most dedicated service. Although not himself an out-and-out pacifist, Fr. Andrew joined the procession to Lambeth Palace in September 1939 to affirm the rights of pacifists in the Church of England.[53] He himself determined to stick to his post at Plaistow. He wrote that during the air-raids, 'I always go into church; it is my duty, I think, to be near the Blessed Sacrament, and it is a very blessed duty.'[54] The church and the parish halls were badly damaged by a bomb in 1940. On 18 November, Fr. Andrew wrote describing the scene:

> I looked into the poor little ruined church. Its roof is split from end to end, some of the windows are boarded up, others are vacant and bare, and the rain was pouring in and great pools of it were shining on the blackened floor. Next door to the church the parish hall . . . is just a pitiful heap of ruins. The parish is full of skeletons of houses from which the souls have fled, for most of my flock are evacuated, and I have to write many letters to them and their country parsons.[55]

The Community found hospitality for worship at St. Andrew's, Fr. Putterill's church. The church was repaired, but in March 1941 it was again badly damaged, by a land-mine. This time, the Community had use of the Nurses' Chapel at the Plaistow Maternity Hospital, and then they were lent a hall by Howard's Road Hospital.[56] Fr. Andrew survived the war by less than a year, dying on 31 March 1946. He

50. Gt. Chap. 8/1/36.
51. ibid. 8/10/41.
52. ibid. 13/8/47, 7/1/48.
53. Anson, op. cit., p. 161. Letter 4/11/39 in Burne.
54. Letter quoted in Burne, pp. 179–80.
55. ibid. pp. 195–96.
56. Gt. Chap. 23/4/41. Anson, op. cit., p. 161.

was succeeded by Fr. Edward, the last Superior of the Community. One of the Society's last works was to prepare the restoration of St. Philip's as a memorial to Fr. Andrew and other past members.

The lack of recruits meant that the Community gradually had to give up long established work. As has been seen, Stanford-le-Hope was relinquished to the Brotherhood of the Holy Cross. The St. Giles' Homes passed to the Sisters of the Sacred Passion.[57] Care of the East London cemetery was given up. But the three priests and two lay-brothers who survived in 1950 still carried on retreats and quiet days, the wardenship of St. Peter's, Woking, and the hospital chaplaincies, as well as the parish work and the watch- and clock-repairing business. By the time of Fr. Edward's death in 1952, the numbers had dropped to two, and if three be the minimum number for a religious community, the Society of the Divine Compassion had ceased to exist. Fr. Barnabas invited the Society of St. Francis to send some friars to help in St. Philip's parish, and Fr. Eric Shipman, Vicar of St. Andrew's, formally invited them to take over.[58] Shortly before his death, Fr. Andrew had said of the Society of St. Francis: 'All that we had hoped for and proposed to do, you seem to be doing. We would have liked it, if we had been able to come closer together in our communities.'[59] One of the first achievements of the Society of St. Francis at Plaistow was to lay the foundation-stone of the new St. Philip's church in February 1954. The new church was consecrated on 15 March 1955. H.R.H. Princess Margaret who had laid the foundation-stone was present at the consecration. The sermon was preached by Fr. Algy Robertson, Guardian of the Society of St. Francis.

The New Testament teaches that in the story of the Church, Christians often reap where others have sown, and sow where others will reap. The Society of the Divine Compassion entered on ground already prepared by the Community of St. Alban, and as Fr. Andrew's words indicate, it was fitting that the Society of St. Francis should take over in turn at Plaistow. For nearly sixty years, the Society of the Divine Compassion ministered at Plaistow, sharing poverty and hardship with their parishioners. As one of the older men's communities in the Church of England, their experience was invaluable to others. Two sometime members of the Community, Brother Giles and Fr. William, broke important new ground where the Society of St. Francis again was ultimately to be the inheritor. Their influence, as will be seen, was important to individualists like A. S. Cripps and Edward Bulstrode.

One can scarcely fail to be conscious that the Society of the Divine Compassion embodied much that was best in Anglicanism.

57. *Church Times* 8/9/50 and below.
58. *Church Times* 20/2/53.
59. S.S.F. Chapter Minute Book 1950–61 pp. 96/8.

Thoroughly committed to the Anglo-Catholic movement, one of the few interruptions to its work was to allow Brethren to attend the Anglo-Catholic Congress.[60] While some of its former members from time to time seceded to Rome, the Community always formally discouraged people from doing so. Fr. Andrew once described Roman Catholicism as a 'spiritual dictatorship' while recognising that it shared some of the advantages as well as disadvantages of dictators.[61] Like many Anglo-Catholics, members of the Society felt uneasy about the establishment of the Church of South India, but discouraged any idea of withdrawing from the Church of England.[62] But if it be true that the Church of England is nothing if not pastoral, the love of souls which was so conspicuous in the ministry of such as Fr. Chappel and Fr. Andrew will remain the Society's greatest memorial.

60. SDC (II) 5/2/23.
61. Burne, op. cit., p. 134.
62. Gt. Chap. 11/4/45.

7

William Sirr

Fr. William Sirr has come to be known as William of Glasshampton from the site in Worcestershire where he attempted to pioneer a contemplative community for men. His earlier training and experience, however, was with the Society of the Divine Compassion, in connection with which he has already been considered.

William Sirr came to the priesthood when he was already in middle life. He spent some years in business before reading to become an Associate of King's College, London. He was ordained in 1897, and served as Curate of All Saints', Camden Town (NW1). Two years later he became Curate of St. Peter's, Vauxhall (SE11) where he remained for three years (1899–1902).[1] He then joined the Society of the Divine Compassion, and in 1906 was elected Superior, holding that office until 1912.

He felt a strong call to the contemplative life. Towards the end of his time as Superior, he became spiritual director to a Miss Butler, a lady who lived as a solitary in Bristol, and his experience in this role strengthened his conviction.[2] Father Andrew, who succeeded him as Superior of the Society of the Divine Compassion, directed him to wait and pray for two years. Then he sent him to test his life as Chaplain to the Sisters of St. Giles at East Hanningfield. In May 1915, he wrote to Fr. Andrew, observing that one essential condition of the monastic life was the complete exclusion of women from the cloister and precincts, something which was quite impossible at East Hanningfield.[3] In the Autumn of 1915, he began six months of strict seclusion under the aegis of the Cowley Fathers. When this period ended, he considered the possibility of living in a cottage at High Easter (Essex) as a 'hermitage', but he returned to live with the Society of the Divine Compassion at East Hanningfield and Stanford-le-Hope. Fr. George, who was Superior 1916–18 did not encourage his desire for the contemplative life, saying that 'profession in a community [involved] a bond to the family of which it becomes a member, the indissolubility

1. Biographical details from *Crockford*.
2. Peter Anson, *Call of the Cloister* (1964) (CC) p. 194.
3. Geoffrey Curtis, C.R., *William of Glasshampton* (1947), p. 48.

of which is the same as that of marriage: one is vowed to it, rather than to the will of God as found within it.'[4] Fr. Barnabas, who was elected Superior in 1918, was more sympathetic, and the Chapter of the Society at last gave its consent.[5]

Fr. William had already found the site for his monastery – the stables of a vanished country house at Glasshampton in Worcestershire. His former protégée Miss Butler left money in 1926 which enabled the necessary alterations to be completed,[6] but Fr. William had managed as best he could since moving there in November 1918. For a time, he lived there alone and in complete poverty. He was at that time nearly sixty,[7] and to begin the contemplative life at that age and in such conditions was a formidable task. He drew up a stern rule. There was to be perpetual and unbroken silence except at worship and as between the Superior and the Brethren. The day was to include five hours manual work, and besides the Divine Office there were to be two hours of mental prayer and intercession.[8] It is said that the Office was recited with 'almost too prayerful slowness'.[9] A number of men tested their vocation sharing this life, but none stayed – ' . . . the majority were the sinful and the failures. Attracted by his personality and compassion, they came not to a *monastery* or a *life* as such, but to the Priest-Religious who had made the monastery.'[10] Fr. William was not a good judge of character – an essential quality in a Superior – but he was a great spiritual counsellor, a kind of *staretz*, consulted by Christian and non-Christian alike.[11] He had a good friend in Ernest Pearce, Bishop of Worcester (1919–31), but rejected his suggestion of joining the Anglican Benedictines who were then at Pershore. They did not fulfil Fr. William's ideal of prayer and manual work. He was quite prepared to carry on alone, fully convinced that an enclosed community of men was the greatest need of the Church of England.[12] As years went by, he sent lay postulants to Cowley or Nashdom (where the Benedictines settled), saying that it was not right for him to receive them at his age as he had no priest-religious with him to carry on when he could no longer do so.[13] He had a special ministry to 'fallen' priests who came to him seeking a way of penitence.

In October 1936, age and ill-health compelled him to give up. He

4. ibid., p. 71.
5. ibid.
6. ibid., pp. 33, 106–07.
7. CC, p. 196.
8. ibid.
9. ibid., pp. 199–200.
10. Fr. Curtis, op. cit., p. 96. Italics original.
11. CC, p. 196.
12. Fr. Curtis, op. cit., p. 131.
13. ibid., p. 133.

retired to the Homes of St. Barnabas at Lingfield (Sussex) where he died in March 1937. One of his most remarkable friendships was with Earl Baldwin, his neighbour in Worcestershire. In 1939, Baldwin was instrumental in arranging for his remains to be removed from Lingfield and reburied at Glasshampton.[14] In 1938, Glasshampton had been purchased by a trust, on condition that it remained a religious house, as a memorial to Fr. William. In 1946, it became a retreat house. Subsequently, it passed into the hands of the Society of St. Francis. It is used now as a house of quiet and contemplation within the Franciscan life, and all novices spend part of their training there. Its present use therefore fulfils at least part of Fr. William's vision.

14. ibid., p. 163.

8

The Society of the Incarnation of the Eternal Son

As well as being the founder of the Society of the Divine Compassion, James Adderley had almost as big a role in establishing a Sisterhood, the Society of the Incarnation of the Eternal Son, and the two communities originally worked side by side. Adderley's part was to inspire and guide the woman around whom the Community grew. This was Gertrude Bromby, daughter of C. H. Bromby, Bishop of Tasmania 1864–83. Her brother, H. B. Bromby, who later became Vicar of All Saints', Clifton, was made Vicar of St. John's, Bethnal Green, in 1885, and Gertrude came to keep house for him. Three years later James Adderley came to live at the Vicarage as Bromby's curate. Gertrude Bromby said nine years later that she had always believed in Adderley's 'great holiness of life'.[1] They had much in common. She too joined the Christian Social Union and was later a keen supporter of the Labour Party. She too was something of a 'Liberal Catholic', which in her case meant that she was more interested in 'practical Christianity' than in either dogma or ritual.[2]

When Adderley went to St. Philip's, Plaistow, in 1893, Miss Bromby moved near-by to 7 Meredith Street. Here she began a remarkable ministry of compassion, visiting the poor, nursing the sick and running a club for boys. Another lady joined her in 1894. The following year, Sister Gertrude, as she then became, received the habit. Development as a community came during the next three years. Three other sisters were clothed in 1896. On the Feast of the Epiphany, 6 January, 1898, Mandell Creighton, Bishop of London, received Gertrude's profession as Mother of the Community. The Sisterhood was very close in spirit to the Society of the Divine Compassion, but the two communities worked alongside each other while retaining their separate identity.[3] The Sisters lived in great poverty, sometimes uncertain how they were

1. Letter 17.9.97. See appendix.
2. CC p. 468.
3. SDC Chapter Minutes 2.7.97.

63

going to pay for the next meal. Nevertheless, their simple dwelling was crowded with poor people coming to them for relief.[4]

Adderley left his community in 1897 and moved from Plaistow to a new ministry in Mayfair. Mother Gertrude and her community followed him. In a letter to Fr. Henry Chappell, (see Appendix I) she made it clear that she stood on principle – for her, the reluctance of the Society to be guided by Fr. Adderley's wishes was 'to disobey the voice of God'.[5] There is little doubt that personal devotion to Fr. Adderley also played its part, however unconsciously, for the Sisterhood was later to follow him from Mayfair to Marylebone and thence to Birmingham. These successive moves created fresh problems for the Sisters. Part of their work in London was to run a hostel for working boys in Munster Square. The two Sisters at the hostel remained in London when the rest moved to Birmingham in 1905. With the Bishop of London's permission, they left the community. Later they went to the mission field in Pondoland where they ran an Anglican boarding school.[6]

It was Bishop Gore who urged the Sisters to move to Birmingham. After five years, they moved in 1910 to a house in Alum Rock Road, Birmingham 8, and here they found a permanent home except for five years in the Second World War when they were bombed out. The Sisters worked in Fr. Adderley's parish, St. Saviour's, Saltley, and in four other parishes. Later, they worked with Adderley at St. Gabriel's, Deritend.[7]

Charles Hare designed a chapel for the Sisters which was dedicated by Bishop Russell Wakefield in 1912 'for the greater glory of God and in honour of St. Francis and St. Clare'. After the move to Birmingham, Mother Gertrude assumed the additional name of Clare. The chapel was in some ways intended as a memorial to her family.[8] D. T. Jenkins has observed that the building of this special chapel is unusual among the Franciscan communities, where the custom has been to adapt existing buildings rather than to build afresh. A Chaplain was appointed to the community in 1913, the Rev. Arthur Herbert Hitchcock.[9]

The Sisterhood was ·the first Franciscan community to work in

4. CC p. 469.
5. Letter 17.9.97.
6. Hilfield archives F. 120.
7. ibid.
8. CC p. 470.
9. Hilfield archives F. 120. Hitchcock is listed in *Crockford* until 1920 as Curate of All Saints', Clifton (from 1900). He was trained at Lichfield Theological College and ordained in 1884 to a curacy at Golden Hill, Staffs. From 1891–97 he was Curate of St. Frideswide's, Poplar, when he probably met Mother Gertrude, though her brother was his vicar at Clifton.

Birmingham.[10] In 1907, they were joined at Saltley by John Hawes, or Brother Jerome (q.v.) as he had become. Fr. Adderley put him in charge of a mission church dedicated to St. Francis. As related elsewhere, for a short time he attempted to establish a community of men in two converted slum cottages as his 'friary'. Not long afterwards he went to the Bahamas, and subsequently went over to Rome.

One of Mother Gertrude's achievements in Birmingham was to open an orphanage where poor boys from the workhouses could be brought up in a Christian environment. The civic authorities were only persuaded with reluctance to support her work. She has been described as a 'real mother' to the hundreds of boys who came into her care.[11] In London and Birmingham, care for poor boys, in club, hostel or orphanage, was a conspicuous part of the Sisters' work. In 1915, they began a new venture – short retreats for working class girls. These took place once a fortnight, the Sisters giving up their cells to the retreatants and sleeping where they could.[12] The spirit of poverty was still very much with them. They could not afford coal in the early days, and one Sister has described them as 'very detached from £.s.d.'[13] The Sisters always aimed to share the poverty of the people among whom they worked. They sought to overcome class distinctions, drawing recruits from all classes and making no differentiation of 'choir' and 'lay' sisters.[14] Mother Gertrude's debt to the Christian Social Union is apparent in her declaration that the community was 'to show by word and deed that it believes our Lord to be the answer to all social questions.' She also said, 'To pray sincerely one should know something about the object or cause prayed for; therefore social conditions must be studied.'[15]

Despite their high ideals and the quality of their work among the poor, the Sisterhood met adversity in Birmingham which in the long run they failed to overcome. Bishop Gore was translated to Oxford in 1911. His successor, Russell Wakefield (1911–24) was also a good friend to the community. It was otherwise with Bishop Barnes (1924–53), who forbade the Sisters to have any 'rebel' priest to celebrate the Eucharist for them – and many Catholic-minded priests in his diocese were driven to become rebels. Worse, he refused to receive the profession of any Sister, and numbers consequently declined.[16] Dr. Barnes later modified his attitude, but the damage was already done.

10. CC p. 470.
11. ibid.
12. Hilfield archives F. 120.
13. ibid.
14. CC p. 471.
15. ibid.
16. Hilfield archives F. 120.

The indomitable Mother Gertrude died in 1930. Her successor, Mother Alice Christine, had been one of the first members of the Community; unfortunately, she developed cancer during her second term of office. During an air raid in November 1940, the convent was hit by a bomb. For the duration of the war, the Sisterhood separated. Two Sisters stayed in Birmingham, some went to Warwick, others to Temple Balsall, where Edward Bulstrode (q.v.) had once found a home. After the war, the community failed to regain its vitality. From 1964, the surviving Sisters were taken under the care of the Community of the Holy Name, Malvern, and lived under their rule.[17]

17. ibid.

9

The Community of St. Giles

Shortly before the Great War, the Government became concerned about the care of the small number of leprosy patients in England, and it has been related in Chapter 5 how the Society of the Divine Compassion, as it became consolidated and began to expand, undertook spiritual responsibility for their care. A charitable trust was established which took on the financial responsibility. A suitable site for a Home was found at East Hanningfield, near Chelmsford, in 1914[1] – a small farm standing on 23 acres of land which offered reasonable seclusion. Three nursing sisters had the actual care of the patients. In time, these were joined by others, not all of them trained nurses, and under the influence of Fr. Andrew and the Community at Plaistow, these women developed the desire to become a religious community.

The settlement was known as St. Giles' Home, and the Sisterhood became the Community of St. Giles. One of the nurses, Sister Clare, became Mother of the Community. They adopted a regular life of prayer, using *Day Hours* as their Office Book, though they made enquiries of the American Order of St. Francis for a suitable breviary (see Chapter 22). But despite the dedicated nature of their work, they were only loosely constituted as a religious community. They kept a simple rule, and renewed their vows annually, but none of the original Sisters had been trained in the religious life, and the later recruits did not go through a proper novitiate. Probably for this reason, a number of nurses came and went. Some, with a genuine vocation to the religious life left to fulfil it in the Roman Catholic Church.

However, there were signs in the 1920s that the Community of St. Giles might become firmly established and begin to expand. It was the only women's community to belong to the Fellowship of the Way, and its Chaplain, Fr. Peter Hardy, represented it on the Chapter of the Fellowship.[2] In 1931, the Sisters discussed with the Brotherhood

1. Peter Anson, CC p. 160.
2. Hilfield Archives C. 600. Peter de Haviland Hardy was a graduate of Hertford College, Oxford, and trained for the ministry at Westcott House, Cambridge. He was Curate of Havant, Hants., 1928–30 and then joined the Brotherhood of St. Francis of Assisi. He was Chaplain of St. Giles' Home 1931–35. He became Vicar of Netley, Hants., in 1935.

of St. Francis of Assisi the possibility of their taking charge of a house in Essex where old and infirm wayfarers could be looked after.[3] Nothing came of this project, and in the years which followed, the problem became not one of expanding in new directions, but of maintaining the work already in hand.

In 1936, only five Sisters remained in the Community. The care of leprosy patients had expanded considerably in twenty years, and had become beyond the capacity of this small Sisterhood. The Trust invited the Community of the Sacred Passion to take over their work. This Sisterhood had been founded in Zanzibar in 1910 under the influence of Bishop Frank Weston and had subsequently moved to Magila on the mainland. In East Africa, they had gained experience in the care of sufferers from leprosy.[4] The Sisters took care of the patients at East Hanningfield, and the five surviving Sisters from the Community of St. Giles were absorbed into the Community of the Sacred Passion. The Trust remained responsible for the buildings, with their heating and lighting. These included the old barn which had been converted into a chapel by Father Andrew and the Brothers from Plaistow.

The Community of St. Giles survived a little over twenty years as a separate religious community. Its work continues in the hands of its successors. The care of those afflicted with leprosy was a special concern of St. Francis. A particular interest will always attach to the Community of St. Giles as an English Sisterhood founded specifically for that work.

3. B.S.F.A. Chapter Minute 20.5.31.
4. CC pp. 529, 581. Peter Anson gives an account of the Community of the Sacred Passion on pp. 581–83.

10

Pioneers and Prophets

1. Arthur Shearly Cripps

Arthur Shearly Cripps was never a religious, nor did he feel a call to the religious life.[1] He was a saintly parish priest and missionary, in contact with the Franciscan pioneers in England, who chose to live a Franciscan life-style among the Africans in Rhodesia (Zimbabwe).

Cripps was born in 1869, the seventh of eight children of a solicitor at Tunbridge Wells (Kent). He was educated at Charterhouse before going up to Trinity College, Oxford, in 1887. There he read Classics Mods. and Modern History. At Oxford, he came under the influence of Charles Gore, and decided to take Holy Orders.[2] He was impressed by the support which Gore and Scott Holland gave to the dockers in the great strike of 1889, and joined the Christian Social Union.

Cripps took his B.A. in 1891 with second class honours. He trained at Cuddesdon, and was ordained in the Diocese of Chichester to serve as Curate of Icklesham near Winchelsea. In 1894, Trinity College presented him to the living of Ford End near Chelmsford. Next year, he met James Adderley who came to conduct a mission in his parish. The two became close friends between 1895 and 1900, sometimes going on 'tramping missions' together.[3] Just before Cripps left for Rhodesia, Adderley preached for him again, and Cripps stayed with him at Saltley in 1906 when he first came home on furlough. Cripps became a Poor Law Guardian between 1898 and 1900, and felt concern for the welfare of tramps. He saw the disastrous effects alcohol could have on them, and this made him a strong teetotaller.[4] Cripps enjoyed some distinction as a poet, and two of his poems from the years 1898–1900 were inspired by saints noted for their compassion for the poor – St. Vincent de Paul and St. Francis of Assisi.

One of Cripps' friends at Oxford had been Frank Weston. Influenced by Adderley and others, Weston went out to Zanzibar in 1898 where

1. Douglas V. Steere, *God's Irregular: Arthur Shearly Cripps* (1973), p. 7.
2. ibid., p. 4.
3. ibid., p. 10.
4. ibid., p. 34.

he was to win fame as Bishop (1908–25). His example probably led Cripps to volunteer for the mission field, and in 1900 the Society for the Propagation of the Gospel sent him out to Mashonaland in Rhodesia.[5] Cripps served as an army chaplain during the Great War, and he again became Rector of Ford End 1926–30. Otherwise, apart from furlough, he spent the rest of his life in Southern Rhodesia (as it was then known) until his death in 1952. He dedicated himself to the service of the Africans. Even before going out, he had been influenced by Olive Schreiner's novel *Trooper Peter Hallett of Mashonaland*. This book depicted Cecil Rhodes as 'the Rhodesian Ahab . . . seizing the vineyard of the poor black Naboth',[6] and it determined him 'to place a few years of his own life in the scale-pan on the side of the African.'[7]

The story of those 'few years' which turned out to be nearly half a century has been told by his biographer Douglas Steere in *God's Irregular*. He struggled against the reduction of land in the native reservations, against injustice to Africans in the courts and ill-treatment of black servants. He came into conflict, not only with the European settlers and the Government of Rhodesia but often with the Church authorities as well. He opposed Government aid for (and therefore control over) Church schools,[8] which was Church policy to make education more widely available. For most of his service 1900–26, Cripps was at the mission station at Wreningham, for a time the only Anglican priest there. When he left, his work was taken over by the Society of the Divine Compassion (q.v.). His very isolation at Wreningham drew him closer to missionaries of other churches – John White, a Methodist, Pastor Liebenburg of the Dutch Reformed Church, and also Roman Catholics. He declared on occasion that he was at heart an Evangelical or even a Quaker, but he recognised that the Church must have some frontiers – 'the river that has no banks is a swamp.'[9]

With the progress of the Ecumenical Movement, his attitude hardly seems very remarkable, but he was far ahead of his time. When he returned to Rhodesia in 1930, it was without official backing and without the licence of his Bishop, E. F. Paget. He worked with the Society of the Divine Compassion at Wreningham until they left in 1933 and later took on a truly Franciscan work looking after a colony of sufferers from venereal disease.[10]

Apart from his work as a missionary and his role as spokesman and

5. ibid., p. 15.
6. ibid.
7. ibid., p. 16.
8. ibid., p. 124.
9. ibid., p. 111.
10. ibid., p. 125.

champion of the Shona people, he impressed his friends and acquaintances by his simple life-style and his vision as a poet. His friend John White felt attracted to him by three things – his devotion to Christ, 'his simple Franciscan life' and his championship of the African.[11] It was White who described Cripps as 'our modern Francis of Assisi – in many respects a worthy successor of that great saint.'[12] White says that 'Year in, year out, he lives as closely as possible to the African mode of life, in all its simplicity, dwelling in an African hut and eating the simple food which Africans usually eat. With an inner joy and peace, he brings happiness out of every discomfort.'[13]

Cripps was a lover of nature. He was inspired by his native Kent,[14] and much of his poetry was inspired by the beautiful countryside in Rhodesia. As English poetry had been nourished by discovery of the Classics, so he hoped that African poetry would be nourished by English classics without losing its true identity. He wrote in his introduction to *Rhodesian Verse 1888–1938* (Oxford 1938):

> Let us Europeans, who love Mother Africa as her loyal guests, try our very best to help her to keep all of hers that is worth keeping! Moreover let us try to show any Africans who have learned our New Learning (if they would seem to have been born Poets) that they would be well advised to shape their songs with the love of their own country in their hearts, and with the noble rhymes and music and dances of their own country running in their heads.[15]

His own poem from that anthology, *A Mashona Husbandman*, recognises the natural dignity of his subject:

> You find him listless; of but little worth
> To drudge for you, and dull to understand?
> Come watch him hoe his own rain-mellowed land –
> See how the man outbulks his body's girth!

Those who regard him as a visionary and a prophet might well quote from *Great Zimbabwe*:[16]

> Thro' all a world His wind is free
> To blow at will man's embers hot:
> In colour-blind perversity
> He gave to us His Vision's glee –

---

11. C. F. Andrews, *John White of Mashonaland* (1935), p. 117.
12. ibid., p. 123.
13. ibid., p. 119.
14. See, for instance, his *Magic Casements* (1905).
15. op. cit., p. 19.
16. Then still only the name of a ruined temple.

Vision our children have forgot,
Vision they yet again may see.

'Will not Providence be providing a Southern Rhodesian Africans'
Poetry Anthology soon – in a very few years' time now?'[17] he asked.

Douglas Steere has used the phrase which more than any captures
his spirit – God's Irregular. He was an unbriefed advocate of the
Shona people, a missionary in his latter years without home support,
a Franciscan with neither habit nor rule. Among the disciples of Gore
and Adderley, he realised their ideals, not in community, but in his
personal life.

2. George Martin

George Martin came from an impeccable clerical background. His
father, also called George, was a Doctor of Divinity and Vicar of St.
Breward near Bodmin (Cornwall). George junior was born in 1864,
and after an education at Blundell's School, Tiverton, he went up to
St. John's College, Cambridge, where he took his B.A. in 1886. Next
year, he was ordained by the Bishop of Truro (George Howard Wilk-
inson) and served as Curate of Duloe near Liskeard (1887–91) and
Marhamchurch near Bude (1891–93). He then was appointed Rector
of Caerhays near St. Austell.[18]

After six years at Caerhays (1893–99), he gave up his living. As a
friend put it, he offered 'all that he was and all that he had to the then
Bishop of London (Mandell Creighton) to become a leader in Church
work among men';[19] more specific details are not available, but 'when
his proposal was refused, he gave himself up to living in the slums of
south-east London, occupying one miserable top attic in the scarcely
habitable purlieus of Southwark'[20] Three addresses for him are on
record – in Blackfriars Road (1901), Maze Pond (1920–30) and the
Bethel Estate (1940).[21] He combined poverty or even squalor with a
life of prayer, rising for his devotions at six o'clock and observing
silence on Fridays for the three hours of the Crucifixion.[22] He neglected
his person and his clothes to the point of making himself unfit for
'ordinary society'. His way of life led many, including Peter Anson,[23]
to conclude that he had parted with his considerable fortune, but when

17. *Rhodesian Verse 1888–1938* (Oxford 1938), p. 16.
18. For biographical details see John Venn and J. H. Venn, *Alumni Cantabrigiensis*.
19. *Church Times*, 27.12.46.
20. ibid.
21. *Crockford*.
22. *Church Times*, 27.12.46.
23. Peter Anson, The Call of the Cloister (CC) (1964), p. 163.

he died in 1946, he left £1,000 to St. John's College to assist students from Cornwall reading for Holy Orders and £22,000 to the Bishop and Mayor of Southwark for the poor of the borough.[24] He supported himself working as a porter at Borough Market, and walked to the hop-fields to work with the East Enders in summer – a ministry where Brother Giles and Edward Bulstrode also pioneered.

On one occasion, he was in trouble with the police when he set light to some scaffolding which had been erected outside a church for spectators to watch a royal progress.[25] In July 1934 when he was 70, he was injured by a lorry and never fully recovered.[26] He spent his old age in a London workhouse, where he shared a large common ward with many unfortunates.[27]

The love which he showed to the poor of Southwark and received in return from them is apparent not only from his obituary and the notice he receives in *The Call of the Cloister* but also in *Alumni Cantabrigiensis*. The last named, often a rather impersonal summary of careers, speaks of 'an influence almost hypnotic and a power for good that was irresistible' which he possessed. 'When the memory of his saintliness and good deeds has perished, there will remain the massive granite cross, which he erected on Dodman Point as a sacred reminder to seamen who pass along the south coast of Cornwall.'[28] Yet so obscure was his life that the *Church Times* was only able to record that he had died 'recently'. Of all those who attempted to follow the Way of St. Francis, none, perhaps, has embraced poverty so completely or for so long as George Martin.

3. John Cyril Hawes

John Cyril Hawes was born on 7 September 1876, the third son of a London solicitor. He was educated at King's School, Canterbury, where one of his contemporaries was Henry Joy Fynes-Clinton, who later became famous as Rector of St. Magnus Martyr, London Bridge. John Hawes was still young when he developed an interest in architecture which never left him. At sixteen, he was articled to a firm of architects in London. Here he first discovered Anglo-Catholicism. His family background was strongly Evangelical, and respect for his family for some time deterred him from going over to Rome. Already at this age he had a sense of vocation, and when he was a young man of

24. *Alumni Cantabrigiensis.*
25. *Church Times*, 27.12.46.
26. *Alumni Cantabrigiensis.*
27. *Church Times*, 27.12.46.
28. ibid.

twenty-two, a sermon at St. Thomas', Regent Street, so moved him that he offered himself for service with the Universities Mission to Central Africa. He was unable to go, on medical grounds.[29]

At this point he encountered James Adderley at the Berkeley Chapel. Adderley introduced him to St. Francis and to Christian Socialism. Hawes read various books on St. Francis, including Sabatier's life, which he read in an evening,[30] and *The Commonwealth*, the Christian Social Union's monthly publication. He also met Wilfred Hornby, former Bishop of Nyasaland, who commissioned him to design a church at Gunnerton in Northumberland. Hawes already felt a calling to the priesthood before this, and Bishop Hornby encouraged him to try taking services and catechism and visiting farms near Gunnerton. In 1901, he persuaded him to begin training at Lincoln Theological College. He was ordained in 1903 to a curacy at the Holy Redeemer, Clerkenwell, again through Bishop Hornby's influence. He was offered a stipend of £150 p.a., but accepted only £90, giving away as much as he could and working among the poor of the parish.[31] He already felt a calling to the Franciscan life. In the parish of the Holy Redeemer, he encountered the Sisters of Bethany who had been working there since 1888. Hawes became friendly with Sister Rosina, and he influenced her and three other sisters in their decision to leave the Sisters of Bethany and found their own community on the lines of the Poor Clares. Sister Rosina and her companions settled at Sculcoates, near Hull (see Chapter 11). In seeking a Franciscan life for men, Hawes naturally became interested in the Society of the Divine Compassion. He disapproved of their wearing a black habit (though this was worn by the Friars Minor Conventual) and their saying the Office in English.[32]

In 1906, Hawes left Clerkenwell and joined Aelred Carlyle at Caldey Island. He had already come across him when his Benedictine Community was at Painsthorpe, Yorks. Abbot Aelred was prepared to train him in the religious life though as a Franciscan, not to join his Community. Hawes' skill as an architect was used to design monastic buildings at Caldey which Hawes nevertheless found too grandiose for his Franciscan tastes.[33] He was clothed as a novice and took the religious name Jerome, but he was allowed to live as a hermit in a limestone cave on Caldey Island. He completed his novitiate at Caldey, but left without being professed (1907). He went first to the Society of the Divine Compassion, but Fr. William Sirr, who was then Superior,

29. Peter Anson, *The Hermit of Cat Island* (1958), p. 7.
30. ibid., p. 9.
31. ibid., p. 14.
32. ibid., p. 17.
33. ibid.

refused to profess him or to accept his probation at Caldey. On St. Francis' Day 1907 he set out on a tramping pilgrimage. He mixed with tramps on the roads and slept in casual wards and common lodging houses. He made his way to Sister Rosina at Hull, and then returned to London.

Next he encountered John Goldie-Taubman, an eccentric squire from Braddan in the Isle of Man, who invited him to become his Domestic Chaplain. Hawes' plan was to use the Chaplain's house, which he 'wasted no time in making as uncomfortable as possible',[34] the site of a new community. Brother Cuthbert, who also had been a novice at Caldey, joined him. Squire Taubman seems to have found his Chaplain rather too much to endure, and Jerome and Cuthbert left and joined Fr. Adderley, then at Saltley, where Jerome (Hawes) became his curate. With Bishop Gore's permission, Hawes made his profession to Adderley. There was, therefore, a real possibility of a new Franciscan community coming into being at Saltley. Cuthbert, however, left and became a priest in the United States. Another postulant came who only stayed a few weeks. Jerome expressed himself 'very disgusted with the ritualistic, socialistic and incipient modernism of most of the clergy at Saltley.'[35] He went off on another tramping pilgrimage, this time round the Black Country, preaching with some success in the open air. Adderley suggested that he should join George Martin (q.v.) at Southwark, but he said, 'I could not bring myself to make such an utter surrender, involving having no church and not being able to celebrate Mass daily . . . I just could not face giving up wearing my brown habit.'[36]

Bishop Hornby again guided him, this time to become Rector of St. Paul, Long Island, Bahamas. He took up his appointment in January 1909. He resumed his Franciscan habit[37] which he had discarded while tramping. Long Island had been devastated by a hurricane, and Bishop Hornby hoped that his architectural skills could be put to good use repairing the damage. In fact, Hawes stayed only two years. He left on 25 January 1911 after keeping the patronal festival. He made his way to the Society of the Atonement at Graymoor, New York (q.v.) which had corporately gone over to Rome. Hawes was received into the Roman obedience on 19 March 1911.[38] The rest of his story has been recounted by Peter Anson in *The Hermit of Cat Island*. He found fulfilment in the Roman Catholic Church for his vocation as a Franciscan and for his skill as an architect, and this must diminish the

34. ibid., p. 23.
35. ibid., p. 25.
36. ibid., p. 26.
37. ibid., p. 28.
38. ibid., p. 33.

regrets over his loss to the Church of England. His career between 1898 and 1911 showed the difficulty for a man with a genuine vocation to the Franciscan life who was unable to accept the framework of an existing community (and at that time the Society of the Divine Compassion was the only Franciscan community for men) and who in practice was unable to carry through the difficulties of launching a new venture in the religious life.

4. Edward Bulstrode

Edward Bulstrode, or Brother Edward as he was known, came from a well-to-do middle class family. He was the fourteenth and youngest child of William and Jane Bulstrode, born in 1885. His grandfather had kept a shop in Marylebone High Street. His father managed a mill in Wandsworth (SW15) and lived in Croydon (Surrey). He also owned a farm in Berkshire. Edward was sent to Haileybury in 1900. He was not a keen games player, and was not happy at school. From Haileybury he went up to Keble College, Oxford, in 1904.

His religious outlook was formed at Oxford. Twice while he was at Keble he visited Oxford House, Bethnal Green, in which Arthur Winnington-Ingram, by then Bishop of London, still took a keen interest. Winnington-Ingram and Oxford House influenced him away from his Evangelical home background in the direction of the Catholic Movement. He came to a spiritual turning-point one Holy Week in his student days, and made his first confession on Easter Eve.[39] He spent more time at Oxford House between going down from Keble in 1907 and beginning his training for the sacred ministry at Ely Theological College the following year. In 1909 he was ordained by Bishop Jacob of St. Alban's and became Curate of St. Columba's, Stratford (E15).

After two years as a curate, he felt drawn to the religious life. The ideal of poverty had a strong appeal to him: when he inherited £3,000 from his father, he distributed it among former employees of his father's mill, candidates for Holy Orders and poor widows; on one occasion he referred to covetousness as 'the besetting sin of our day'.[40] Fr. Andrew of the Society of the Divine Compassion attracted him, and he spent two nights at Plaistow, but the Superior, Fr. William Sirr, persuaded him rather to try the Cowley Fathers. At Cowley, he became a novice, but conflicts within himself, perhaps from his Evangelical background, came to the surface. He felt convinced that he had a vocation to preach

39. Kenneth Packard, *Brother Edward* (1955), p. 22.
40. ibid., p. 53.

to the poor, and this became his main mission in life. But he could not reconcile this calling to obedience to the Society of St. John the Evangelist, and he left Cowley in July 1913. He wrote, 'I should like to see one great big Community . . . all under discipline, and liable to be sent where needed.'[41] But not long afterwards, he wrote of the religious life as being Judaistic (presumably as tending to Justification by Works) – 'the sort of danger that St. Paul contended against in Galatians.'[42] He did not regard the vow of obedience as one of the counsels of perfection.

After leaving Cowley, he wandered. For a time, he thought of becoming a wandering friar in the Diocese of Oxford, but Gore (then Bishop of Oxford) did not encourage him.[43] He met Brother Giles, and went off with him to Kent to work among the hop-pickers, a work he resumed twenty years later.[44] In the Great War, he served for a time as an army chaplain at Horsham (Sussex), but left in 1915 after a disagreement with the military authorities.[45]

In June 1915, perhaps for the first time since leaving Oxford, Edward Bulstrode found some stability. Frank and Sophia Fairbairn were in charge of some almshouses at Temple Balsall, Hampton-in-Arden (Warwicks.) which they ran on the lines of Nicholas Ferrar's Community at Little Gidding.[46] Bulstrode used this as a base between 1915 and 1929, and Bishop Wakefield of Birmingham gave him permission to officiate at Temple Balsall. He regarded himself as in some sense a religious, and began to call himself Brother Edward. Like Douglas, he preferred to be known as 'Brother' rather than 'Father'.[47] In 1929, he tried to gather a Community together. He took two cottages at Westcote in the Cotswolds, where Bishop A.C. Headlam of Gloucester gave him permission to officiate.[48] One cottage, named Nazareth, was for men, and here Edward was joined by his brother Frank, a young Scot called Brother Donald, and Edward's sister Alice who kept house for them. The other cottage, Bethlehem, was for women. It was run by Geraldine Mott (Sister Geraldine) as a Sisterhood, with a Rule devised by Brother Edward.[49] For a time, all went well. Edward was joined in 1929 by a priest, Malcolm Buchanan, and by two laymen, Joseph and Martin. Buchanan had been Warden of the Edmonton

41. ibid., p. 66.
42. ibid., p. 67.
43. ibid., p. 57.
44. ibid., p. 61.
45. ibid., p. 77.
46. ibid., p. 80.
47. ibid., p. 82n.
48. *Crockford*.
49. Packard, op. cit., p. 93.

Missionary Brotherhood in Canada (1922–24) and then Vicar of Stainton-in-Cleveland, Yorks., 1925–29.[50]

However, to Edward, Westcote, like Temple Balsall, was not so much a community where the religious life could be practised as a base from which to set forth on evangelistic work. From his days at Temple Balsall, Edward had worked in the parish of St. Aidan, Small Heath, Birmingham, where he gathered little groups around him to study the Bible. These he formed in 1933 into the Disciples of Jesus of Nazareth. These could be compared to Companions rather than Tertiaries. Edward prepared their Bible Notes, and until 1951, they regularly held a retreat-conference at the College of the Ascension, Selly Oak.[51] Edward also had a 'prophet's room', as he called it, at St. Silas', Pentonville (N1), another church where he had permission to officiate between 1927 and 1929.[52]

Edward and his brother Frank were frequently away from Westcote; Alice Bulstrode moved to Slough where she became an important figure in the League of Our Father (see Chapter 24). Malcolm Buchanan left after a year to become Curate of Whitby (Yorks.).[53] The main burden of keeping Westcote going fell on Brother Donald, and after two years, he began to have serious doubts. He had thoughts of joining Christa Seva Sangha, but was turned down by Jack Winslow; Brother Edward discouraged him from proceeding to Holy Orders. He became a tramp preacher, but when his health broke down, he joined the Society of St. John the Evangelist as a lay brother, and remained with them five years.[54]

In 1932, Edward began to work regularly among the hop-pickers at Beltring near Paddock Wood in Kent. He and others – Giles, Douglas, George Potter, George Martin – had already made this a special work; Edward's achievement was to make it an annual mission. He shared evangelism with the Salvation Army. This part of his work at least outlasted him, for when he had to give up in 1947, the Society of St. Francis took over from him.[55]

He will also be remembered for organising the Village Evangelists in 1949. After the Second World War, he realised – a generation before most – the need to encourage and support the clergy in the villages, many of whom were lonely and dispirited, though the rural areas remained outposts of Christian commitment. For years, he had been

50. *Crockford.*
51. Packard, op. cit., p. 87.
52. ibid., p. 135; *Crockford.*
53. *Crockford.*
54. Packard, op. cit., p. 129.
55. ibid., p. 137.

preaching on village greens and street corners,[56] and his dream was to build up teams of like-minded men who, with the consent of the clergy, would help them to preach the Gospel while living in apostolic simplicity. He had the support of Walter Carey, formerly Bishop of Bloemfontein (1921–34) who became Co-Warden of the Village Evangelists with Brother Edward.[57] The Village Evangelists were twenty-four priests who, under Brother Edward's inspiration took the name the Servants of Jesus of Nazareth, a name which recalled both the Community at Westcote and the Disciples in Birmingham. As well as helping the clergy, the Evangelists were linked with the work of the Society of St. Francis.[58]

It was a prophetic vision, but it was begun when Edward was already advancing in years and becoming increasingly occupied with the Second Coming. His health began to fail. As early as 1935, he had been rushed to hospital at Chelmsford with a perforated gastric ulcer. In 1949, he had suspected cancer, but again recovered.[59] His health finally collapsed in 1952, and he died on 25 March 1953.

His obituary said that 'He combined in a wonderful way the contemplative and active aspects of the spiritual life, and clothed his great powers with the beautiful gift of self-effacement.' The writer saw him as a 'magnificent missioner' and one who had played a great part in reviving the evangelistic zeal in the Anglican Communion.[60] The Village Evangelists were described as a 'worthy living memorial'. Despite the continuing need, that work has not endured. His love for humanity and for the Church remain his two chief claims to sanctity.[61]

56. CC p. 164n.
57. ibid.; *Crockford*.
58. Society of St. Francis Chapter Minute 20/21.1.47.
59. Packard, op. cit., p. 137.
60. *Church Times*, 10.4.53.
61. ibid.

PART II

COMMUNITIES IN THE BRITISH COMMONWEALTH

11

The Community of St. Francis

The Community of St. Francis is the oldest of the Franciscan communities still extant in the Church of England, and the earliest foundation to be a member of the Society of St. Francis, though it was affiliated as recently as 1964. Its members are now the only women in any part of the Christian Church to belong to a Franciscan First Order. The Community evolved from an existing Sisterhood which was not specifically Franciscan. It came into being through the spiritual friendship of a priest and a religious sister, both of whom subsequently went over to Rome.

The Sisters of Bethany, now at Bournemouth, were founded in 1866, and worked first in the parish of St. Philip, Clerkenwell (EC1),[1] but they became attached to the more Anglo-Catholic Church of the Holy Redeemer from its consecration in 1888. Before this, in 1882, Rosina Rice (Sister Rosina), a lady who was to develop a deep devotion to St. Francis and St. Clare,[2] joined the Community. In 1903, John Hawes (q.v.) became Curate of Holy Redeemer parish. Through his friendship with Sister Rosina, she was encouraged to think of withdrawing from the Sisters of Bethany to found a Franciscan community – Fr. Hawes hoped that he might found a brother community for men. He and Sister Rosina together drew up a Rule based on the Rule of St. Clare but also drawing on the Rule of St. Francis (1223) but modifying the Clares' Rule to suit an active rather than an enclosed community.[3] One professed Sister of Bethany and two others, probably novices, joined Sister Rosina[4] when in 1905 she went to live with the Sisters of the Holy Comforter.[5]

In 1906, Sister Rosina and her companions were invited to work in the parish of St. Mary, Sculcoates, in the dockland area of Hull. They rented a small house which they named St. Damian's Convent. They adopted a Franciscan brown habit with a knotted cord, black veil and

---

1. CC, p. 408.
2. ibid., p. 495.
3. Sister Joyce, C.S.F., *Short History* (privately printed).
4. Three others, according to Peter Anson, CC, p. 495.
5. At Edmonton (North London); the community is now at West Malling, CC, p. 465.

sandals. Their devoted work among dockers and sailors and their families drew other recruits, and their numbers grew between 1906 and the Summer of 1908 when they returned to London to the Parish of St. Philip, Dalston. Fr. Hawes visited them at Sculcoates on his tramping pilgrimage in 1907.

After the move to Dalston, Cosmo Gordon Lang, then Bishop of Stepney, became Visitor, approved their Rule, and professed the first novices. The Sisters attended the Eucharist in St. Philip's Church; the Vicar, Charles Thornely, became their Chaplain. They recited the Office in the oratory of their convent.[6] In 1909, they took a larger house in Richmond Road, Dalston, where they remained until 1962. The Sisters supported themselves by working in the parish, caring for the sick and dying, and also ran a laundry, where the lack of facilities meant intense hard work.[7]

They were by now beginning to become settled when the Community was hit by a spiritual crisis. Sister Rosina pondered whether loyalty to St. Francis did not imply submission to the Pope. The secession of the American Society of the Atonement (q.v.) precipitated a decision. Sister Rosina and five other Sisters crossed the Atlantic and were received into the Church of Rome at Graymoor on 26 November 1910.[8] Fr. Hawes followed them into the Roman obedience, also at Graymoor, four months later.

Three Sisters, however, remained at Dalston, including Sister Helen Elizabeth, who had already made her life profession. Fr. Thornely appointed her Mother Superior; his support, and that of Bishop Paget (who had replaced Dr. Lang at Stepney), was invaluable in seeing the Community through the crisis.[9] The life of poverty was very exacting, and it has been reckoned that during the Great War, the Sisters were living on 2/6 ($12\frac{1}{2}$p) per head per week, eating meat only on Sundays.[10] Nevertheless, new recruits joined the Community. In 1920, they were given the house next door. They turned it into a home for incurable and bedridden women. Equipment was obtained free from an old military hospital. A trained nurse was hired, but the Sisters took turns of night duty.[11]

Mother Helen Elizabeth built a separate chapel with its own cloister and garden. This was dedicated by Bishop Henry Mosley of Stepney in May 1924. As well as being used for the daily Office, a festal

6. Sister Joyce, op. cit.
7. ibid.
8. ibid. Sister Rosina had been in touch with Mother Lurana of the Society of the Atonement since the latter's visit to the Sisters of Bethany in 1897.
9. ibid.
10. ibid.
11. ibid.

Eucharist was celebrated in the chapel on the Feast of the Dedication, Easter, St. Francis' Day and Christmas, but the Sisters continued to attend the parish church for the daily Eucharist.[12]

During the Great Depression, the Sisters undertook a special ministry to the down-and-out, providing food, clothing, rest and occasionally work for the men who called at their door. Recruits to the Community were fewer at this stage. Nevertheless, the Community had fostered a Third Order. Two women tertiaries shared the life of the Community for many years, and in 1923 a tertiary priest, Fr. George Ford, became Chaplain.[13]

The Sisters' convent and St. Francis' Home have been described as

two adjacent, very ordinary mid-Victorian dwelling-houses [which stood] out from their neighbours because of the fresh dark-brown and pale-cream paint on windows and doors. In summer time the green leaves of a tall acacia tree provide[d] a note of contrast. Here it [was] easy for the Community to live a hidden life, without attracting much attention. It [was] the realism, not the romance of St. Francis, that one [found] at this convent in north-east London.[14]

Any romance was shattered by the blitz in the Second World War. First the Convent then both Convent and Home were damaged, while St. Philip's Church was wrecked. Mother Helen Elizabeth and three Sisters moved back into the Convent when part of it was made habitable and the chapel could be used. Three Sisters and the patients from the home were housed at Singleton Rectory near Chichester for the duration of the war.[15]

An important development took place during the war when Fr. Algy became Chaplain.[16] The Society of St. Francis had already come into being.[17] Fr. Algy was anxious to involve at least one community of women in the Society so that something resembling the traditional three Franciscan orders could emerge.

The Sisters and their patients returned from Singleton in 1945, and the following year St. Francis' Home was repaired and ready for reoccupation. At the end of the war, there were six Sisters in the Community, and they looked after ten patients. Mother Helen Elizabeth's last achievement was to revitalise the Community. One of the patients at the home has spoken of 'her sublime faith . . . her words of comfort

12. ibid.
13. ibid.
14. CC, p. 497. Peter Anson was writing before the Sisters moved from Dalston.
15. Sister Joyce, op. cit.
16. ibid.
17. See Chapter 24.

. . . her keen sense of humour . . . her love of music.' After nearly forty years as Superior, she died on 7 March 1950.[18]

She was succeeded by Sister Agnes Mary. Recruitment to the Community picked up, and a new constitution was adopted. A friar of the Society of St. Francis was to be Warden, and there was to be a three year period of simple profession before life vows. Although there were fewer down-and-outs to provide for under the Welfare State, new work opened up for the Sisters in the parish of St. Mary, Hackney Wick. In 1957, three Sisters went to live in a wing of St. Mary's clergy house. When the Society of St. Francis took over St. Philip's, Plaistow, a priest-friar came regularly to celebrate the Eucharist in the Sisters' chapel, while the Sisters helped with evangelistic missions and from time to time helped in the Franciscan parishes at Plaistow and St. Mary's, Cable Street (E1).

The years 1958–62 were critical ones for the Community. The London County Council planned development in Dalston which involved demolishing many houses, including the Convent. The Sisters found themselves a new home in rural Somerset at Compton Durville near Yeovil. The old manor house had been used from 1952 to 1959 by the Sisters of the Sacred Cross.[19] The Community of St. Francis moved in August 1962. Foundations for a new home and chapel were laid in April 1963, and dedicated by Bishop Edward Henderson of Bath and Wells, the Visitor to the Community, a year later.[20]

In 1964, the Community became formally affiliated to the Society of St. Francis, but retained its own Chapter and Constitution. The Rule, based on that of St. Clare, which the Sisters had followed since 1905, was replaced by the Principles of the Society of St. Francis which the Chapter adopted. The Third Order of the Community was united with that of the Society of St. Francis.[21] Sister Elizabeth succeeded Sister Agnes Mary as Superior in 1971. Until 1964, the Sisters had used *Day Hours* for the Divine Office. In 1964, Prayer Book Mattins and Evensong replaced Lauds and Vespers, and the Monastic Diurnal was used for the Lesser Hours. In 1972, however, the Sisters adopted the Office Book of the Society of St. Francis with its four-fold office of Morning, Midday, Evening and Night Prayer. With their tradition of a Rule based on that of St. Clare, it is natural that the Community of St. Francis should often have been thought of as a Franciscan Second Order. But they could not entirely fill such a role as they were active

18. Sister Joyce, op. cit.
19. CC, p. 497.
20. ibid.; Sister Joyce, op. cit.
21. Sister Joyce, op. cit.

and unenclosed. In 1973, the First Order Brothers' Chapter recognised the Sisters as members of the First Order of St. Francis.[22]

The new St. Francis' Home at Compton Durville was built with accommodation for sixteen patients in pleasant and spacious surroundings. The work of nursing the elderly continues there, but on a smaller scale. Many of the more recent recruits to the Community have not been trained nurses, and modern health regulations are, rightly, exacting as regards nurse/patient ratio and the requirement of buildings. Sisters have found new spheres of ministry.[23] In 1967, a new guest house was opened for conferences, retreats and quiet holidays, converted from the old barn. From 1967–74, two Sisters worked at the Mission Station at Fiwila, Zambia. From 1971, Sisters helped on an individual basis in Birmingham with care of girls at risk. This work had originally started in London under Father Joe Williamson.[24] Since 1976, this work of the Wellclose Square Fund Charity has been fully staffed by the Sisters. In 1974, two new ventures began. The Sisters took over a house in San Francisco owned by the Diocese of California. Each of the Sisters has a ministry in a parish or in social work, and the house is self-supporting. American Sisters have now been recruited. The same year, the Sisters opened a house at Newcastle-under-Lyme (Staffs.) for retreats and small groups seeking spiritual renewal. Sisters also work in the Diocese (Lichfield) and on evangelistic missions in parishes, usually working with the Franciscan Brothers. In 1976, they took over a house in Dover (Kent) previously run by two Companions of the Society, providing temporary accommodation to people in need. Other Sisters from the house are engaged in pastoral work. These new openings show that the Community has moved towards diversification, but until 1977, Sister Mary Francis kept up links with the East End of London, where the Community's work had begun, working in the parish of St. Mary, Hackney Wick (E9).

An account of the life and history of the Community of St. Francis has recently been written by Mother Elizabeth called *Corn of Wheat* (Becket Publications 1981). The book tells the lively and very human story of this Community and sets its place in the Franciscan movement.

22. Sister Joyce, op. cit.
23. *Third Order Chronicle*, June 1979.
24. Joseph Williamson was particularly well known in his last ministry as Vicar of St. Paul with St. Mark, Whitechapel (E1) 1952–62.

12

The Order of St. Elizabeth of Hungary

The origins and early history of this Community are related by its foundress and first Superior, Mother Elizabeth, in two of her books, *Into the Deep* and *Letting Down the Nets*. Each covers about five years, respectively 1912–17 and 1918–23. Mother Elizabeth tells how she and a friend were on holiday in Sussex on the fifth Sunday after Trinity and heard the opening of St. Luke Chapter Five as the Gospel with its challenging command, 'Launch out into the deep', and this became their motto.[1] These two ladies and another friend were drawn together in 1903 to offer themselves for parish work at St. Alban's, a church in a poor district of Fulham. Dr. Ridgway, the Bishop of Kensington, was encouraging, but other plans were on foot for the area, and the idea was dropped. Mother Elizabeth and one of her friends entered existing religious orders, respectively in 1904 and 1907. The third, later to become Sister Agnes, was for the moment looking after her aged mother.[2] Until 1912, Mother Elizabeth was occupied with missionary work in Cardiff.

The next move came through a retreat in July 1912 where the life of St. Francis was a subject of meditation. Mother Elizabeth was present and felt moved to seek the guidance of the Holy Spirit, and prayed, 'Baptize us, O God, with the Holy Ghost, and kindle in our hearts the fire of Thy Love.' They agreed to use this prayer and to form an association which took the name, the *Confraternity of the Divine Love*. Within a fortnight, over twenty people had joined them,[3] 'with the understanding that if God opened the way, an order of Sisters should be formed'.[4] Mother Elizabeth felt that she must leave her existing order, which she did with their consent rather than approval on 8 April 1913.[5] Unexpectedly, the chance came for mission work at

1. Mother Elizabeth, *Into the Deep* (ITD) (revised edition 1967), p. 1.
2. ITD p. 61.
3. ITD p. 4; CC p. 503.
4. Hilfield Archives F.115; CC p. 503.
5. ITD p. 7. It was the Society of St. Margaret, East Grinstead.

St. Alban's, Fulham, where Mother Elizabeth had first received her inspiration.[6]

Until 1916, she and the ladies who joined her simply worked within the Confraternity of the Divine Love. It was a 'wide and simple body', not burdened with rules over intercession.[7] Within the Confraternity, Mother Elizabeth and two Sisters (increased to eight by 1916) began to evolve as a community. In following the ideal of poverty, they pledged themselves to have no invested funds, to accept no payment for services rendered, not to distribute money to others and to spend whatever was given them.[8] A gift of £50 from a friend made it possible for them to begin – in a three-room flat in the poorest quarter of Fulham. The Rev. Gilbert Elliott, Vicar of St. Alban's, Fulham, welcomed them to the parish, and they were soon officially recognised by the Bishop of London as women workers.[9] They wore a habit of grey and brown – 'St. Francis' colours' – and were known among themselves as 'the sparrows'.[10] They visited from house to house, taught girls and called on and nursed the sick; they also opened their doors to anyone in distress or loneliness.[11] Fortunately, they were able to make two moves to bigger premises, and after the second move they had enough room for their own simple oratory.

In July 1914, they took a house in Uxbridge Road, Hanwell, and worked in the parish of St. Mellitus, where they worshipped. They named their house St. Elizabeth – many of the locals, who had never heard of the saintly Hungarian Queen who was given St. Francis' cloak, thought it was named after the Reverend Mother! But the links with Fulham were kept. A hostel was opened in Earl's Court, dedicated on St. Francis' Day 1915. The Sisters owed much to the guidance of Fr. Willoughby Carter, Vicar of St. Matthias', Earl's Court, who became Chaplain to the Confraternity. It was possibly his influence which led the Sisters to adopt a fruitarian diet, on which they seem to have flourished better than he did.[12]

The Sisters offered themselves for service in the Great War, but were advised that they would be better occupied continuing their work on the home front. One of the earliest associates of the Confraternity, Frederick Brown, was killed serving with the R.A.M.C. in 1915, and likewise James Langdale in 1916; other associates, both men and

6. ITD p. 16; CC p. 503.
7. ITD p. 10.
8. ITD pp. 11–12.
9. ITD p. 17.
10. ibid.
11. Hilfield Archives F. 115.
12. Mother Elizabeth, *Letting Down the Nets* (LDN) Chapter IX in original edition (1923).

The Order of St. Elizabeth of Hungary

women, served in the war and were sent overseas. The Sisters discovered their special vocation in caring for poor children. At first, they looked after a few for a short time for sick or poor parents, but the work soon expanded, and two homes were opened in Hanwell, St. Michael's for boys and St. Gabriel's for girls. The atmosphere really was that of a home and not an orphanage, with children in groups of ten, the older ones helping to look after the younger. Chapter VII ('The Children') of *Into the Deep* radiates with Mother Elizabeth's love and care for these young ones.

In 1916, the Sisterhood numbered nine (Mother Elizabeth and eight novices) and two probationers.[13] Mother Elizabeth was already under profession from her former community, and on 19 November (the Feast of St. Elizabeth of Hungary) the two Sisters who had shared her life since 1913 were professed in the Lady Chapel at St. Matthias', Earl's Court. At this point, therefore, they formally became a Community. After the novitiate, the other Sisters were to serve five years in simple vows before proceeding to solemn profession.[14] They continued their practice of keeping only enough money in the bank for about one month's expenses. As well as following St. Francis' principle of poverty, they adopted that of St. Teresa of Avila of having not more than thirteen Sisters in one house.[15] It was appropriate that they should have chosen St. Elizabeth of Hungary as their patron saint, one of the greatest of Franciscan tertiaries. Not only did they share her compassion for the poor, but their Community resembled those of women tertiaries regular in the Church of Rome.[16] In 1921, the Bishop of London's advisory council gave formal approval of their rule and constitution, and the Bishop (Dr. Winnington-Ingram) installed Mother Elizabeth at a service at St. Matthias', Earl's Court on 4 March.[17]

Meanwhile the Confraternity continued to develop. It had already grown to about 250 members by 1918.[18] The associates were bound only by their baptismal vows, and prayer for the guidance of the Spirit. But as well as the Sisterhood, third orders were envisaged – the Company of St. Gertrude for women, that of St. John of the Cross for men.[19] In formal terms, the Confraternity was to consist of companions

---

13. ITD p. 52.
14. ibid.
15. CC p. 504.
16. ibid.
17. LDN (revised edition) p. 57.
18. ITD (original edition 1917) p. 69.
19. LDN (original edition) p. 11. The Third Order for men in fact never came into being. That for women was short-lived – members either joined the Order or returned to the Confraternity.

(or associates), separate third orders of men and women, and women tertiaries regular.

As the Sisterhood grew in numbers and maturity, fresh work was taken on. From 1916, the Sisters went on missions, beginning in Passion Week at Hayes, Middlesex, but they felt an especial call to the villages.[20] 'We are absolutely and entirely against the ministry of women within the actual church building,' Mother Elizabeth wrote, 'but this does not preclude us from teaching in the halls and homes, and sometimes a woman, even though a Sister, will be listened to, and may say things which they will not brook from their poor long-suffering priest!'[21] In more recent years, however, Sisters have exercised a ministry in church. In Australia, they have conducted services and preached, especially when churches have been without a priest. In England they have preached. Nevertheless, most of the present Community are opposed to the ordination of women.

In that crucial year 1916, a house was taken at Heathfield in Sussex. Here the Sisters could rest, and here Sister Agnes, one of the original members, died in 1916.[22] The house was named St. Mary's. An adjacent house, St. Margaret's, was used from 1921 for retreats and conferences of associates. The first such conference took place earlier in August 1917. 'It is one of our great desires to combine the study of sociology with the spiritual problems which the Church has to face', Mother Elizabeth wrote.[23] Her fruitarian views were held with deep conviction. 'We believe it to be one of the really missionary works God has given us to do.'[24] She pays tribute to Bishop Gore in her writings, but it is not clear how close his influence was. Towards the end of *Into the Deep* she writes: 'This is the "socialism" we long to see; not the evasion of the gift of birth, nor the ignoring of the good of education, but the sharing of all in the inspiration of a common love.'[25] Among her writings is a spiritual guide, *We would see Jesus* in which she reflects thus on Anglo-Catholicism:

> There are those among us who would prefer, and will state that they prefer, the intellectual stagnation and sentimentalism of certain foreign literature to the works of minds of our own Church noted for their beauty of philosophical thought, and soundness of theology; just because they do not bear certain superficial marks of modern Catholicism.[26]

20. ITD (revised) Chapter 8.
21. ITD (original edition) p. 65.
22. ITD (revised) Chapter 12.
23. ITD (original) p. 81.
24. LDN (original) p. 86.
25. op. cit. (original) p. 105.
26. op. cit. (original) p. 36.

She saw the English Church as having a special vocation to meet the intellectual challenge of the day. Christ's work was to lift us heavenwards:

> . . . true Christianity [is] the lifting up of our souls away from materialism, while decadent religion has the tendency to add to the number and uses of material things as aids to devotion; in reality detracting from spiritual values.[27]

She had short shrift for the disrepute brought on holy things by the flippancy of the younger clergy.[28]

Apart from the works already quoted, Mother Elizabeth wrote a number of others. An early one was *The Dawn of Vocation* (1919). *The Vocation of the Soul* was a series of devotional addresses. Other devotional writings were *When thou prayest* and the *Sacrament of Penance*. Later she wrote *Fruit of the Spirit* (1942) and *Living Stones* (1948), both on the work of the Holy Spirit. Her last work was *Growth in Vocation* (1962). In one of her earlier works, *Restoration to the Sacred Heart*, Willoughby Carter wrote of Christianity offering 'complete restoration to every soul that seriously desires it'. Every chapter concerns restoration – to love, grace, sacramental life, light, holiness, union with God, vision. Mother Elizabeth had a particular devotion to the Sacred Heart.[29] These books show her to have been a spiritual guide of no small importance, and most of them are still in print, including *Into the Deep* (revised 1967) and an early booklet of short stories, *Delphiniums*.

Meantime, the Order continued its practical work. In 1921, the Sisters took over Oakhurst House at Erith which they ran as a retreat house for the Diocese of Rochester; the Bishop (J. R. Harmer) came to bless the house in March 1922.[30] In 1923, a colony or group of homes for children, St. Mary-in-the-Fields, was established at Mayfield, and dedicated by the Bishop of Lewes (H. K. Southwell) on 11 June 1923. The children in care included four Russian refugees who were Orthodox.[31] The children shared the Sisters' fruitarian diet and seemed to thrive on it. Hostels were opened in London, Heathfield and Eastbourne where members of the Confraternity could meet and where churchpeople could share fellowship.[32] When girls grew up from the children's homes, they were admitted as associates of the Confraternity, and could stay for two years at the hostels while training for

---

27. Mother Elizabeth, *We would see Jesus* (original edition 1932), p. 39.
28. ibid. p. 58.
29. ITD (original) p. 68.
30. LDN (original) pp. 73–74.
31. ibid., pp. 45–8.
32. ibid., p. 14.

work which might take them away from the protective wing of the Order.[33] Cottages were also provided for elderly ladies at Heathfield.[34]

In 1927, the Sisters' work expanded overseas, when they took charge of St. George's Hospital at Christchurch, New Zealand. Lady Campion, wife of the Governor of Western Australia, invited them to work in the province, and at Whitsun 1928 their new home at Bunbury was blessed. Here they continued to work until 1957. In 1931, their work in Western Australia was extended to Busselton and Margaret River.[35]

Since the 1950s, the Community has retrenched its work. From their earliest days, the Sisters declared themselves 'devoted to the work of bringing the love of God to the lapsed, friendless and lost of every class.'[36] New times bring new opportunities. Their traditional policy of opening their doors to those in need has in recent years provided a home for 'young people in difficulty, alone in a big city with no one to turn to', and a special concern has been shown for young drug addicts.[37]

Mother Elizabeth retired from office in 1949 and went to live at Heathfield where she died in February 1960. She was succeeded as Reverend Mother by Sister Angela, who held office until 1970. Frances was Mother 1970–73 and then Mother Rachel, who holds office at the time of writing. The first two Mothers (Elizabeth and Angela) each had two Deputy Mothers, and Mother Frances had one, but with the contraction of the Order, the office has been dropped.

Mother Angela sent out her Deputy Mother, Mary, to Australia along with Sister Frances who was to take charge there. Shortage of numbers meant that the Australian house had to be closed down, and the Sisters returned to England in May 1957. It had been in Australia that the fruitarian diet was first modified because of the different climate and shortage of fresh vegetables. The Sisters in England changed their diet at the beginning of the Second World War when the shortage of food meant that any variation from the standard rationed food, except a full vegetarian diet, would be very expensive and inadequately nourishing. Some of the Sisters had already been advised to eat meat for health reasons.

The London house at 94 Radcliffe Gardens, Kensington, was given up in 1970, and Heathfield became the Mother House.[38] The property was sold to a local group concerned with rehabilitating former drug addicts. The Order sold it to them on favourable terms as a contri-

33. ibid., p. 45.
34. Hilfield Archives F. 115.
35. ibid. CC p. 503.
36. Hilfield Archives F. 115.
37. ibid.
38. ibid.

bution to their work, which still carries on. With the move to Heathfield, St. Mary's became the Convent and St. Margaret's the Guest House. For the convenience of the older Sisters, the old conservatory adjoining St. Margaret's was converted into a small chapel for use in the winter months. In September 1966, a new chapel at St. Mary's was completed, the Eucharist celebrated there for the first time on 2 September. The altar was moved there from the old log chapel. The smaller chapel at St. Margaret's was converted into a library. Under Mother Angela, the Order achieved greater financial stability. Their existing investments were sold out, and the money was placed in a deposit fund with the Central Board of Finance of the Church of England. The interest on this investment is used for the upkeep of the Community and the maintenance of its buildings.[39] This had the approval of the Visitor (Edward Roberts, Bishop of Kensington, later of Ely) in 1961 and an amendment was written into the Constitution in 1963.

The prayer for the Baptism of the Spirit used since 1912 had been intended with the meaning of John the Baptist's promise in St. Luke 3, v. 16. The phrase 'Baptism in the Spirit' came to take on a more specialised meaning, particularly connected with Speaking in Tongues, as a result of the Charismatic Movement. In 1973–74, Mother Rachel and other of the Sisters became involved in the movement for Charismatic Renewal. The Order and the Confraternity of Divine Love wisely avoided the theological arguments which have arisen in some circles over this movement. To avoid contention, the hallowed prayer was reworded, 'Fulfil us, O God, with the Holy Spirit, and kindle in our hearts the fire of thy love.'

To the outsider, the years from 1950 might appear to be a gradual story of withdrawal. The closure of the railway line to Heathfield in 1965 meant that an important means of communication was no longer available. But this is only one side of the story. Sisters have gone on pilgrimage to Walsingham and the Holy Land. In 1964 and again in 1966, Sisters visited Roman Catholic Franciscans in France who shared a devotion to the Sacred Heart. They had corresponded for some time before this, and support for the cause of Christian Unity has become an important part of the Sisters' concern. Although the Order has not become part of the Society of St. Francis, the revised Franciscan Office Book was adopted in July 1977. Franciscan tertiaries in the area have for a number of years made their annual retreat at Heathfield. Contraction of work, therefore, has only been the background to a widening of vision.

39. ITD (revised) p. 86.

13

Neither Purse nor Scrip

The Society of the Divine Compassion proved to be, if not the parent, then the godparent, of the Brotherhood of St. Francis of Assisi at Hilfield, and so of the Society of St. Francis. The family link came through a man and a mission. The man was Edward Kelly Evans. The mission was the apostolate to the wayfarers.

Edward Kelly Evans was born in King's County in Southern Ireland (now County Offaly, Eire) in 1879. He was over thirty when he went to test his vocation with the Society of the Divine Compassion in 1911, and he is better known by the name he took in religion, Brother Giles. The Society of the Divine Compassion already had a tradition of 'road missions'. James Adderley himself from time to time 'took to the road', so far as is known wearing a habit when he went tramping and dossing, emptying his pocket before setting out to share the life more completely.[1] After he left the Community, the Brothers continued the tradition, going on foot on preaching tours through the Essex villages.[2] Brother Giles did not settle to community life at Plaistow, but found his special vocation on the road, 'going from tramp ward to tramp ward'. He began his wayfaring from Stanford-le-Hope in 1913. Soon he became a detached religious. Bishop Gore and the Cowley Fathers again played their part, the former in giving his blessing to Brother Giles' work. The Cowley Fathers provided both spiritual direction and physical support. The rigours of wayfaring brought Brother Giles more than once to the verge of collapse, and the Cowley Fathers nursed him back to health.[3]

The Great War interrupted his work. In 1915, he enlisted in the Royal Army Medical Corps and served as a stretcher-bearer in France. In 1917, he took a commission in the King's African Rifles and served in East Africa. Here he contracted malaria, which contributed to his breakdown in health in 1922.[4] But in 1919, in conditions aggravated

1. Stevens, op. cit., p. 28 f.
2. Fr. Francis, *Brother Douglas* (1974), p. 40.
3. ibid., p. 41.
4. ibid., p. 43.

by the disruption of war, Brother Giles returned to his work on the road.

In March that year, he encountered J. R. Fox, who was later to join him as Brother Roger. Fox, then an undergraduate at New College, Oxford, had heard about 'the man who dressed in brown and talked to tramps', and met him at the Cowley Fathers' church. He describes him at that time as 'slightly bald though not yet forty, with his brown habit, Franciscan cord and sandals'.[5] That summer, Fox joined him on another of his missions – to the hop-pickers in Kent. By their own choice, Giles and Fox lived in a loft of a stable at the farm near Maidstone where they worked. They gathered straw to make a bed. They rose early each day, lit a fire and washed in the pond. They worked eight hours a day. At the end of the week, they received about 11d. each ($4^{1}/_{2}$p), but in those days it was enough to buy bread, jam, bacon, kippers and a little meat. They shared the stable with other hop-pickers, and brought them at least to talk about the Christian faith. To Brother Giles, a stable was hallowed by association with Bethlehem. He had two oleographs, of the Crucifixion and the Nativity, before which he said his prayers. He and Fox used to sit under an apple tree to say the Office early in the morning.[6] Fox seems to have been Giles' first disciple, but it was on another hop-picking mission in September 1921 that Giles had a fateful encounter with Douglas Downes.

Life was hard in the hop-fields, but at least it had the wholesome cleanness of the countryside in contrast to the life Giles shared in the 'casual' or 'tramp' wards. The Poor Law still in operation in the 1920s forbade tramps to beg, though they were allowed to work. When they arrived at a casual ward, they were allowed supper, lodging for that and the following night, with a hard day's work between, such as sawing wood or picking oakum; the meals were of the quality of prison fare; on their departure, they received an allowance of bread. These harsh conditions were less damaging than the loss of personal dignity. Tramps had any tobacco, matches or similar small possessions locked away for their time in the 'casual'.[7] They received a necessary bath, usually cold. Their clothes were exchanged for an institutional night-shirt, and they were locked away for the night either in a ward or a cell – the latter often overcrowded.[8] 'St. Francis, were he in England

5. J. R. Fox, Memoir.
6. ibid.
7. One is reminded of King Lear's passionate outburst (Act II, Scene iv):
   Oh reason not the need: our basest beggars
   Are in the poorest thing superfluous.
   Allow not nature more than nature needs,
   Man's life is cheap as beast's.
8. Fr. Francis, op. cit., p. 56.

now, would go to a tramp ward.' In that saying, Brother Giles summed up his special calling, one in which Roger, Douglas and others followed in his footsteps. Giles carried virtually nothing with him when he went wayfaring except the Cowley Office Book and the clothes he stood up in, 'neither purse nor scrip', according to the precept of the Gospel. 'Say the Divine Office in the tramp ward. Think of Our Lord's Passion when you have to cut wood with them, or pick oakum.'[9] Yet he regarded the vocation of a Friar as only a fuller carrying out of the vows every Christian makes at baptism. Poverty, chastity and obedience were for him the logical conclusion of renouncing the world, the flesh and the devil.

When he went down from Oxford, Roger Fox determined to join Brother Giles. In July 1921, they met at Burnham, Bucks. (Nashdom Abbey). Fox's father got Bishop Gore to try to talk him out of his resolve, but in vain. On St. Francis' Day (4 October 1921) at the Eton College Mission, Hackney Wick, Fox – or Brother Roger as he now became – was clothed as a Franciscan novice by the Superior of the Cowley Fathers. Brother Giles was absent, ill-health already telling on him, but among those present were Dom Gregory Dix[10] and Douglas Downes.[11] Already before this, a new prospect had opened.

On his wayfaring, Brother Giles had encountered the Earl of Sandwich[12] at his home, Hinchinbrook, near Huntingdon. Lord Sandwich himself was deeply concerned that the Poor Law should be reformed, a concern fully shared by his wife, an American, née Alberta Sturgess. Lord Sandwich had been aroused by his experience as a visitor of Aylesbury Gaol, and he and his wife had taken an interest in modern methods of treating young delinquents in the U.S.A. In 1912, an experiment was launched of training delinquent boys and girls at Flowers Farm on the Sandwich family estates at Hilfield in Dorset. An American, Homer Lane, was put in charge, and he ran the home as a self-governing and self-disciplining community which was given the name, *The Little Commonwealth*. Lane had not been entirely successful in running a school for delinquent boys in Detroit, and the experiment at Flowers Farm folded up in 1916, Lane diverting his main interest to psycho-analysis.[13] At the end of the war, Dorset County Council took over Flowers Farm for a time to train demobilised soldiers in agriculture.

In 1921, Lord Sandwich wrote to Brother Giles, offering Flowers

9. J. R. Fox, Memoir.
10. Of Nashdom Abbey, author of *The Shape of the Liturgy*, etc.
11. J. R. Fox, Memoir.
12. George Charles Montagu, 9th Earl of Sandwich; grandson of the 7th and nephew of the 8th Earl. Conservative M.P. for Hunts. South, 1900–06.
13. Fr. Francis, op. cit., p. 42. Fr. Denis, op. cit., pp. 121 ff.

Farm for an experiment in reclaiming men from the life of the road. Giles himself at this time was thinking of establishing a centre for this purpose near Oxford, and had the Bartlemas Chapel in mind as a possibility. He hoped to draw men such as Fox and Downes from the university into his work. Douglas Downes was at that time Chaplain of Worcester College. He had already joined Brother Giles on some of his missions. In September, he and Giles were hop-picking together in Kent when Giles showed him Lord Sandwich's letter. It was Downes who persuaded him to accept, seeing at once that work on the land was a way to reclaim the wayfarer.

The project needed capital, but when it seemed viable, Lord Sandwich made an interest-free loan of £1,000 to stock the farm and meet preliminary expenses. A committee of supporters was formed at Cambridge, chaired by the Master of Jesus College.[14] The historian G. G. Coulton was a member of this committee.

Brother Giles and Roger Fox were joined by Charles Boyd, an Australian who had tried his vocation with the Community at Caldey Island, remaining in the Church of England when Aelred Carlyle and most of his monks went over to Rome. Boyd had then joined the Anglican Community at Pershore, but was never entirely at home in the Benedictine life. Two important meetings took place at the Cowley Fathers' house, St. Edward's, Westminster. One was between Roger Fox and Charles Boyd. The other was between Fox, Boyd and Major (later Colonel) A. M. Lloyd, who was there on a day retreat. The first encounter led Boyd to join the venture at Flowers Farm. The second found for the venture a friend who brought it humanity, practicality and stability. Lloyd became the first treasurer of the home, and took up residence at Flowers Farm with his family. Both Major Lloyd and Douglas Downes, in their different ways, had been moved by their experience of suffering in the Great War to dedicate their lives after it to compassion for their fellow men.

The Brothers moved in at Flowers Farm in mid December 1921, travelling by train to Evershot and jogging over the remaining three miles of country road with the farm bailiff in the dog cart. The site consisted of four empty brick houses which had first to be cleared out, the farm buildings, vegetable gardens and fields. Although great changes have taken place, this original pattern is still discernible in the lay-out of the present Friary. Word soon got round that Flowers Farm was to be a refuge for wayfarers. At Christmas 1921, the 'family' at the home had risen to sixteen, Brothers, helpers and wayfarers.

One of Brother Giles' sayings was, 'No work is pleasing to God without prayer.' Almost at once, a room was fitted out as an oratory

14. Arthur Gray, Master of Jesus College 1912–40.

with an altar, frontal, crucifix and candlesticks. Flowers Farm was in the parish of Batcombe; Giles, Roger and Charles were all lay brothers, and worshipped at the parish church on Sundays. On Tuesdays, the Vicar (Rev. J. Pullibank) came to the home to celebrate Holy Communion. But the Divine Office was a vital part of their life. They rose at 5.40 a.m., said the Angelus at 6.00 a.m. followed by Lauds and Prime from the Cowley Office Book. They kept silent prayer in the morning and again after Vespers. Most of the day was spent in manual work. At first, meals were taken in silence, but this was relaxed for the sake of the unemployed and wayfarers who joined them and shared their meals.[15]

It might have seemed, early in 1922, as though the man, the place and the work had met in the way that brings religious communities to birth. But within a year, the enterprise nearly foundered. Roger Fox says that Brother Giles 'did not have a clear idea whether the place was to be a Franciscan novitiate, or a home for tramps – or both.'[16] Surveying his career from 1911 to 1922, it would seem that Brother Giles did not find settled community life congenial, and his special gift lay in getting alongside the wayfarer and sharing his life rather than in winning him from it. His very success in attracting the support of Roger and Charles and Major Lloyd, by making the Flowers Farm project possible, diverted him from his true mission. In September 1922, he 'disappeared' from Flowers Farm. The physical strain of illness and hardship, combined with the mental strain of work to which he could not adapt, seems to have undermined him. For a time, he returned to Southern Ireland, but after 1925 his former associates lost contact with him.[17] In human terms, it was probably a mistake for Brother Giles to accept the work at Hilfield. His achievement was to inspire others to imitate his example and carry on his work.

Its survival was remarkable. The Cambridge committee, concluding that the project was not financially viable, withdrew its support. St. Clair Donaldson, Bishop of Salisbury, however, stood firm behind the little community. He talked over the situation with Brother Roger, who felt too inexperienced to take charge himself. Roger discussed matters with the Superior at Cowley. The outcome was that Lord Sandwich invited Douglas Downes to take charge. He accepted with reluctance, not because it meant exchanging a chaplaincy at Oxford for work among the down-and-outs, but out of simple doubt of his own ability. 'I'm only taking this on till someone better steps in,' he said.[18] The work was to make him a legend in his own lifetime. Brother Roger

15. J. R. Fox, Memoir.
16. ibid.
17. Letter of Major Lloyd, 12 November (No year).
18. Fr. Francis, op. cit., p. 43.

did not remain at Hilfield. He joined the Church of Rome and became an Augustinian canon at the Abbaye St. Maurice in Switzerland. Brother Charles remained, and soon new recruits came. The steady support of both Lord Sandwich and Major Lloyd was invaluable in seeing the project through this crisis.

Robert Douglas Downes who took over at Hilfield in 1922 was born at Brighton in April 1878. His father was at one time a Methodist minister, but disagreeing with the Methodist Council on the subject of eternal punishment, he took up writing for a living. Douglas' mother was an Anglican who took him to worship at St. John's, Upper Norwood. Here he first encountered Anglo-Catholicism, but until middle age, Evangelical influences on him were stronger. His biographer records a remarkable experience of his boyhood. Douglas lost his watch, and promised his life to Christ if he found it. He saw it glittering in a dry ditch and 'gave himself to the Lord.' It was his 'Fleece of Gideon'. Douglas was confirmed at the age of seventeen while still at school at Dulwich College. There too he read the lives of St. Francis by Mrs. Oliphant and Paul Sabatier. In 1896, he went up to Corpus Christi College, Oxford, where after a third in Classical Mods. he ended with second class honours in Modern History.

He prepared for the sacred ministry at Wycliffe Hall, Oxford, but before presenting himself for ordination, he taught for a short time, first at Smyrna, then at an English prep. school. He was ordained in 1903 and served as a curate, first in Walthamstow (E17), then in Lambeth (SE1). In 1908, he went to India as Vice-Principal of the Society for the Propagation of the Gospel's College at Trichinopoly, remaining there until 1914. He returned to his old parish in Lambeth for a short while before volunteering as an army chaplain, and served in Egypt during the Great War. In 1918, he joined the Oxford Pastorate, and was Chaplain of University College 1919–20 and then Worcester College.[19]

It was in these post-war years at Oxford that he encountered Brother Giles. But it was not the first time that he had worked among tramps, or 'wayfarers' as both Giles and Douglas preferred in their courtesy to call them. As an undergraduate, he had worked among them with the Oxford Christian Union, taking part in services in a lodging-house in St. Ebbe's parish.[20] At the time he came to Hilfield, Douglas Downes was regarded as an Evangelical or Low Churchman. But like many of the Franciscans, his career shows how meaningless such party labels can be. His zeal for souls was truly Evangelical, but experience made him a strong believer in sacramental confession.[21] In worship, he

19. Fr. Francis, op. cit., for biographical details.
20. ibid., p. 9.
21. ibid., p. 50.

valued simplicity and sincerity more than ritual, like St. Francis himself.

He came to Hilfield in his forties, well seasoned by experience. This, his simple trust in Providence, and his great practicality were all needed. His biographer has said that Brother Douglas – as he should now be called – 'was a genius for making something out of nothing', whether it were men or things.[22]

Lord Sandwich had generously allowed the farm the first year rent free. Thereafter, it was to rise from £70, then £100 to a maximum of £200. These terms were met, and the Earl's original loan of £1,000 was also repaid in 1926. That year, the farm itself was given up, having failed to pay its way, but the rest of the site was retained. Two more profitable occupations were undertaken – market-gardening and handicrafts. Printing, weaving, basket-making and wood-carving were all begun. The garden area at Hilfield was good for produce which was sold at a stall kept by the home at Dorchester market. Transporting it, a distance of fourteen miles, presented a problem. While Major Lloyd was living at the home, he loaned his car. When he left, they used their donkey, Madam, to take it by cart to Evershot station whence it went by train. Later, undergraduates collected £20 to buy an old Ford car, the first of many vehicles owned by the home, held all the more in affection on account of their ricketiness.

Individual well-wishers were generous in their support. Among neighbours were St. John Hornby of W. H. Smith's who gave the printing-press, Lady Lilian Digby and Mrs. Cary Batten. Another friend was Mrs. Garton of Banstead Wood, Surrey. The donkey and cart were the gift of Mrs. Berkeley Portman.[23]

Brother Giles had stressed the importance of prayer to work. But 'Work with Brother Douglas was always a priority even over formal prayer.'[24] The economics of Hilfield made this necessary, but Douglas was aware of the creative and recreative powers of work for the men to be rescued from the road, whose downfall so often was their inability to find work or their alienation from the habit of it. If Giles taught that 'to pray is to work', Douglas taught that 'to work is to pray'.

The first new recruit to join Brother Douglas was a much older man, Brother Arthur. Arthur de Winton, as he was in the world, came from a good family in Brecknockshire, and followed a career in banking. When over fifty, he was inspired by Frank Weston, Bishop of Zanzibar, to volunteer for service with The Universities Mission to Central Africa. It was after his return in 1925 that he met Brother Douglas and joined him at Hilfield. In due course, Major Lloyd gave

22. ibid., p. 44.
23. BSFA Chapter Minute Book 30.5.24.
24. Fr. Francis, op. cit., p. 47.

up as Treasurer of the home, though he continued his devoted co-operation in its work. Brother Arthur's experience made him the ideal Treasurer to succeed him.

Soon after Arthur came Brother Kenneth. In the Brotherhood of St. Francis, all the members were known as Brother whether they were ordained or not. This changed in 1937 when the custom of the Brotherhood of the Love of Christ was adopted though Douglas, a priest since 1904, continued to the end of his life to be called Brother. In the 1960s the Society of St. Francis (as they had become) felt it to be more true to the Franciscan spirit to call every member Brother – Friars (fratres or fratri) being simply, 'brothers'. Kenneth was for long senior among the unordained Brothers, and after Douglas's death, senior of all.

The Home of St. Francis – to give the establishment its proper name – was geared to reclaiming men from the life of the road by training them in the habit of hard, sustained work. The shortcoming of the unreformed Poor Law was that it treated all wayfarers alike. The experience gained by Giles, Douglas and their companions showed that this was a disastrous mistake. Among wayfarers there were those who genuinely sought work and began to walk from place to place to find it. Some were still young, strong and capable of work. But as Father Denis wrote, 'Wayfaring is a disease which saps a man's strength, moral, physical and spiritual.' Lack of settled home and work drove such men into the company of 'old lags' among the tramps, whose worst habits, almost of necessity, they picked up. The old lags were men often physically or mentally handicapped, or through the habit of years virtually incapable of work; but they deserved less harshness and more compassion than the system allowed them. In dealing with them, Douglas separated the two. The younger ones were

> not tramps at all, in the strictest sense of the word. They are youths whom misfortune or ill-chance has driven on the roads . . . We try to give them a short training, and accustom them to an eight-hour day again, so that they can win back a habit of steady work.[25]

The short training in fact lasted several months, during which men could sometimes be taught a trade. Douglas never asked – or expected – a real old tramp to be anything but a good old tramp. But he worked devotedly to improve the lot of the 'good old tramp'.

The importance attached by Brother Douglas to work did not mean that he undervalued prayer. The pattern of life at Hilfield remained much as it was in Brother Giles' time, with the Brothers rising at 5.30 a.m. and saying the seven-fold Office daily. The Offices were open to all at the Home, though attendance at Compline (9.30 p.m.) was no

25. Fr. Algy in *Church Times*, 10.3.39.

longer expected of all. In the winter months from 1923–24, the Angelus was rung at 7.00 a.m. instead of 6.00 a.m. With Brother Douglas as a resident priest, it was possible to have a regular celebration of the Eucharist at the Home on Sundays at 8.00 or 8.30 a.m. When the living of Batcombe became vacant in 1923, Brother Douglas was placed temporarily in charge, and the stipend was a useful contribution towards the rent.[26] From 1929, Brother Kenneth's proposal was followed of each member involved in the work of the Home taking off a quiet day once a month and going on retreat once a year.[27]

Douglas and his companions continued Giles' work on the roads, sharing the casual wards and the common lodging houses. If going to the former, they went literally penniless. If going to the latter, they took 2/- (10p) a day – 14/- a week, compared with the 13/9d. received by men on the dole. The lodging houses preserved more of the decencies of life, but were sometimes less hygienic than the casual wards. 'It was necessary to search the beds for possible vermin,' Brother Kenneth recalls. 'One was always glad to get back to the Friary for the privilege of a hot bath and clean underclothes.'[28] Brother Giles had always gone to the casual wards dressed in his habit. At first, Brother Douglas wore a boiler suit, but soon, he too came to wear the habit. He and his companions met abuse and blasphemy, but this changed when the wayfarers discovered their love and their willingness to share hardship. Douglas broke stones with the other tramps, and accepted their gifts of bread as well as sharing his own.[29] Bread broken with the poor was for him 'almost a sacrament'.[30]

Douglas' purpose in wayfaring was primarily evangelistic. He went to bring a message of compassion and even hope to men who often were totally alienated from the Church and from society and who might be complete atheists. Douglas sought to bring them the message that God really did care. He had some spectacular successes. One was Leslie Rose, who turned up at Hilfield seeming respectable and intelligent, but with a record of imprisonment for cat burglary and house breaking. After meeting Brother Douglas, he was moved to repentence, sacramental confession and amendment of life. Despite a stammer, he testified to his conversion at an open-air meeting conducted by the Brothers in Yeovil market. He afterwards tried to win some of his former associates from their ways, but he developed tuberculosis and died soon after. A memorial plaque was placed to him in the Friary

26. BSFA Chapter Minute Book, 10.10.22, 5.10.23, 23.11.23.
27. ibid., 12.7.29.
28. Br. Kenneth, Memoir.
29. Fr. Francis, op. cit., p. 58.
30. *Isis*, 8.3.39.

chapel with the simple inscription, 'Lost and Found.'[31] There were many failures too. Brother Douglas had once to dismiss a man from the home who struck one of his fellows with a hoe. 'I came to God's house,' he said as he went, 'and God took me in. Now God turns me out, and that puts the tin hat on God.'[32]

The experiences which Douglas and the others shared with wayfarers made it possible for them to appeal to public opinion for reform of the Poor Law. Unease on the subject was not new, as readers of Dickens' *Oliver Twist* must be well aware. As early as 1866, Government Vagrancy Committees had urged reform. Difficulty arose from the fact that standards in the casual wards had been the responsibility of local authorities, or were even left to the discretion of ward masters. The first requisite was a common minimum standard. The Great War had temporarily shelved the problem by drawing the men off the roads, but in 1919, the situation was worse than ever. Some advance was made by the Casual Poor Relief Order of 1925, which laid down that there should be warm baths, clothes were to be disinfected, there was to be proper sleeping accommodation and better food. Brother Douglas and his companions were able to testify from first-hand experience how bad conditions still were – often a less attractive prospect than prison.

In June 1925, Brother Douglas, with Mary Higgs (later known as Mother Mary) and Major Lloyd, founded the Vagrancy Reform Society. They publicised the need for reform, and advocated specific measures. They drew on the experience of the Danish labour colonies, which made a proper distinction between those who sought work, the physically or mentally handicapped, wastrels and criminals. A journalist who lived for a time in the home at Hilfield and made two long journeys on the road publicised his findings, first in newspaper articles and then in a book. From the interest aroused, fresh steps towards reform were taken in 1928. The Vagrancy Reform Society gained the interest of a Conservative M.P., Lord Henry Cavendish Bentinck.[33] Other members of Parliament and peers who gave their support were Sir John, later Lord Simon, George Lansbury, Susan Lawrence and the Bishops of Exeter and Southwark.[34] Neville Chamberlain, then

31. Fr. Francis, op. cit., pp. 49–51.
32. ibid., p. 47 f.
33. Lord Henry Cavendish-Bentinck, son of the 6th Duke of Portland by his second marriage; Conservative M.P. for Nottingham South, 1895–1906 and 1910–29.
34. Lord William Cecil, Bishop of Exeter 1916–36; Cyril Forster Garbett, Bishop of Southwark 1919–32, later Bishop of Winchester and Archbishop of York; Susan Lawrence, Labour M.P. for East Ham North, 1923–24 and 1926–31, Parliamentary Secretary to Arthur Greenwood as Minister of Health, 1929–31; Sir John Simon, sat as M.P. for Yorks., Spen Valley, as a Liberal, 1922–31 and as a National Liberal 1931–40, created Viscount Simon in 1940; George Lansbury, Labour M.P. for Bow and Bromley, 1910–12 and 1922–40, leader of the Labour Party, 1931–35.

Minister of Health, received an all-party deputation to press for reform. He felt that the country was still recovering from the General Strike of 1926, and confined action to directing that the existing regulations, including those for better food, should be exactly carried out. Arthur Greenwood, who succeeded Chamberlain in the Labour Government of 1929, went further, and took up Mary Higgs' suggestion of re-appointing the Commission of Inquiry which had reported in 1906, but whose findings had been shelved. Members of the Vagrancy Reform Society were called to give evidence to the commission. As a result of the evidence brought to light, Greenwood introduced definite reforms in the casual wards in November 1930. Separate cubicles and screened baths were introduced, work was restricted to four hours in the morning and again in the afternoon, food was further to be improved, there were to be services on Sunday. Responsibility for carrying out these reforms rested with the Vagrancy Committees and the Poor Law Conference, who were responsible to the local authorities. Not the least important was that public opinion had been roused to reform, even though it was at the time of the Great Depression.

While these improvements were being carried out, a number of hostels were set up which extended the work at Hilfield in rehabilitating wayfarers. The first was not far away at Sherborne in 1928. Local supporters included the Vicar of Sherborne, Col. Wingfield-Digby of Sherborne Castle, and the Headmaster and boys of Sherborne School. Gradually, a new pattern emerged. Brother Douglas' ambition was to see a home in every county and a hostel in every town. Hilfield was to be a mother house to train men capable of running the hostels on the lines established there. The expansion of the work was as follows:

Blackborough Hill, Cullompton, Devon (1928): This hotel was promoted by the Rev. Ernest Field[35] a friend of the Brotherhood at Hilfield, and encouraged by Lord William Cecil, Bishop of Exeter, the supporter of the Vagrancy Reform Society, who himself had slept in the casual wards.[36] It was converted from a derelict mansion.

Walcrock, Ticehurst, Sussex (1932): a farm property of 21 acres which was made into a home for 36 men. An oast house was converted into a chapel. Dr. Bell, Bishop of Chichester, was chairman of the supporting diocesan committee.

Middlebank, near Rosyth, Scotland (1932): This was a smaller venture and of short duration. It was the only home under the auspices of the Brotherhood of St. Francis north of the border. (See also below.)

Lockeridge, Wilts. (1932): This began in a converted army hut, and at

35. Rev. Ernest Field, Rector of Pulham St. Mary, Norfolk, from 1917.
36. Fr. Francis, op. cit., p. 57.

first, conditions were difficult, especially in the winter of 1932–33. In due course, the home was equipped to cater for a dozen men.

Holywell Hyde, near Welwyn Garden City, Herts. (1932): This was converted from a derelict farm formerly nicknamed 'Holywell Hidden'. One of Brother Douglas' sayings was, 'Put the waste man on the waste land'. Holywell Hyde was a good example of trying to reclaim both.

Bryn Llewellyn, near Blaenau Ffestiniog (1932): This was the first venture in North Wales. An anchoress lived in the cottage at the entrance to the home. The services in the chapel were always well attended, and several men were prepared for confirmation. The men were occupied making rugs and baskets and keeping poultry. The site of the North Welsh home was later transferred to *Cors-y-Gedol, Dyffryn, Merioneth.*

Tyn-y-cae, near Brecon (1933): This was a property in the hands of the de Winton family. Brother Arthur inherited it, and gave it to the Brotherhood as a wayfarers' home, himself becoming the first Warden. It accommodated only twelve men, but kept a flock of nineteen sheep.

Bodrean, Truro, Cornwall (1933): This hostel was the generous gift of a Miss Brodie who herself worked to convert it to a home for wayfarers.

Goodworth Clatford, Andover, Hants. (1934): A hostel was made here out of an untenanted property threatened with demolition. It helped to cater for the very large number of casuals passing through central Hants., many of them on the Bristol-Southampton route. Brother Hugh was Warden, and Brother David taught the men carpentry, making candlesticks and toys to sell.

These homes aimed, like Hilfield, to rehabilitate wayfarers through a prolonged period of training. Naturally, casuals were attracted to them, and these were not to be turned away, though they were encouraged to go to the casual wards if any were near by, and they were not to interfere with the main work of the homes.[37] The spiritual guidance offered in the homes was of great importance, and although financial support from local authorities was invaluable, the voluntary and religious nature of the work was not to be compromised.[38] The homes received grants from Public Assistance ranging from £25 to £300 p.a. It was policy to pay up to 2/6 (12$\frac{1}{2}$p) per week pocket money to men in the homes, and a grant of between 1/- (5p) and 10/- (50p) a week at the discretion of the Warden when a man went to an approved job. The discipline of the homes made it necessary that the grants made by the county committees and the Unemployment Assistance Board should go to the authorities of the homes and not to the individual men.[39]

The age-limit of men admitted to the homes was left to the discretion

37. BSFA Executive and Finance Committee Minute Book, 22.2.34, 20.6.34.
38. ibid., 22.6.37.
39. ibid., 15.5.35, 29.8.35.

of the warden, but the emphasis was on 'a Christian Home where those who are young in vagrant life can recover hope and be trained in self-support'.[40] Brother Douglas himself regarded those up to the age of twenty-five as the most promising material for rehabilitation.[41] The Central Association for Young Wayfarers' Hostels and the Unemployment Assistance Board paid 15/- (75p) a week for men over sixteen remaining at a home for at least four weeks.

Statistics are a poor guide to human conditions, but figures from the first year at two hostels are worth quoting. Lockeridge had 136 admissions in 1932. Thirty-eight left to employment and the same number to seek employment, twenty-two to other agencies, four were repatriated and three admitted to hospital. The remainder were 'casuals' of one night's residence, or remained in some hostel, or were found unsuitable.[42] Middlebank in Scotland in a period of six months took seven men for less than a week and twenty-seven for more. Of the latter, two found jobs, seven left to seek work, two left without notice, five were sent away and eleven remained in the home.[43] A more human account than these statistics is given by the account of Christmas at Middlebank in 1932. 'Few had ever celebrated the Festival, and hardly any had ever received a Christmas present.' But that year they ate Christmas turkey and listened to King George V's broadcast, and each man received from the Christmas tree a tie and a handkerchief with a shilling (5p) wrapped in the corner. They shared some of their crackers, mince-pies and fruits with children of the next village, many of whom were down with chicken-pox.[44]

The various homes were opened under the auspices of the Brotherhood of St. Francis of Assisi, often with one of the Brothers in charge as Warden. But it was policy to hand over control to local or county committees.[45] Though this involved a risk of compromising Brother Douglas' ideals, it was only possible thus to draw in the resources of good-will and support necessary for the work. Douglas and his companions gave the inspiration, but they could not solve the problem of the wayfarers alone. Though not directly the work of the Brotherhood, homes similar to theirs were set up in Durham, Essex, Gloucestershire, Kent and Somerset. In 1931, the Brotherhood took over the work of the League of Our Father (see Chapter 24) who since 1902 had been caring for wayfarers.[46]

40. ibid., 15.5.35.
41. Fr. Francis, op. cit., p. 56.
42. Statement 31.12.32.
43. Statement 30.11.32.
44. Hilfield Archives. Undated, presumed 1932.
45. Fr. Francis, op. cit., p. 76.
46. Fr. Francis, op. cit., p. 76.

By the late 1930s, the problem of wayfaring was being, if not permanently solved, at least transformed by the approach of the Second World War. After the war, the problem was set in a different context with the introduction of the Welfare State. With fewer wayfarers to rehabilitate, the homes were adapted to other uses. Tyn-y-cae and Bodrean were used for refugees, and after the war, Tyn-y-cae was taken over by the Youth Hostels Association. But it would be the greatest mistake to suppose that the mission had been accomplished. The hardest lesson to learn from Brother Douglas' life is that legislation, however humane and enlightened, will never do away with the need to get alongside the poorest of our brethren, to love and to share with them. In 1939, when the homes were closing or finding other uses, Brother Douglas wrote: 'We must keep ourselves and others awake to the wrongness of our present social and economic order. Secondly, some of us must do as St. Francis did, share the life of the poor.'[47] Those two sentences summed up a lifetime of compassion.

47. *Isis*, 8.3.39.

14

The Brotherhood of St. Francis of Assisi
1921–37

The mission to the wayfarers by Giles and Douglas in the previous chapter has been considered apart from the development of the Brotherhood of St. Francis of Assisi as a religious community. Logic has been preferred here to chronology. It has already been remarked that Brother Giles 'did not have a clear idea whether [the Home of St. Francis at Flowers Farm] was to be a Franciscan novitiate, or a home for tramps – or both.'[1] Likewise, 'Brother Douglas would have been the first to admit that he did not set out with the idea of founding a religious community.'[2] But the Community at Hilfield was not alone or even unusual in the Church of England in having evolved from a work of mercy rather than from a specific intention of establishing the religious life.

As has been said, Giles and Douglas placed value on both prayer and work. The special character of the Community at Flowers Farm was that it was not an association of religious who ministered to wayfarers; it was a community of *both* wayfarers *and* religious. As the Provisional Rule of 1927 stated, 'The Community consists of (1) Homeless Wayfarers who are able and willing to work and (2) Religious Brothers living under a Simple Rule of Life.'[3] Nor were these empty words. One Edward Thomas Furse was referred to as 'Brother Furse' even when he was up before Quarter Sessions charged with stealing gunpowder, fuses and chemicals from the store at the Friary. Brother Douglas gave evidence on his behalf which got him off, and brought him back to the Friary.[4] To the present day, one feature of life at the Friary is that all who live there, the Brothers, guests and wayfarers, share the same table and join together in work. That this was an expression of a truly Franciscan spirit is obvious enough, but it did not make it any easier to establish a Franciscan religious community. Fr. Hubert Northcott of Mirfield when visiting the Friary in

1. See above.
2. Fr. Francis, op. cit., p. 78.
3. Provisional Rule (1927).
4. BSFA Diary ff. 256, 263.

1936 commented that it was difficult to train novices there in the detachment usually thought desirable when the really worthwhile recruits would wish above all to share the work and life of the wayfarers.[5] The numbers of professed brothers grew only slowly until the Community was transformed under Fr. Algy. But the refusal to compromise the ideal gave spiritual strength to the Community.

Its survival and growth owed much to the encouragement and guidance of St. Clair Donaldson who was Bishop of Salisbury from 1921 to 1936 – exactly the most critical period of its development. He was not only Diocesan, but became Visitor to the Community; as such, with the Warden, whom he appointed, and the religious brethren meeting in Chapter, he formed the governing body.[6] He approved the Provisional Rule on his visitation on 3 February 1927. The period from then until 14 February 1931 when vows were taken by three of the Brothers was the time of testing as a religious community.

The aim of the Brotherhood was, quite simply, 'to win souls for Christ.' A firm basis of prayer life was provided. As well as Mattins and Evensong, the Brothers said Terce, Sext and None, and had half an hour of private meditation daily. The Eucharist was celebrated on Sundays, and replaced Mattins on Tuesdays, Thursdays and Saints' Days. All members of the home took some share in the prayer life, joining in prayers at 7.25 each morning and 9.30 in the evening. During breakfast there was reading, an address was given at evening prayers, and on Sundays there was a Bible class. Each member was expected to attend one service in the parish church at Batcombe or Hilfield on Sundays.[7] The habit was worn even before the Provisional Rule was drawn up. Both Giles and Douglas had found that when 'on the road', the religious dress at first provoked antagonism but soon won acceptance.

It would be difficult to say exactly when, between December 1921 and February 1931, the Brotherhood of St. Francis actually came into being as a religious community. The approval of the Provisional Rule and the taking of vows mark formal stages in its development. But the first printed number of *The Flowerette* in January 1925[8] already opens with the Constitution of the Brotherhood, and the Provisional Rule clearly developed from this. The aim was then stated to be to rescue the down-and-out men who tramped the roads; the means, providing a Christian home 'where they can obtain work and recover hope',

5. Fr. Denis, *Father Algy* (1964), p. 126.
6. Provisional Rule.
7. ibid.
8. In 1924, the numbers were cyclostyled. The name *Flowerette* seems to be a double reference, to Flowers Farm and to the famous collection, *The Little Flowers of St. Francis.*

sharing their life on the road, and training brothers for this work. It was stated that there was no endowment, but that the work was carried on by the industry of the Community and the generosity of friends. Brothers Douglas, Arthur and Bill Mansell (sometime of the Church Army, who only stayed at Hilfield about eighteen months) were then the only religious members of the Community. The patrons were the Duchess of Atholl, the Earls of Sandwich and Shaftesbury, Bishop Talbot, Bishop Burge of Oxford, Arthur Gray, Basil Levett, St. John Hornby, Mrs. Garton, Mrs. Duke and Mrs. Cary Batten.[9] This article in *The Flowerette* was written to encourage support, and it was stated that the accounts were audited annually. After the near collapse of 1922, it was necessary to restore public confidence.

Bishop Donaldson made an annual visitation of the Friary in February or March, arriving in the late morning or early afternoon and staying until the early evening. In 1928, he addressed the Brothers on the theme, 'I work the work of Him who sent me', stressing that God had a purpose for everyone, and that we were allowed a limited time for our work on earth.[10] In 1929, he blessed the chapel and confirmed two of the men, and spoke on the opportunities of emigration to Australia.[11] In 1930, he agreed to an amplification of the rule, including a provision that new recruits should be trained for two years.[12] At his visitation in 1931, he received the professions of Douglas, Arthur and Kenneth, and clothed another Brother, Charles, as a novice. The Bishop celebrated the Eucharist at which a number of the men communicated and preached on the meaning of the vows of poverty, chastity and obedience which the three Brothers had taken.[12] A year later, he confirmed five men from Hilfield and three from Blackborough.[13] Brother Philip was noviced in 1933, and in 1934 another seven candidates were confirmed.[14] The record of these years is one of slow but steady growth as a community, while its evangelical work was bearing fruit.

The further development of Hilfield as a religious community came about through its association with other ventures in the religious life.

---

9. *The Flowerette*, January 1925. Katherine Marjory née Ramsay was wife of the 8th Duke of Atholl, Conservative M.P. for Kinross and West Perths., 1923–38, Parliamentary Secretary to the Board of Education, 1924–29 – the first woman to hold government office; Anthony Ashley-Cooper, 9th Earl of Shaftesbury, Dorset J.P. and landowner; Edward Stuart Talbot was Bishop of Winchester, 1911–24; Henry Murray Burge was Bishop of Oxford, 1919–25. For Lord Sandwich and St. John Hornby, see above.
10. BSFA Diary ff. 7–8.
11. ibid., f. 98.
12. ibid., ff. 215–16.
13. ibid., f. 288.
14. ibid., f. 361, 417.

If Giles was the pioneer and Douglas the real founder, it was Father Algy who brought the work to completion. The ways of Providence are beyond man's comprehension, but however difficult to understand at the time, it can be seen in retrospect that the history of the Hilfield community would have been different, and almost certainly less fortunate, if illness had not twice intervened – first to replace Giles by Douglas in 1922, then to force Algy Robertson to return from India to which he had gone intending to devote his life there. In 1931, he accepted the living of St. Ives near Huntingdon. There he established the Brotherhood of the Love of Christ, a fourth community of men on Franciscan lines along with those at Plaistow, Hilfield and Peckham. It was not so remarkable that a man of Algy's vision should have envisaged forming a single Franciscan community, but it was a triumph that he was able very largely to bring it about. The history of religious orders has more often seen their branching into separate orders, as the Cluniacs and Cistercians stemmed from the Benedictines, and as the Medieval Franciscans split into Spirituals and Conventuals.

It was not long before contact developed between Hilfield and St. Ives. Algy visited Hilfield in August 1934.[15] He was then still a member of the Christa Seva Sangha (see below). Brother Kenneth, who was then acting Warden, went on retreat to St. Ives in March 1935.[16] These were only preparations for Algy's extended visit to Hilfield in 1936, which was to have momentous consequences. Before continuing the story, it is necessary to turn aside and recount Algy's experience of communities in both India and St. Ives, and also to take note of the wider but looser association which had already brought men and women of common sympathies together – the Fellowship of the Way.

Before leaving the story of Hilfield in its primal simplicity, a little more may be said of the life there. Many distinguished visitors came. James Adderley was there in August 1930 and June 1932.[17] Lord Sandwich stayed the night in August 1932.[18] The Bishops of Southwell (Henry Mosley) and St. Albans (Michael Bolton Furse) came, separately, in August 1933.[19] In 1934, the Trades Union Congress held a commemoration at Dorchester of the centenary of the 'Tolpuddle Martyrs'. George Lansbury, David Grenfell[20] and Mr. Stevenson of the *Daily Herald* took the opportunity of visiting the Friary.[21] A more

15. ibid., f. 447.
16. ibid., f. 453.
17. ibid., ff. 181, 319.
18. ibid., f. 332.
19. ibid., ff. 387–88.
20. David Rhys Grenfell, Labour M.P. for Glamorgan, Gower, 1922–59.
21. BSFA Diary, f. 451.

unusual visitor was a certain 'Francis of Antioch', once a film actor, then a priest of the Syrian Church, who had taken to the roads delivering tracts.[22] But the Hilfield Community was particularly indebted to visitors from older established religious orders who were able to offer helpful guidance. One who should be particularly mentioned is Father Hubert Northcott of Mirfield.

Despite material hardships and the growing pains of a religious community, the Brotherhood of St. Francis had the ability to enjoy life to the full. The Diary of the house abounds in evidence: a Rogationtide procession when the front door had to be barred to keep out the geese;[23] a 'very good tea and sing-song at Wittenden's Café' to round off a very wet outing to Salisbury;[24] a football match against a team from the nearby village of Melbury Osmund – 'They were very badly behaved; injured three of our men, offered to fight two or three of our men and had to be rebuked by the referee.'[25] The quality of life and evidence of the Franciscan spirit of joy comes across as clearly in these times of recreation as in the record of rules and professions.

22. ibid., f. 329.
23. ibid., f. 39.
24. ibid., f. 193.
25. ibid., f. 304.

15

The Brotherhood of the Holy Cross

In his autobiography *Father Potter of Peckham*, George Potter says two
things which give valuable clues to his spirituality:

> It is that dirty towel of humble service – just as we should have
> found it in the Upper Room – which we have made our symbol of
> service.[1]
> I have always loved St. Francis of Assisi. His wholehearted giving
> was so like the perfect selflessness of his Master, Jesus Christ. He
> was indeed in love with the Love of God.[2]

'Humble service'; 'wholehearted giving'; 'perfect selflessness'; much of
Fr. Potter's own work is summed up in these phrases.

It is fortunate that he wrote his two autobiographical works, *Father
Potter of Peckham* and *More Father Potter*. The four lines of his entry in
Crockford tell us less than similar entries about most clergy. The B.H.C.
Quarterly, beginning in December 1931, is one of the chief records of
his Community. His books are chatty and popular in style, but they
convey a picture of the man, though a self-portrait, and fill in many
details of his life.

George Potter came from a more humble background than most of
the other Franciscan pioneers. For him, there was no upbringing at
Public School and Oxbridge. He felt a vocation to the priesthood at
the age of nine.[3] He entered Kelham in 1909, in those days the chief
passage to the Anglican priesthood for boys with little means. He
stayed eighteen months, but developed severe gastric trouble and was
forced to leave. 'For thirty years of my life I have suffered from severe
gastritis,'[4] he wrote later. Nevertheless, he regarded Father Kelly of
Kelham and Father David Jenks, who became Superior in his time
there, as two of the strongest influences on his life.[5] He was able to
complete his training for the priesthood through a two-year course to

1. op. cit., p. 12.
2. ibid., p. 13.
3. ibid., p. 17.
4. ibid., p. 61.
5. *More Father Potter*, p. 34.

become an Associate of King's College, London, anonymous donors helping him to meet the expenses.[6] He was ordained in the diocese of Southwark in 1912, becoming Curate of All Saints', South Wimbledon. This was not, as the district might suggest, a pleasant part of suburbia, but 'a very poor parish'.[7] He served for a year as an army chaplain, but was otherwise at Wimbledon until 1917. Then until 1923 he was at St. Bartholomew's, Bermondsey. In 1923, Bishop Cyril Garbett asked him to take charge of St. Chrysostom's, Peckham. Fr. Potter described it as 'the most derelict parish in the diocese',[8] the Church sadly in disrepair and the Vicarage non-existent. Even so great a spirit as his was daunted, but as he prayed for guidance, he noticed the words written up, 'Christ our Life.'[9] He accepted, and began his ministry camping out with three homeless boys in the parish hall. He recalled in 1931 that three people came to his first service, their total offerings $6^1/_2$d. (about $2^1/_2$p). In 1924, he moved with a layman into a dilapidated public house. Soon, the response he gained from the parish was excellent. 100 people were assigned definite jobs in the parish, and did them. The attendance at the parish communion rose to 200. At the house, a cosy parlour was fitted out, and a cellar where in summer at least local boys could take a cold shower – a luxury in days when most homes in the district were without bathrooms, and public baths were beyond most pockets. The Diocese, seeing that Fr. Potter was making a go of the parish, purchased a proper priest's house in 1926.[10]

By the late 1920s, Fr. Potter had worked for fifteen years in poor parishes of south London. He had to organise sports clubs, concert parties, play the organ, run the choir, scouts, church clubs, act as doctor, nurse, lawyer, shorthand typist, cook, charlady, vet and undertaker as well as visiting and teaching the children. 'A band of self-sacrificing men ready to work eighteen hours a day would be invaluable,' he wrote.[11] Thus was born the Brotherhood of the Holy Cross. Its genesis thus had obvious points of comparison with the Society of the Divine Compassion. Fr. Potter's first achievement was as a parish priest, bringing back to life a church which was spiritually run down and materially almost a wreck. He invites comparison with Fr. Henry Chappel, S.D.C., and with great priests like Frs. Mackonockie and Wainwright.

Fr. Potter's first two recruits to the Brotherhood were Brother John,

6. *Father Potter of Peckham*, p. 18.
7. ibid.
8. ibid., p. 25.
9. ibid., p. 28.
10. B.H.C. Quarterly December 1931.
11. ibid.

formerly handyman at the Order of the Holy Paraclete at Whitby whom Fr. Potter met by chance visiting Kelham, and Brother Francis, lay reader and general factotum at Bermondsey. Francis already knew Fr. Potter and had looked round St. Chrysostom's with him when he was offered the parish. Brother Stephen joined the Brotherhood in 1931 and 'seemed to spend most of his life in the kitchen'.[12]

George Potter had already felt called to the particular work for which he became famous. An encounter with a delinquent boy in his days at South Wimbledon led him to conclude: 'All the boy needed was some affection and discipline. It was then that I decided that I wanted to have a home for youngsters like him.'[13] The care of such boys became the special work of his Community.

Fr. Potter mapped out a life for his Community which demanded real toughness of character. He could not be accused of any lack of warmth in his heart, but his preference for 'muscular Christianity' led to some one-sidedness. 'I did not want "pious" young men for the community,' he wrote, 'I wanted the type of man who makes a good scout-master.'[14] Later he wrote of the 'type of worship which appeals to elderly ladies and a few effeminate youths' and of the 'joy' of having a public school captain or sports captain serving the altar, or scouts serving in the parish or teaching Sunday school.[15] He complained that some postulants to the Brotherhood 'were quite happy when swinging censers, but did not seem so content with a dustpan in their hands.'[16] Fr. Potter was fortunate in having his mother, until her death, and his two sisters to help look after him at Peckham and bring a feminine touch to the place. His sisters later took charge of the hostel at Southwick.

His work for poor boys began with strays without homes and boys sent to him by the magistrates. A derelict factory was taken over and converted into the Hostel of St. Francis for Homeless Boys. Between 1928 and 1931, over seventy boys passed through his care, and by 1931, the hostel had settled down to catering for a regular family of twenty. Fr. Potter's aim was to turn them 'into decent Christians and useful citizens'. Some became servers and Sunday school teachers, and some even began to hope for a life of service to others.[17]

One problem in Peckham was the number of stray, sick and maimed dogs and cats whom nobody wanted or cared for. Fr. Potter undertook to put these down humanely – 'a useful, but not always tasteful, job'

12. *Father Potter of Peckham*, p. 52.
13. ibid., p. 57.
14. ibid., p. 40.
15. *More Father Potter*, p. 39.
16. B.H.C. Quarterly December 1931.
17. ibid.

as he said, 'done in the spirit of St. Francis.' The pelts were sold and the money used to buy a clock for the Boys' Common Room and three habits for the novices.[18]

The Brotherhood grew as its work grew. They began with a very simple routine of daily Eucharist, Mattins, Evensong and Compline. 'I admit that work came first,' Fr. Potter wrote.[19] By 1932, however, a daily pattern of prayer and work had been built up. The Lesser Hours were said, but while some brothers said Prime, others began the day's chores, while even the daily Eucharist was attended only by 'as many brothers as can be spared'. But there was a meditation after Terce, intercessions after Sext, and after 10.15 p.m., about an hour after Compline, talking ceased.[20] The boys in the hostel attended prayers at 7.00 in the morning and 9.30 in the evening.

'We can offer no quiet or contemplation,' Fr. Potter wrote. He often received letters from men who wanted to 'get away from the world' and sought 'the peace and solitude' of the monastic life. 'It always sounds so strange to us, but, of course, we cannot blame the writers . . . we do need men who are . . . "self-contained", i.e. such as have a real vision of Christ and can feel near Him in work and noise, as well as in the peace of the Sanctuary.'[21] Fr. Potter also had to put off men seeking a path to Holy Orders – still not easily attained between the wars by men of limited means. Fr. Potter summed up a lot of their life at Peckham when he said, 'We have to spend more time at the bottom of the Mount of Transfiguration than at the top.'[22]

A Book of Principles was drawn up for recruits and aspirants to the Community, explaining the rule of life and the counsels of poverty, chastity and obedience. 'I will not marry, or seek to marry, so that my affections can rest wholly upon Christ, to whom I desire entirely to devote my life. I will live in holy chastity.'[23] So ran the vow of chastity. Nevertheless, the Book of Principles described the life of celibacy as 'not normal' and the unmarried state as not 'in itself higher than the married'.[24]

But while unsuitable recruits were deterred, the Brotherhood continued to grow. In 1932 it consisted of Fr. Potter, styled Priest Superior; three brothers and five novices. But the hard work strained them to the limit. 'What a joy it will be for them to have a room they can call their own – and some have waited now for seven years!'[25] The strain

18. ibid.
19. *Father Potter of Peckham*, p. 41.
20. B.H.C. Quarterly September 1932.
21. ibid.
22. ibid.
23. *Father Potter of Peckham*, p. 44.
24. *More Father Potter*, pp. 78–9.
25. B.H.C. Quarterly December 1932.

on Fr. Potter himself was considerable, and in September 1932 Brother John became Prior, supervising the work of the Brothers and training the novices and postulants. This left Fr. Potter more free to attend to the parish.[26] The opening in 1933 of the Hostel of St. Martin at Southwick near Shoreham came as a great blessing to the Community. It made it possible for the Brothers to take a holiday by the sea and enjoy the countryside.

Both Cyril Garbett, Bishop of Southwark 1919–32, and his successor Richard Parsons (1932–41) were good friends to the parish and Community. Bishop Parsons visited the hostels in February 1933. In June, he sang Mass at 8 o'clock at St. Chrysostom's. Then in the chapel of St. Francis' Hostel, Fr. Potter was formally installed as Superior; the Brothers and Novices took simple vows. The Community thus gained recognised status. 'Our great day', Fr. Potter called it.[27] Canon Cockin (later Bishop of Bristol) became Warden. A small band of friends were formed into oblates and associates, though tertiaries would have been more appropriate to a Franciscan-type community. The Third Order attached to Christa Seva Sangha and the Brotherhood of the Love of Christ was growing in the 1930s, and tertiary meetings in South London took place at St. Chrysostom's.

Further expansion of the work for boys came through the generosity of Lily Davenport Cancellor. This lady was the widow of a London magistrate, H. L. Cancellor, who founded a hostel at Basingstoke during the Great War for boys on probation. In 1931, the Brotherhood of the Holy Cross were asked to re-organise the work and move the hostel to the London area. In 1933, a house was found at Linden Grove, Nunhead, large enough for forty boys and ten brothers to be accommodated. In 1934, the boys were moved from St. Francis' Hostel to what was appropriately named the Cancellor Memorial Hostel.[28] Tribute was paid in the B.H.C. Quarterly to Mrs. Cancellor when she died in 1938. The maximum number of boys in the hostel rose until at the beginning of the Second World War it reached forty and finally forty-six.

Naturally, the Brotherhood's care for boys in trouble moved others to care for unfortunate girls. Back in 1925, Fr. Potter applied to the South London Church Fund for a grant towards a woman worker to provide leadership for the women and girls in his parish. The worker he got was Molly Lockyer of the Greyladies. For ten years she worked in the parish, living in a flat in a poor area, forsaking peace and comfort as she carried on her work in the Sunday schools and women's clubs. In 1935, Molly Lockyer established a girls' hostel. As Fr. Potter

26. ibid.
27. ibid. June 1933.
28. ibid. December 1934.

wrote, it was not a venture of the Brotherhood but something 'which has grown naturally out of the Franciscan spirit which imbues the parish and workers'.[29] Miss Lockyer went to Cape Town in 1936. Her work was carried on by Miss H. M. Jones, popularly known as 'Jonah', until her retirement in 1954. The Girls' Hostel came to be called St. Clare's. It was moved to Oxford during the war.

When moves were made to draw the Franciscan communities together, the Friary at Peckham became a convenient meeting place. At Whitsun 1934, several members of the Brotherhood of St. Francis joined Christa Seva Sangha and the Brotherhood of the Holy Cross for a three-day retreat conducted by Fr. Talbot of Mirfield.[30] Those present included both Douglas and Algy. Fr. Potter described the gathering as 'most inspiring'. The Chapter of the three Brotherhoods met at Peckham at St. Francistide 1935 to discuss a common rule.[31] In the end, the Brotherhood of the Holy Cross was not to become part of the Society of St. Francis, but the links were sufficiently close in 1937 for Brother Paul to be sent to Hilfield for his novitiate.[32]

As time went on, the combined strain of parish and community began to tell on Fr. Potter. In 1930, he had been allowed an assistant priest, Geoffrey How. After three years, he was replaced by Charles Matthews. But in September 1936, Fr. Potter wrote, 'I wonder sometimes whether I shall be able to carry on both the work in the parish and the Community.' He was at that time attempting to spend three days a week in each.[33] At the end of the year, the Bishop gave him a year's leave of absence from the parish during which he lived at the Friary. At first, a married tertiary priest, Leslie Stephenson, was to take over the parish,[34] but in the event Fr. Denis of the Society of St. Francis took charge.[35] Fr. Potter took treatment for his gastric ulcers. His doctors advised him to give up part of the work. And so in 1938, Fr. Francis, S.S.F. (William Tyndale-Biscoe, formerly of St. Ives) became Vicar of St. Chrysostom's. Fr. Potter in theory became his honorary curate, the Friary now being his chief work. His health was still precarious. He collapsed on Christmas Eve 1938 but managed to struggle through the Midnight Mass. He had an operation early in 1939.[36]

The work of the Friary continued through the blitz and all the

29. ibid. March 1935.
30. ibid. March, June 1934.
31. ibid. December 1935.
32. ibid. December 1937.
33. ibid. September 1936.
34. ibid. December 1936.
35. *Father Potter of Peckham*, pp. 83–4.
36. B.H.C. Quarterly March 1939.

hazards of the Second World War. The number of boys in the hostel dropped to thirty and dwindled to twenty-two by the end of the war. Some auxilliary firemen were billeted on them for a time. The boys' dining room was converted into a shelter. On three occasions in the autumn of 1940, bombs fell in the garden. The boys slept in Anderson shelters until mid-November, and when they were flooded out, in the gymnasium.[37] Fr. Potter slept in the chapel throughout the war, to be near the Blessed Sacrament, and always available.[38] Only two boys were slightly injured during the war. Some of Fr. Potter's old boys served with distinction in the war and received decorations for bravery.

At the end of the Second World War, the Brotherhood consisted of nine Brothers and one oblate.[39] The Brotherhood took over the house at Stanford-le-Hope from the Society of Divine Compassion and made it into the boys' hostel which Brother Stephen looked after. The hostel was later moved again, to Holy Trinity Vicarage, Lee, S.E.13. Two of the Brothers, Martin and Thomas, were engaged in parish work at Hinckley, Leics. Another, Brother Bernard, was in Aden. Men still came forward to test their vocation, but the last to be admitted to life vows were Andrew and Arnold, who were professed by Bishop William Stannard of Woolwich on 23 April 1953.[40]

The failure of men to find their vocation with the Community, and the dispersal of some of the Brothers, reflected how conditions were changing. As Fr. Potter himself recognised, the Welfare State took over responsibility for much of the 'washing of the feet'.[41] He hoped that the changed conditions would make it possible for the Brothers to undertake more parish work. In a sense, the Welfare State had made the Brotherhood the new poor. The Brothers received no salary, though they were allowed 4/- or 5/- (20 or 25p) a week to spend on themselves if need be. They did not pay National Insurance and therefore could not look forward to a state pension. It was hoped to invest a little money for the Brothers' old age.[42] It was perhaps fortunate that the Brotherhood was wound up before having to face such a grim outlook in the inflation of the 1960s and 1970s.

George Potter was made an Honorary Canon of Southwark in 1954, a fit tribute to his long service in the Diocese. He died on 15 February 1960 after receiving the Blessed Sacrament from Fr. Ashby, Vicar of

37. ibid. December 1940.
38. *Father Potter of Peckham*, p. 98.
39. Frs. George, Francis and Giles; Brs. Peter, Stephen, Martin, Thomas, Christopher and Andrew; Br. Lawrence (oblate).
40. Memoir of Br. Arnold.
41. *More Father Potter*, xi.
42. *Father Potter of Peckham*, p. 125.

St. Antholin's, Nunhead. One of the last members of the Community before it was dissolved has written:

> Fr. George was a great priest, easy to talk to, and compassionate. Looking back, however, I would say, he was not cut out to run a regular religious community. B.H.C. was a very informal group, and the tensions that arose at the Friary, Linden Grove, came out of the tug of war that the hankerings for a regular observance brought about. This resulted in Brothers doing their own thing or leaving. Novices couldn't take the strain. Fr. George's personality kept it going. He was an individualist, but a well-loved one. When he died it was only a matter of time for B.H.C. to fold up.[43]

Of those in the Community in its last phase, three found their way into the Sacred Ministry – Francis, who became Rector of Houghton Conquest, Beds., in 1952; Giles who, after a curacy at Clewer, joined the Society of St. Francis; and Bernard who became a parish priest in Lancashire. Stephen and Arnold also joined the Society of St. Francis. The other Brothers left before the Community expired. That three Brothers should find their way into the Society of St. Francis was only a partial realisation of the unification once envisaged. Perhaps Fr. Potter was too much of an individualist to merge his life's work in a wider organisation as Douglas and Algy had done. The Brotherhood of the Holy Cross was very much his personal *tour de force*.

43. Memoir of Br. Arnold.

16

Jack Winslow and Christa Seva Sangha

An important development in the Franciscan movement took place in India in the 1920s. It was native to Indian soil, though the stimulus came from English missionaries. Like the Society of the Divine Compassion, it did not begin, but became Franciscan. Indirectly, it led to the drawing together of English Franciscan communities and to the formation of a Third Order in England.

The inspiration came from Jack Winslow, son of the Rector of Hanworth in Middlesex. He was related to Charringtons, the wealthy brewers, and more distantly to one of the Pilgrim Fathers.[1] He was a colleger at Eton. 'I was not really happy there,' he wrote,[2] and went up from there to Balliol College, Oxford, where he took second class honours in Classical Mods. and Greats. After taking his B.A. in 1906, he made a short visit to India and also spent some time at Oxford House. He trained for the sacred ministry at Wells, and was ordained in the diocese of Southwark to serve as Curate of Wimbledon from 1907 to 1911.[3] Then until 1913, he was a lecturer at St. Augustine's, Canterbury. He left for India on New Year's Day, 1914, which was to be his base for the next twenty years.

Winslow has recorded his experiences in two books. *Christa Seva Sangha* was written in 1930 when he was still in the midst of his Indian ministry. *The Eyelids of the Dawn* was written in 1954, twenty years after his return. Both are largely autobiographical, but they are the main source for an account of the community he founded.

From 1914 to 1922, Winslow served as a missionary with the Society for the Propagation of the Gospel at Dapoli, Ahmadnagar and Kolhar.[4] His experience in those years led him to conclude, 'I must become an Indian to the Indians.'[5] He felt the influence of the great missionary,

1. Jack Winslow: *The Eyelids of the Dawn* (ED) for autobiographical details.
2. ibid., p. 31.
3. He almost overlapped with George Potter who was ordained to the adjacent parish of South Wimbledon in 1912.
4. *Crockford.*
5. ED, p. 75.

Charles Freer Andrews,[6] whose initials the Indians adopted to stand for 'Christ's Faithful Apostle'. Winslow believed that the Christian missionaries had failed 'to offer [the Indians] the gift of real love and equal friendship'.[7] Winslow was impressed by the ancient tradition of asceticism among the Indian sages and their distinctive community, the ashram. The ashram was in vogue at the time. Gandhi set up one at Ahmedabad where he lived in the traditional style with his disciples. S. Jesudason and Ernest Forrester-Paton[8] set up one at Tirupattur in 1921.[9] It was while Winslow was on furlough in England in 1919 that the inspiration occurred to him. On 12 August, he had a mystical experience as of an 'imperious voice' and saw what had to come into being.[10] It was nearly three years later on St. Barnabas' Day (11 June) 1922 that, with the approval of the Bishop E. J. Palmer of Bombay, his Community was formed. Bishop Palmer conducted a service of inauguration at St. Barnabas' church, Miri, an outstation of the S.P.G. Mission at Ahmadnagar. With the association of day and church, it was hardly surprising that St. Barnabas should have been chosen as patron saint for the Community – a saint who has always inspired both missionaries and religious.

The Community was called Christa Seva Sangha, literally Christ-Service-Society, or as Winslow rendered it, Society of Servants belonging to Christ. The original members were Winslow himself and five Indians. Their ideal was 'A life of common service and equal fellowship for Indians and Europeans, and the development of Indian ways for the expression of Christian life and worship.'[11] Winslow believed that the great obstacle to missionary work was that it presented 'the water of life in a Western cup'.[12] His dream was that English brothers in the Community would bring the Catholic tradition of the Church while the Indian brothers would pare away whatever was accidental, temporary and local in Western Christianity.

As well as the tradition of the ashram, the Community revered the model of the *sannaysi*, the ascetic, wandering religious teacher. The sannaysi wore a saffron robe. The Brothers of the Sangha wore a robe

6. Charles Freer Andrews, graduate and later chaplain and fellow of Pembroke College, Cambridge. Member of the Cambridge University Mission Brotherhood at Delhi 1904–15.
7. Jack Winslow: *Christa Seva Sangha* (CSS), p. 11.
8. S. Jesudason, a Tamil Christian, and Forrester-Paton, a Scottish Presbyterian, were medical doctors together at the Scottish Hospital in Poona before starting the ashram at Tirupattur. Jesudason was known as Periannan (Big Brother) and Forrester-Paton as Chinannan (Little Brother).
9. ED, p. 78.
10. CSS, p. 18.
11. ibid., p. 10.
12. ibid., p. 16.

of plain white cloth with a saffron girdle. The saffron girdle was later adopted by the Brotherhood of the Love of Christ in England.

The Community began in a small house in the mission compound at Miri. They had a constitution approved by Bishop Palmer. Winslow was elected head of the community, styled *acharya*. Bishop Palmer acted as visitor until he resigned as Bishop of Bombay in 1929. The Community aspired to complete simplicity of life, sharing their few possessions. They slept on bedding on the verandah. The food was strictly vegetarian – a necessity with the various prohibitions on meat among the Indians. The fare was to be the cheapest available in the villages costing only 6d. $(2^1/_2p)$ a day, consisting mainly of unleavened cakes, green vegetables, rice, lentils, oil and butter. Christa Seva Sangha differed from the Western tradition in that it was not, as such, composed of celibates. One of the original Indian brothers was married, and lived in a tiny separate house adjoining that of the brothers. Postulants wore a dhoti[13] and shirt. Celibate brothers who dedicated their lives to religion and renunciation were allowed to adopt the full saffron dress, thus identifying themselves with the life of the sannaysi.[14]

In the way of life, *bhakti* came first – devotion to Our Lord, and the full life of prayer. Study, particularly of the Scriptures, came next. Finally came the life of service to the sick, suffering and needy, the showing forth of the beauty of Christ in word and life. It is here that Christa Seva Sangha departed most radically from Hindu ideals, by associating renunciation with service, and affirming the goodness of the material creation.[15]

Before the Sangha was founded, Winslow had co-operated with the great liturgical scholar E. C. Ratcliffe[16] and others in drawing up *The Eucharist in India* which was published in 1920. Ratcliffe used his extensive knowledge of Christian traditions in the East in preparing it. The Liturgy which they drew up was used in the Sangha in Marathi and English. The spiritual life of the ashram attempted to blend some of the best from European and Oriental rites. The hours of morning and evening twilight were used for meditation. Specifically Western traditions were not excluded. The procession of lights at Candlemas, of palms on Palm Sunday, and the washing of feet on Maundy Thursday, appealed to the Indian mind.[17] Evangelistic work as such received less stress than living the Christian life, and service. Winslow quoted

13. Dhoti: Hindu loin-cloth.
14. CSS, p. 21.
15. ibid.
16. ED, p. 82. Ratcliffe, a great liturgical scholar, became Vice-Principal of Westcott House (1924–30). He later became Ely Professor of Divinity at Cambridge (1947) and Regius Professor (1958).
17. CSS, pp. 23–4.

the Indian proverb, 'Those who are thirsty will go to the river: the river need not go to them.'[18]

The first six years 1922–28 were the time of testing. The Community shared in the evangelistic work of the Ahmadnagar district, and had particular success among the outcastes. Orthodox Hindus approved of their work which could hardly fail to raise the desperately low standards among the least fortunate members of society.[19] The community remained at Miri for a year, then moved to an unoccupied bungalow at Junnar, fifty miles north of Poona, again for a year. Then for two years they were at Ahmadnagar, occupying what once had been a Muslim tomb. This was a better centre than the villages, and the Community established friendly contact with both Hindus and Muslims.

The years 1926–27 marked a watershed. The Community was still without a permanent base, and two of the original members left. A small legacy came to the Community, and the four remaining members used it to go on pilgrimage to the Holy Land. Winslow as acharya went on to London, and as a result of his visit, two essential needs were met. Dame Monica Wills gave £1,000,[20] sufficient to purchase five and a half acres of land outside Poona where a permanent ashram could be created. Winslow also met a number of young men, mostly Oxbridge graduates, interested in missionary work. Three of them returned with him to India in 1927; five others followed later in the year. Among the new recruits was Algy Robertson (see following chapter). Two others who went out with Algy perhaps deserve special mention. One was Oliver Fielding Clarke who after staying at Poona until the end of 1928 did a further two years service in Bombay before returning to England. The other was Verrier Elwin who dedicated the rest of his life to India. In 1933, he and an Indian member of the Sangha, Shamras Hivale, made their own settlement at Karanjia where they had a chapel dedicated to St. Francis and where Elwin wrote his *Hours of St. Francis* and life of St. Francis. By then he had become an ardent political disciple of Gandhi and drifted away, not only from the Christian ministry but from the Church altogether. This was a preparation for his work in Indian anthropology which was to win him international recognition. Of the eight new members, four were priests and four laymen, and three of each remained in the Community. Fresh Indian recruits also joined, and when Winslow was writing *Christa Seva Sangha* in 1930, the Community numbered about twenty.[21]

'When you bring Christ to us, bring Him to us not as a civilised

18. ibid., p. 25.
19. ibid., p. 32.
20. ED, p. 89.
21. CSS, pp. 40–1.

European, but as an Asian ascetic, whose wealth is communion and whose riches are prayers.' With such a longing among Indians, the appeal of St. Francis to the religious Hindu is understandable. When the rule of the Sangha was amplified in 1928, St. Francis became joint patron saint with St. Barnabas – a move in which Algy Robertson was influential; it is from this time that the Community was more formally Franciscan. The spirit of the Community also drew on the Orthodox tradition of monasticism developed by St. Basil.[22]

Another step in the Franciscan direction was to divide Christa Seva Sangha into a First and Third Order. Six years of experience as a mixed community were now behind them. The First Order were henceforth specifically members of the Poona ashram. The Third Order, at least to begin with, were closely connected with the work of the ashram, but it soon took on the character of other Third Orders: they shared the ideals of the ashram, knowledge of Christ, simplicity of life, and the brotherhood of mankind, while not necessarily joining in their work.[23]

Poona is one of the great intellectual centres of India, and an advantage of the Ashram's location was that the Community could work among Indian students. It provided for the first time a hostel for Indian Christian students.[24] The Cowley Fathers had already been at work for some time in Poona, and once again their wisdom and experience proved invaluable. The Presbyterians helped by sharing their hall for lectures and Bible study.[25]

For eight months, the Community lived in tents while the ashram was being built,[26] but gradually the buildings and the life of the Community took shape. Bishop Palmer blessed the ashram on Michaelmas Day 1928. On Bishop Palmer's resignation in 1929, his place as Visitor of the Community was taken by Bishop Azariah of Dornakal – the first Indian bishop of the Anglican communion. The student hostel was begun in two separate hired bungalows each about half a mile from the ashram; a third bungalow was added later. About twenty students were accommodated, including Christians, Hindus and Muslims. They dined together, and their food was vegetarian. It was hoped that the common meal would establish a sacramental bond of fellowship.[27] A room was used as a chapel at the hostel with a daily Eucharist and morning and evening prayers. This was mainly for the Christian students, but though worship was not compulsory, students of other

22. ibid., p. 40.
23. ibid.
24. ibid., p. 35.
25. ibid., p. 37.
26. Fr. Denis, op. cit., p. 82.
27. CSS, p. 51.

faiths often joined in. Great emphasis was placed on service. Schools for poor children were run by the hostel students, one for the children of Muslim students, another for children of untouchables. Bible circles were arranged for Christian students which were not confined to those at the hostel, and women students were admitted – a bold step in the circumstances.[28] Largely through the enthusiasm of Brother Bernard Fox, the hostel formed a cricket XI of which they were duly proud. A member of the Sangha, either of the First or the Third Order, was generally Warden of the Hostel. It is one part of Jack Winslow's work which has survived to the present day.[29]

The student hostel became an important work of the Community, but their other work continued. A weekly visit was made by members to a leper asylum six miles away.[30] On great religious festivals, the Brothers followed the Indian custom of giving a feast to poor and outcaste children.[31] They worked in the villages, trying to spread knowledge of hygiene as well as preaching the Gospel.[32] The importance of the life was still emphasised. 'Unless the Church can produce Christian Yogis,' Winslow wrote, 'masters in the spiritual life, who are competent to direct others in the discipline and science of the mystical way, she will fail to attract the choicest spirits of Hinduism.'[33]

Algy Robertson, who had had a remarkable influence on Christa Seva Sangha in a very few years, was forced through ill-health to return to England in 1930 (see below). But an important new recruit in 1932 was W. Q. ('Bill') Lash who joined the Community after serving his title at St. Mary's, Portsea; later, from 1947 to 1961, he was to be Bishop of Bombay.

When the Community was reorganised in 1928, the ashram continued to be open to both celibate and married members. This was in the Indian tradition, and as the Indian Brothers for the most part wished to be open to the possibilities of marriage, this was a necessary provision if the Community were to retain its joint English-Indian composition. A more serious problem was that the original group from 1922 found it difficult to fit into the pattern of life at Poona. In 1932, this was met by establishing a separate village ashram at Aundh which better suited their needs, while the Franciscan style of life at Poona could continue to develop. In 1934, Jack Winslow decided to leave India and return to England. On his departure, it was decided to separate the two. The Community at Aundh retained the name Christa

28. Fr. Denis, op. cit., p. 89.
29. ibid., p. 91; CSS, p. 53.
30. CSS, p. 49.
31. ibid., p. 51.
32. ibid., p. 55.
33. ibid., p. 47.

Seva Sangha, and a married Indian member, Shankarao Wairagar, took charge. Those at Poona took the modified name Christa Prema Seva Sangha – Society of the Ministry of the Love of Christ. The celibate members continued to live in the ashram at Poona. Its Third Order, some of whose members were in England where they helped to foster the vocation of tertiaries, continued. Fr. Lash became acharya of the Poona Community. Apart from a short time when Fr. Harold Satchell, tragically killed in an accident, took over, Fr. Lash remained acharya until he left India in 1961. Even after becoming Bishop of Bombay, he spent a month each year in the ashram in the rainy season. Life in the ashram was modified during the Second World War. The difference between the First and Third Orders was abolished. Though the unmarried members continued under a regular rule, they were allowed to earn money for the support of the ashram – necessary when less financial support from England was forthcoming. Jack Winslow continued to support Christa Seva Sangha, but the English Committee of supporters transferred to Christa Prema Seva Sangha. The English Community at St. Ives (see next chapter) which had begun as a branch house of Christa Seva Sangha, declared in June 1934 that the parent body was no longer a religious community, but a fellowship working in a village area.[34]

An account of Winslow's work in India must take account of two interests he had very deeply at heart. One was his commitment to the movement for independence, which rapidly gathered strength in the 1930s. 'We of the Sangha', he wrote, 'were heart and soul with India in her aspirations.'[35] His sympathies, however, did not extend to the Muslim movement for an independent Pakistan. Jinnah's campaign, which Gandhi himself came to recognise as inevitable, Winslow dismissed as 'disastrous'.[36]

Jack Winslow continued his remarkable career after leaving India. In 1932, he had become associated with the Oxford Group Movement. When he came to England in 1934, he attended one of their house parties, and it was then that he decided that he could no longer remain acharya of the Sangha.[37] The Oxford Group continued to be his main interest in the 1930s.[38] He served a number of curacies in England including one from 1939 to 1942 at his father's old parish of Hanworth. He had two sessions, 1942–43 and 1944–48, as Chaplain of Bryanston School. But his most important role in his later years was as Chaplain of Lee Abbey, a position he held from 1948 to 1962. However different

34. Brotherhood of the Love of Christ Chapter Minute 9.6.34.
35. ED, p. 108.
36. ibid., p. 117.
37. Fr. Denis, op. cit., pp. 109–10.
38. ED, pp. 139–41.

from Poona, Lee Abbey was another community of both married and single people with a vision – in this case, of the renewal of the Church.[39] This accorded with his other work in India, for he had taken part while there in the first discussions towards the formation of the Church of South India.[40]

Jack Winslow may be compared to James Adderley in that he began a work where others were to reap the harvest. But he was a leading member of Christa Seva Sangha for twelve years, far longer than Adderley stayed with the Society of the Divine Compassion. The Community which he founded he also led and guided through the difficult stages of its growth and development. It did not long survive his departure. The hostel at Poona continued until 1963. Christa Seva Sangha was the grain of wheat which fell into the earth and perished only to bear much fruit.[41]

39. ibid., p. 148.
40. Fr. Denis, op. cit., pp. 85–6.
41. St. John, 12, v. 24.

17

The Brotherhood of the Love of Christ

William Strowan Algernon Amherst Robertson became known to thousands as Father Algy. The full story of his life has been told by his colleague, Father Denis. In the story of the Anglican Franciscans, he has a four-fold importance. He was a member of Christa Seva Sangha in India. On his return, he founded the Brotherhood of the Love of Christ. He was largely instrumental in uniting his own Community with the Brotherhood of St. Francis of Assisi to form the Society of St. Francis. And as Guardian of the Society he played a major part in building up the Third Order and in founding the Community of St. Clare.

He was born in Ealing in 1894, the son of a liveryman of the Carpenters Company. His family were Congregationalists,[1] but soon after entering Westminster School in 1908, he was confirmed. He remained a member of the Crusaders, and like many of the Franciscans, his spirituality was both Catholic and Evangelical. He went up to Queens' College, Cambridge, in 1913 and took his degree in 1916. At Cambridge he came under the influence both of the Oratory of the Good Shepherd and the Student Christian Movement. Through the Oratory he came into contact with John How, Edward Wynn and Eric Milner White, and through S.C.M. with William Temple who was then Headmaster of Repton. Algy failed the medical examination for the Officers Training Corps, and unlike most of his contemporaries did not do military service. He won the Winchester Prize for Public Reading, and when he went down from Cambridge he took a three-year appointment as Lecturer in History and English Literature at St. Paul's College, Calcutta. Another contact at Cambridge had been Frank Weston, Bishop of Zanzibar, who first aroused his interest in the mission field.[2] From his time at Calcutta (1917–19) he gained a great love for India and its people, and his return there was virtually certain.

He returned to England to read for Holy Orders at Westcott House,

1. Father Denis, *Father Algy* (1964), p. 18.
2. ibid., p. 31.

Cambridge. He was ordained in 1921 to serve as Curate of St. George's, Cullercoates, near Whitley Bay in Northumberland. In 1924, he became for three years travelling secretary for the Student Christian Movement to the theological colleges.

His work with the Theological Department of S.C.M., his experience of working with unemployed boys from Tyneside and Wearside at the annual camp at Wooler (Northumberland), and his contacts at and via Cambridge, seem to have combined to direct him back to India in 1927.[3] One of his last works before leaving England was to plan the Anglo-Russian Conference at St. Alban's which led to the formation of the Fellowship of St. Alban and St. Sergius – a body which has done so much to promote understanding between Anglicans and Orthodox.

It has been related (Chapter 16) how he met Jack Winslow on his visit to England. In November 1926, he was admitted as a postulant of Christa Seva Sangha at the Oratory House in Cambridge, together with Bernard Gurney Fox and Oliver Fielding Clarke. He went out to India the following year with the vision of transforming the Sangha into a Franciscan religious community, and he felt clearly by this time that he was called to the Franciscan Way.[4] His influence on the development of the Sangha was a remarkable achievement in his short ministry. His other great success was his work at the hostel in Poona. The gifts he had already shown in work with scouts, students and unemployed boys came fully into play. But his biographer has written,

> Algy has been criticised for attracting to the mission field brilliant young men whose zeal was bound to be imprudent. It has been said that those first recruits were altogether too gifted to give any hope of permanence to the Sangha with its small band of Indian initiates. Perhaps the Englishmen were all in too much of a hurry, and could not therefore take account of how differently they all envisaged the future of the Sangha.[5]

Algy never enjoyed a really good physique, and he was not in good health for two years even before leaving England.[6] He looked forward to sharing Indian food and at first his health seemed to improve. But within a year, he began to be seriously ill. By January 1930, his condition was such that his doctor ordered him home to England. He left India aboard the S.S. *Aquilea* in April. It was with great reluctance that he accepted this as the end of his missionary service. 'It is terribly sad to leave India. I must come back somehow.'[7] Back in England, he

3. Bishop John Ramsbotham, Letter 29.5.71 in Hilfield Archives.
4. Fr. Denis, op. cit., pp. 77–8.
5. ibid., p. 81.
6. ibid., p. 82.
7. ibid., p. 93.

was treated for sprue at the Hospital for Tropical Diseases and then took a long convalescence at his mother's home in Ealing. But he suffered for the rest of his life from chronic colitis, and his achievements were made in the context of an unending struggle with ill-health. Both the resort of his mother's home and the support of his devoted followers were necessary to see him through it.

In 1931, the Guild of All Souls offered him the living of St. Ives, Hunts., a parish which had a strong Anglo-Catholic tradition. Algy was at first reluctant to accept, still hoping no doubt to return to India, but Christa Seva Sangha persuaded him to take it when the offer was renewed.[8] He held the living for six years, during which he put tremendous energy into his work as a country priest. At the same time, he established a new Franciscan community and then united it with the Brotherhood at Hilfield. Although forced to leave India, Algy still regarded himself as a member of the Community at Poona.[9] St. Ives was only twelve miles from Cambridge, near enough to be in contact with the Oratory of the Good Shepherd. His old friends like Wilfred Knox and Eric Milner-White encouraged Algy to build up the new Community in his Vicarage.[10]

From 1931 to 1934, Fr. Algy and his colleagues at St. Ives were an English branch of an Indian community. His parishioners were bewildered at the strange collection of young men, English and Indian, at the Vicarage.[11] Lakdasa de Mel, who became Bishop of Calcutta in 1962, preached at Algy's first Harvest Thanksgiving. But Algy won the confidence of his parishioners by maintaining the tradition of services and by encouraging the Brothers fully to join in the life of the town. He brought to his pulpit such distinguished preachers as Professor Charles Raven and Conrad Noel, the great Socialist Vicar of Thaxted.

In 1932, William Lash came to St. Ives to test his vocation to Christa Seva Sangha. When the Poona Community divided in 1934, Fr. Algy and his Brothers continued to support Fr. Lash in India and Christa Prema Seva Sangha.[12]

By that time, community life had already been established in St. Ives Vicarage. Algy had two other priests and three lay Brothers with him. In their daily time-table, an hour was set aside in the morning for study and for lectures on the religious life, the Bible, liturgy and doctrine. Algy drew on the spiritual teaching of Fr. Benson of Cowley and Fr. Strong of the Oxford Mission to Calcutta in finding material

8. ibid., pp. 95–6.
9. ibid., p. 105.
10. ibid., p. 98.
11. ibid., pp. 100–1.
12. ibid., pp. 107, 110.

for his lectures. The Brothers did their own housework, though tertiaries living at the Vicarage helped them with it.[13] They ate three meals a day of good, plain food, though on fast days a main meal was not taken until 6.0 p.m. The Eucharist was celebrated daily in the parish church, Prayer Book Mattins and Evensong were said, and also the Lesser Hours, with a thirty-five-minute meditation after Terce. The Greater Silence was kept from 10.45 p.m. to 10.15 a.m., Lesser Silence until lunch, but on Fridays it was extended until the lecture after None. About once a month, a visiting priest came to conduct a Quiet Day.[14] The Brothers were allowed to smoke, but not in public.[15] A rest was offered at the Vicarage to wayfarers between 11.30 a.m. and 3.30 p.m. on weekdays, and casual wards in the area were notified to that effect.[16] 'Hunger Marchers' from Blaydon on Tyneside stopped by in 1936. They were received in the schools, and volunteers gave medical attention and provided bedding.[17] Brothers visited the nearby sanatoria at Papworth weekly and Wyton fortnightly.[18] Fr. Algy encouraged his Community to maintain their interest in the wider world and in the local area. Articles were read at mealtimes from the *Times*, the *Manchester Guardian* and the *New Statesman* though they were not always found to be very intelligible or constructively Christian.[19] But involvement in the local community included playing tennis, swimming at the baths and supporting the local football club.[20]

As long as Christa Seva Sangha at Poona retained its identity, the Brothers at St. Ives could continue as part of it. The division of the Indian Community raised problems, for while supporting the Prema, it was not logical to be a First Order attached to a Third, as Christa Prema Seva Sangha in fact became. The Chapter at St. Ives discussed the matter on 9 June 1934,[21] taking account of the changes which had taken place in India and the lack of experience of the Poona Community. Algy already favoured the idea of building up the life of his Community within a larger society of Franciscans. To express their continuing support, £50 was sent as a loan to the Poona Hostel.[22] Algy was to be Commissary for the Poona ashram, and English recruits were to be trained at St. Ives for India.[23] But they no longer wished

13. Brotherhood of the Love of Christ, Chapter Minute 13.1.36.
14. Fr. Denis, op. cit., pp. 108–9.
15. Chapter Minute 11.5.36.
16. ibid., 25.3.35.
17. ibid., 30.11.35; Fr. Denis, op. cit., p. 105.
18. Chapter Minutes 11.2.35, 1.4.35.
19. ibid., 30.3.36.
20. ibid., passim.
21. ibid.
22. ibid., 20.7.34.
23. ibid., 29.7.34.

to be linked too closely with the work in Poona. Algy considered how to adapt the Rule of Christa Seva Sangha for an English community. They considered taking the name, 'Brotherhood of the Servants of Jesus',[24] which recalled the meaning of Christa Seva Sangha, but this was dropped in favour of the 'Brotherhood of the Love of Christ'.[25] Both the novices and professed Brethren continued to wear the saffron girdle.

The development of the Brotherhood of the Love of Christ as a separate community took place as the movement grew to unite the Franciscan societies. This is discussed in a later chapter. But as early as 1933, discussions had begun with the Brotherhood of St. Francis of Assisi, the Brotherhood of the Holy Cross and the Franciscan Sisters of Jesus and Mary. In May 1934, representatives of the four communities met at Fr. Potter's Priory at Peckham, and members of the three Brotherhoods shared a retreat at Peckham.[26] They formed the intention of uniting as a Society of St. Francis, with the members of the three Brotherhoods constituting the First Order. The Brotherhood of the Love of Christ gave its assent to the essential steps in 1936. One matter to be decided was the habit of the First Order, and it may noted that the St. Ives Community approved the colour as 'nigger brown'.[27]

The discussions between the Brotherhoods made it clear that by far the best site for training novices was at Hilfield with its atmosphere of detachment and peace. Algy's exceptional gifts as a trainer of men made him the obvious choice as Novice Master. He therefore obtained a year's leave of absence from his Bishop (Bernard Heywood) and spent the time 1936–37 at Hilfield, training the novices and re-organising the Community. By way of exchange, Brother Douglas came to St. Ives in Lent 1937 to admit the novices there.[28]

Recruits were still coming forward, but the proposed merger naturally caused some heart-searching. Tension between the religious life and the life of the parish were felt at St. Ives as at Plaistow and Peckham. After his year's absence, it was almost inevitable that Fr. Algy should resign as Vicar of St. Ives. He celebrated the Eucharist there for the last time on 9 October 1937.[29] The three priest-Brothers, Algy, Francis and Denis, all found their place in the Society of St.

24. ibid., 20.7.34.
25. ibid., 22.10.34.
26. Fr. Denis, op. cit., p. 113.
27. Chapter Minute 5.10.36. The words are underlined. The word was then thought more affectionate than disrespectful, as in 'Nigger Minstrels' and Dvořák's 'Nigger Quartet'.
28. Chapter Minute 8.2.37.
29. Fr. Denis, op. cit., p. 119.

Francis and a new life at Hilfield and beyond. The three lay Brothers, however, decided not to continue after the merger. The last Chapter Meeting was held at St. Ives on 27 September 1937 with Fr. Francis in the chair.

While at St. Ives, Algy, like Jack Winslow, was much influenced by the Oxford Group and Moral Re-armament.

For a time, everything had to be *put under guidance* or *shared*, and there is no doubt that a tremendous sense of fellowship . . . was experienced by those who were caught up in the numberless group meetings that were held. Men and women of all walks of life were drawn into a living fellowship whose influence pervaded the countryside for miles around.[30]

Moral Re-armament appealed to the Evangelical side of Algy's spirituality. It engendered a spirit of renewal in St. Ives parish, but it also aroused antagonism. It shows how closely Algy was in touch with the main currents of life in the Church.

30. ibid., p. 109. Italics original.

18

The Franciscan Servants of Jesus and Mary

The moving spirit behind the foundation of this Community was Grace Emily Costin, known in religion as Mother Teresa. She was born at Folkestone (Kent) on 27 October 1888. She had an unhappy childhood dogged with ill-health, and she was twenty when she had a religious experience which marked a turning-point in her life, though as a girl she had attended a mission service conducted by Father Ignatius of Llanthony.[1] But in Holy Week 1909, she attended a series of evening addresses given by Father Andrew of the Society of the Divine Compassion, and on Maundy Thursday made her confession to him.[2] From that experience, she sought to dedicate her life to the service of God and her fellow-men, though it was over ten years later when she settled to the religious life. Between 1911 and 1914, she was engaged in various forms of social work, including a colony for women inebriates begun by Lady Henry Somerset.[3] Through Lady Henry, she came into contact with two ladies, Sister Ivy and Sister Rosanna, who lived as anchoresses, and Sister Ivy particularly influenced her as a spiritual guide and teacher in the art of prayer.[4] Later, when these ladies had grown old, Mother Teresa and her Community helped to look after them.[5] Lady Henry Somerset dissuaded Miss Costin from settling down permanently to work with the colony, and encouraged her to go to the United States where she remained until the autumn of 1916. In America, she worked as a Travellers' Aid agent, helped at a school run by the Community of St. Mary and acted as a governess. She also stayed for a time with the Sisters of St. Anne in Boston (Massachusetts) where she met Father Powell of the Society of St. John the Evangelist (see Chapter 22). Both of these helped to foster her vocation to the religious life.

1. Obituary, *Church Times* 15.6.79.
2. *Mother Teresa and the Franciscan Sisters of Jesus and Mary* (Posbury St. Francis, 1980), p. 1.
3. Lady Isabella Caroline, daughter of the 3rd Earl Somers; married Lord Henry Somerset (1849–1932), 2nd son of the 9th Duke of Beaufort.
4. *Mother Teresa*, p. 1.
5. ibid., p. 8.

First, however, she returned to England, and as her contribution to
the war effort volunteered for the Women's Police Service. She served
at Gretna Green, helping to police a cordite factory, then in Oxford,
where she was the first policewoman to serve. Later, she became the
first woman to sit in the Church Assembly.[6]

After the Great War had ended, she tested her vocation with the
Order of St. Anne at their English house at Emsworth, Hants. The
Community was Benedictine in ethos, and although she was happy
during the eighteen months or so that she was with them, it was not
there that her true vocation lay. It was at her clothing on 25 August
1919 that she first took the name Teresa. She left about a year later,
and her next move was back to social work under the auspices of the
Fellowship of Reconciliation. At a conference of the Fellowship she
met Father Bernard Walke, Vicar of St. Hilary near Marazion in
Cornwall. Through Father Walke, she took charge of a small home for
children in care at St. Hilary.[7] In 1925, Teresa had to have a major
operation. She gave up her work at the home and for the time being
rented a cottage at Blisland near Bodmin with a Scottish lady. Her
companion put her in touch with Father Robert Andrews of Paisley,
Renfrewshire, and one of his parishioners, a widow, Mrs. Margaret
Pearce. In November 1924, Teresa had had a further experience which
encouraged her to seek life in community.[8] Mrs. Pearce was already
prepared to help Fr. Andrews in parish work at Paisley, and Teresa
and her companion joined her to try to begin the religious life together.
They shared a small flat, trained Sunday School teachers, ran a Bible
Class and visited, living in great simplicity, keeping silence and times
of prayer. Fr. Andrews acted as their spiritual director.[9] The experiment lasted nearly two years. Only Teresa and Margaret Pearce persisted, the latter taking the name Margaret of Mary Immaculate.

Teresa and Margaret began again at St. Agnes in Cornwall where
they resumed involvement in parish life. It was at this time that they
became definitely Franciscan. Teresa discovered inspiration in the
ideals of St. Francis. She and Margaret adopted a brown habit instead
of the navy blue they had worn at Paisley. They also made a pilgrimage
to Assisi in April 1930. With the permission of Walter Frere, Bishop
of Truro, they took Simple Vows on 16 July 1930.[10] They planned at
first that their vows should be for five years, but this period was later

6. *Church Times* 15.6.79.
7. Father Walke writes of this home in his autobiographical *Twenty Years at St. Hilary*
   (1935).
8. *Mother Teresa*, p. 3.
9. ibid., p. 4.
10. ibid., pp. 4–5.

reduced to three, with yearly renewals.[11] As well as parish work, they also conducted small missions, speaking on the village greens. They continued in the same style when they moved to Hinton Martel near Wimborne (Dorset) for a year, September 1931–32.[12]

Between 1932 and 1937, the Sisters worked in the parish of St. Matthew's, Finsbury (City Road, E.C.1). In 1935, Mother Teresa and Sister Margaret took life vows before Charles Curzon, Bishop of Stepney. Other women came to test their vocation, but only one of those who joined them at Finsbury stayed on.[13] While at St. Matthew's, the Sisters became acquainted with Fr. Algy Robertson. Algy hoped to establish a Second Order of St. Francis in the Church of England – a dream ultimately fulfilled by the Community of St. Clare at Freeland. Mother Teresa's community were too dedicated to an active life to become Poor Clares, and in fact were never drawn into the Society of St. Francis.[14] In 1937, the Sisters moved to Whitwell in the Isle of Wight, and in 1942 to Posbury near Crediton. One of the difficulties in their first 16 years was the Community's desire to follow the spirit of poverty by owning no home of their own. This was in the spirit of the first Franciscans, but it made them tenants-at-will wherever they happened to be. In 1942 they had the opportunity of buying a suitable house at Posbury, and settled for a permanent home. They continued to take ownership of property very seriously. Many religious communities place their property with the Fidelity Trust, but Posbury remained the property and responsibility of the Community. 'Our thought was that God had given us the place and we had to be both now and at the judgment responsible and answerable for it.'[15] The responsibility was the more serious in that the Community refused on principle to hold invested funds; any bequeathed to them were at once sold. The Community had to be self-supporting.

By the time they settled at Posbury, the Community had grown to five Sisters and one resident tertiary.[16] Peter Anson described their life as 'more domestic and "family" than conventual'.[17] The preservation of its closely knit character has been more important than growth in numbers. From the varied experience of their early years, they were able to evolve their distinctive life-style. In London, they had found that regular parish work was not to be their main undertaking, though they held themselves ready to help in parishes. The Bishop of Exeter

11. Memoir of Mother Teresa, Hilfield Archives.
12. *Mother Teresa*, p. 5.
13. Memoir.
14. ibid.
15. ibid.
16. Or extern. See below.
17. CC p. 52.

has given them permission to speak at meetings, to preach and to conduct missions in his diocese by invitation of the incumbent, and they have also helped out when livings have been vacant. But their main work has been a distinctive life in which a balance of prayer and active work was established, with prayer predominating. The daily Eucharist and the day Hours of course formed the basis, with an hour and a half of private prayer and half an hour's spiritual reading daily. The chapel, like that at Hilfield, was converted from a stable, a reminder of the Nativity at Bethlehem. It is dedicated to the Most Precious Blood. Gardening and manual work were of necessity undertaken to support the Community, but were nevertheless seen as 'spiritual' in the way that sacraments are spiritual. The work of Posbury as a retreat- and guest-house was also very important, priests, women and girls being welcomed as guests as well as retreatants. (For a time, a cottage was used for children in need of a holiday.) While keeping up their strenuous life of prayer and work, the Sisters have genuinely shared the life of their home with their guests; Mother Teresa was a real pioneer in this sharing of life.[18] The Community run a flourishing Sunday school for the parish of St. Luke, Posbury. For about thirty-five years, the Sisters visited in two hospitals in Exeter.

The Community 'has taken St. Francis of Assisi . . . as the pattern and inspiration in both prayer and labour.' They wear a brown habit with a red cross and cord. Mother Teresa said that it was impossible to follow the whole spirit of St. Francis whom she described as 'a whole world of charity' in himself. The attitude of the Community to property has been described. The distinctive feature which has been stressed is 'to follow on in the way of peace'. The whole Community is pledged to pacifism, and also not to go to law to recover things taken from them, or to take out a mortgage. The Community aims at the 'good measure of disciplined freedom' characteristic of a family, and has two principal objectives:
1. The conversion of each individual life to God under the three-fold vows of poverty, chastity and obedience, for His glory and for the sanctification of 'ourselves, our souls and bodies in His holy service';
2. Corporate witness to the Love of God and the salvation of the world which is accomplished in and through that Love.

Mother Teresa resigned as Superior in 1963, and was replaced by Mother Hilary. Mother Teresa lived on at Posbury until her death in 1979 at the age of ninety, 'her remarkable mind clear to the last'.[19]

As well as the Sisters living under vows, the Community has a number of 'externs' or 'tertiaries', nearly forty women and three men.

18. *Church Times* 15.6.79.
19. ibid.

'Extern' was a term suggested by Fr. Algy when the Posbury Community was not drawn into the Society of St. Francis, to avoid confusion with the latter's Third Order. Since one of them lived with the Community, 'extern' was also misleading, and the term 'tertiary' is now often used. Like tertiaries, the externs live out the spirit of the Community in the world. They make no specific pledge with regard to possessions, but promise to practise simplicity and sobriety, avoid extravagance and not buy 'sweated' goods. The externs, like the professed sisters, pledge themselves to be peacemakers and repudiate modern war as not under the theological definition of 'just'. They have a rule of prayer-life and make a retreat once a year, usually at Posbury. While visiting the Community, they wear a scapular and cord. Like all Franciscans, they particularly observe the two festivals of St. Francis, 17 September (the Stigmata) and 4 October.

Sister Margaret, Mother Teresa's co-founder, pre-deceased her on 25 April 1977. Both missed, by a year or two, their Golden Jubilee in the religious life which would have coincided with that of the Community in July 1980. So closely was she identified with the Community that her spirit is very much alive in it.[20] Those who share Franciscan ideals will appreciate her great longing

> to be allowed to make by prayer, work and love, in the beauty of the Devon countryside, a place of peace and joy, in which the veil between this world and the new earth which is promised to us, may be transparent enough to reveal to the eyes of all who come, something of the immortal loveliness of that country which is our true home.[21]

20. *Mother Teresa*, p. 24.
21. ibid., p. 22.

19

The Daughters of St. Clare, Brisbane

The Community of the Daughters of St. Clare was the first indigenous Australian religious community in the Franciscan tradition.[1] It was largely inspired by an Australian priest, Robert Bartlett Bates, who after training at Melbourne served with distinction in the First World War.[2] After the war, he studied at Merton College, Oxford, and Cuddesdon, was ordained in the diocese of London and served a curacy at St. Andrew's, Bethnal Green, before returning to Australia, first as Vicar of Copmanhurst, New South Wales (1924–26), then as Rector of All Saints', Brisbane, where he remained until 1944.[3] In 1928, he encouraged Dr. Margaret Aileen Williams and three companions to test their vocation to the religious life in a small cottage next door to the Mission of St. Francis of Assisi near Brisbane. In April 1930, three ladies made their profession; the fourth was noviced and Dr. Williams became Superior as Sister Margaret Mary. 'The purpose of the Community was to seek the Glory of God by a life of prayer and work under a Rule of absolute poverty.'[4] A novice and two postulants joined them in 1931. An important part of their work was to care for the aged – originally three old ladies, then when they moved into a larger house, nine, and in due course both men and women. They came to have care of two homes or 'Houses of Rest' – St. John's for men and St. Clare's for women. They also undertook parish work and retreats, for a time ran a dispensary, made altar breads, and took care of boys at a farm school (St. Christopher's Lodge). But they regarded prayer as their chief work.

Margaret Mary was installed as Mother Superior on 22 March 1932. But in spite of the progress of the first few years, recruits were few. A number of women tested their vocation, but there were never more than three professed in the Community at any one time, and only five were professed altogether. Two Sisters went to Fairacres,

---

1. Communities of other traditions preceded it. The earliest women's society to start life in Australia was the Community of the Holy Name (1888).
2. He was awarded the Military Medal in 1915 and bar 1916.
3. For biographical details see *Crockford*.
4. CC p. 589.

hoping ultimately to found an enclosed community in Australia. Fr. Bates had hoped to found a companion community for men. He tested his vocation with the Cowley Fathers, but was dissuaded from the religious life and subsequently married.

In 1948, it was decided that it would be unrealistic for the Community to continue. The Sisters who still remained were absorbed into the Society of the Sacred Advent. This also was an indigenous Australian community, founded in 1892, with its Community House at Albion, Brisbane. One of the characteristics of the Society was that the Sisters were widely scattered in charge of various homes and institutions, but gathered in the Community House twice a year for chapter and retreat.[5] Of the work undertaken by the Daughters of St. Clare, only the making of altar breads was continued. Fifteen years later, however, in 1963, the Society of St. Francis took over the site of St. Christopher's Lodge at Brookfield, and made it their Friary in Brisbane.[6] So as with the Society of the Divine Compassion at Plaistow and Fr. William at Glasshampton, the Society of St. Francis entered on an inheritance at Brisbane where others had been the pioneers.

'Perhaps we aimed too high or perhaps we made the life too hard,'[7] a member of the Community has written. Although it lasted only twenty years (1928–48), the Community of the Daughters of St. Clare has a permanent importance as an indigenous Australian Franciscan community. When the Society of St. Francis took over at St. Christopher's in 1963 they expressed the wish for a 'genuine Australian foundation'.[8] The development of a native Australian tradition would be a worthy memorial to the Sisterhood.

5. CC p. 588.
6. S.S.F. Chapter Minute 8.10.63.
7. Hilfield Archive F. 130.
8. S.S.F. Chapter Minute 8.10.63.

20

The Brotherhood of St. Francis, Saskatchewan

The Anglican Church in Canada has produced one indigenous community in the Franciscan tradition. The Brotherhood of St. Francis, as it was called, was one of a number of Brotherhoods, all of them short-lived, formed in the Diocese of Qu'Appelle in the Canadian mid-West. Great distances, scattered population, the need for fellowship, made it suitable territory for communities similar to the Bush Brotherhoods in Australia and those in the mid-West of the United States mentioned in Chapters 21 and 22. Before the First World War, at least two such Brotherhoods arose. One was the Prairie Brotherhood based at Mossbank. Little is known about it, though it seems to have worked successfully until the war.[1] There was also the Railway Mission. From its base at Regina, the men worked along the railway lines in a way similar to the South African Railway Mission. The Community also had a rest centre, St. Cuthbert's House.[2] Between the wars, a second Prairie Brotherhood was formed. It was directed by the Rev. Frank Syme.[3] It was a loosely knit fellowship with a house at Milestone, from which the members ministered to small congregations in the Centre and South of the Diocese. It lasted from 1934 to 1943.[4] There was also a Clergy House at Mortlach where for a time a group of two or three priests and a layman served an area of 8,000 square miles.[5]

The Brotherhood of St. Francis was inspired by Michael Coleman, who was Bishop of Qu'Appelle 1950–60. In 1952, he encouraged a small group of priests and laymen to live together under a simple rule while ministering to parishes in the South of the Diocese. Their main centre was at Assiniboia, but they also had houses at Avonlea and Ogema. They did not take vows, but members bound themselves to

1. Hilfield Archives F. 150.
2. ibid.
3. F. H. Syme is listed in *Crockford* (1935) as incumbent of Rouleau, Milestone. In 1936 he is listed as priest-in-charge with J. C. A. Cole as incumbent. He is not listed in the following years.
4. Hilfield Archives F. 150.
5. ibid.

a common life for three years. Their ministry among the small congregations tended to disperse them, but they gathered each month for
two days at Assiniboia where they also held their annual retreat and
Chapter. Their spiritual life was based on the Prayer Book Offices and
Compline, with a daily Eucharist wherever they were.[6] Their simple
rule was Franciscan in character.[7] 'This tentative experiment', as Peter
Anson describes it, came to an end in April 1957. One member of the
Brotherhood joined the Society of St. Francis.[8] George Jackson, who
became Bishop of Qu'Appelle in 1960 has said, 'I suspect that lack of
experience and a firm enough rule may have had some effect on the
stability of these groups.'[9]

The Franciscan presence in the Canadian Church is now confined
to tertiaries of the American Province, where there has been a long-
standing link with Fr. Joseph's Order of St. Francis (see Chapter 22).
The record of Roman Catholic Franciscans in evangelising Canada
was outstanding (see Chapter 1). As the Third Order in Canada grows
in strength, it may be that others will be encouraged to begin Franciscan community life, drawing on the experience already gained.

6. CC p. 577.
7. Hilfield Archives F. 150.
8. ibid.
9. ibid. Letter 27.4.71.

PART III

COMMUNITIES OF AMERICAN ORIGIN

21

The Society of the Atonement

The Society of the Atonement was the first Franciscan community to be founded in the Protestant Episcopal Church of the U.S.A. It was contemporary with the first Anglican Franciscan Brotherhoods and Sisterhoods,[1] and arose quite independently of them. It is remarkable in that it began in a province of the Anglican Communion, but came to full flowering only after corporately submitting to Rome. In this it may be compared to the Benedictine Community of Caldey Island. The Community arose from the deep spiritual friendship of a man and a woman, known in religion as Father Paul and Mother Lurana. Their aim from the beginning was to found a community with the three-fold Franciscan orders of Brothers, Sisters and tertiaries.

Father Paul was born Lewis Thomas Wattson on 16 January 1863, the third son of an Episcopalian priest, the Rev. Joseph Newton Wattson, Rector of Millington, Maryland. Joseph Wattson was expelled from the General Seminary in New York for his outspoken acceptance of Tractarian doctrines. He was nevertheless ordained by the Bishop of Baltimore, and proved to be a devoted pastor.[2] Lewis followed his father into the Sacred Ministry. His passage was smoother. After three years at the General Seminary (1882–85) he was ordained deacon and in the following year (1886) priest. Though only twenty-three, he was put in charge of St. James's, Port Deposit (Maryland), and was allowed to proceed to the priesthood under the canonical age of twenty-four. Later, he took charge of St. John's, Kingston (New York). Fr. Wattson was urged by his parishioners to marry, but his own inclinations from early years had been towards the religious life. His father inspired him with the idea of founding a preaching order like the Roman Catholic Society of St. Paul[3] – the Apostle of the Gentiles always seems to have been one of his favourite saints. But in 1893, he fell under the spell of St. Francis of Assisi who, he said later, 'has always exercised a strong

1. Apart from Ascot Priory. See Chapter 2.
2. David Gannon, *Father Paul of Graymoor* (New York 1959), pp. 13 ff.
3. An order founded in New York State in 1858.

appeal to the Episcopalian mind,'[4] and whom he saw thenceforth as his ideal of a monk and missionary preacher.[5]

In 1895, he received an unexpected invitation from the Bishop of Nebraska to become Superior of a group of unmarried priests at Omaha called the Associate Mission. This he undertook, but it soon became apparent that while they wished to remain secular celibate priests, Fr. Wattson wanted to form them into a religious community.[6] He left and returned to New York State.

He had at this time been corresponding for two years with Lurana Mary White, daughter of a wealthy New York Episcopalian family. She was seven years younger than he, and looked to him for guidance in following her own call to the religious life. She became acquainted with the Community of the Holy Child at Albany when attending her finishing school, and returned to join them as a postulant in 1894.[7] Lurana had a strong attachment to the ideal of poverty, though the Community took vows only of chastity and obedience. The Dean of Albany advised her to take a private and personal vow of poverty, and she proceeded to become a probationer (the equivalent of novice) but never really settled in the Community. After leaving, she had the opportunity in 1897 of accompanying her aunt and uncle on a visit to England. She took with her a letter of introduction to Mother Etheldreda of the Sisters of Bethany who allowed her to stay with them and receive a training in the novitiate. Lurana visited Paris and Assisi before returning to the U.S.A. She was given a rosary in Assisi which she wore for the rest of her life.[8]

Sister Lurana (as she had now become) was joined on her return to America by two other ladies (Sisters Ruth and Martha), and together they formed the nucleus of a community and recited the Day Hours. Bishop Worthington of Nebraska invited them to go out to Omaha. Fr. Howard had by then replaced Fr. Wattson as Superior of the Associate Mission, and Sister Lurana felt that he was too little dedicated to the ideal of poverty for her to join him. Sister Ruth and Sister Martha, however, left her to go out to Omaha.[9] Sister Lurana remained at her parents' home at Warwick (New York) where she and Fr. Wattson at last met. With his devotion to St. Francis, Fr. Wattson fulfilled Sister Lurana's ideal of poverty. At St. Francistide, 1898, Fr. Wattson and Sister Lurana offered themselves to God to found a Society of the Atonement. Fr. Wattson placed himself under the Order

4. Gannon, op. cit., p. 88.
5. Sister Mary Celine, *A Woman of Unity* (New York 1956), p. 25.
6. Gannon, op. cit., pp. 39–40.
7. Sister Mary Celine, op. cit., p. 13.
8. ibid., p. 36.
9. ibid., pp. 42–5.

of the Holy Cross at Westminster (Maryland) to be trained in the religious life.[10]

The opportunity soon came to found a community. Three Episcopalian ladies, the Misses Alice and Sally Elliot and Miss Julia Chadwick, all devotees of St. Francis, restored a deserted church, St. John-in-the-Wilderness (New York) which they renamed Graymoor after a former priest (Dr. Gray) and a benefactor (Professor Moore of Columbia University).[11] In 1899, Fr. Wattson was made Chaplain at Graymoor, which he envisaged as a site where the three traditional Franciscan orders could be established, which were to be under the patronage respectively of St. Paul, St. Francis and St. John the Baptist. The Blessed Virgin Mary was to be the patron of the Society of the Atonement as a whole.[12] Fr. Wattson took the vows of poverty, chastity and obedience before Bishop Coleman of Delaware on 27 July 1900. He had already on St. Paul's Day (25 January) assumed a grey-brown habit made for him by Sister Lurana. He was now a religious, and took the name Fr. Paul James of the Atonement, but was always known from that time as Fr. Paul. He took up residence at Graymoor in true Franciscan style in a shack with a leaking roof which he called 'The Palace of Lady Poverty.'[13]

Lurana was already in residence at Graymoor, having become 'Mistress Guardian' in 1899. She was installed as Mother Superior of the Second Order on 4 October 1900. She had already been clothed in a brown Franciscan habit by Fr. Hollings of the Society of St. John the Evangelist.[14] She lived at first at Graymoor with her godchild Violet (or Viola) Carr who was her companion rather than an aspirant. Sister Martha joined her for a time but in 1902 left for Colorado, partly for reasons of health. Mother Lurana had to carry on for a time with only a postulant.[15] She had inherited 750 dollars which she devoted to building the convent. The rest of the money needed came from friends, notably from Dr. Taylor, an English surgeon of Anglo-Catholic views, and his wife, who found the money to purchase the adjacent site for the Friary.[16] Bishop Coleman dedicated the Sisters' convent on St. Francis' Day 1899.[17]

The project of establishing a three-fold Franciscan society was scarcely achieved in their Episcopalian days. Fr. Paul had only one

10. Gannon, op. cit., p. 53.
11. ibid., p. 60.
12. ibid., p. 74.
13. ibid., pp. 87–9.
14. Sister Mary Celine, op. cit., p. 25.
15. ibid., p. 80.
16. Gannon, op. cit., p. 77.
17. ibid., p. 85.

companion in the First Order, Brother Jacob (Paul Jacob), though others came to test their vocation. Brother Jacob was born Ferdinand Wallerstein, and was a Jew by birth, whom Mother Lurana converted to Christianity.[18] There were four Sisters with Mother Lurana in the Second Order when they went over to Rome. Ten tertiaries were converted with them.[19]

Fr. Paul's original vision was of an evangelistic order on Franciscan or Paulist lines. This became subordinate in his thinking to the promotion of corporate union between the Roman Catholic and Anglican Churches. As early as 1900, Fr. Paul was firmly convinced that this should be the Society's main vocation, and all members of the Society, including tertiaries, were obliged to sign a declaration accepting the faith and authority of the See of Rome.[20] It was a brave stance to take up, particularly at that time. Hopes for corporate union had been set back by Leo XIII's *Apostolicae curae* (1896) which rejected the validity of Anglican orders. It required great courage on Fr. Paul's part openly to proclaim his views, but his ministry took on almost a prophetic character. He was a great and popular preacher, but soon there was a marked fall in the number of invitations to preach. Thereupon he turned more to the written word, and published a magazine, *The Lamp*, in which he put forward his convictions. Sister Martha left the Second Order in 1902 partly at least because of the Society's 'romanising' tendencies.[21] Mother Lurana, however, was unwavering in her support of Fr. Paul, but she played a true sister's part in warning him that he was exposing the Society to 'persecutions, ostracism and peril of annihilation'. He replied, 'If our witness is from God, sooner or later it will prevail.'[22]

Fr. Paul sought unity in part at least as a bulwark against the rise of Modernism, which at the turn of the century threatened to engulf both the Anglican and Roman Catholic Churches. In the American Episcopalian Church, many of the more conservative and Catholic-minded clergy suffered a crisis of conscience when non-Episcopalian clergy were admitted to the pulpit. Episcopal ordination had been looked upon by many of them as a safeguard of sound doctrine. A number of individual conversions to Rome took place. One was William McGarvey, Rector of St. Elizabeth's, Philadelphia, Superior of a company of celibate priests living under rule called the Companions of the Holy Saviour. Another was Mother Edith of the Sisterhood of

18. Sister Mary Celine, op. cit., p. 63.
19. Gannon, op. cit., p. 161.
20. ibid., p. 91.
21. Sister Mary Celine, op. cit., p. 104.
22. ibid., p. 93.

St. Mary at Peekshill (New York).[23] It would hardly be an exaggeration to say that the turn of the century saw a crisis for Anglo-Catholicism on both sides of the Atlantic, and the Franciscan communities were not immune to it. Sister Rosina and some of the Community of St. Francis went over to Rome as did John Hawes. All of these crossed the Atlantic and made their submission at Graymoor shortly after the Society of the Atonement had gone over (see Chapter 11).

Those who accused Fr. Paul of disloyalty to the Episcopalian Church (and they were many) scarcely gave him credit for trying to meet the critical situation in the Church in· a creative way. He discouraged individual submission.[24] He exchanged letters with Spencer Jones, Rector of Moreton-in-Marsh, Gloucestershire.[25] Spencer Jones was author of a book called *England and the Holy See* in which he urged that Roman Catholic claims and practices should be accepted as a step towards union. Encouraged by Mother Lurana, Fr. Paul and Spencer Jones co-operated to write *The Prince of the Apostles*. In February 1908, a group was formed called Anglo-Roman Union, whose name speaks for itself.[26]

Such was the background to one of Fr. Paul's outstanding achievements, the observance of 18–25 January as the Week of Prayer for Christian Unity. He chose the feasts of St. Peter's Chair at Rome and the Conversion of St. Paul to mark the beginning and the end, showing where he drew his own inspiration. The observance of this week first took place in January 1908. It survived his conversion to Rome – indeed, this was a step towards the wide observance by which it has come to be marked, particularly since the Second World War.

It is impossible to know whether Fr. Paul and Mother Lurana could have continued a life-long campaign for unity while remaining in the Episcopalian Church. From 1904, they made it their policy to send one cent of every dollar they received to the Papacy as Peter's Pence.[27] This shows the strength of their convictions, for even in the Middle Ages, Papal taxation had aroused bitter criticism. Bishop Kinsman of Delaware, who had been a great friend and supporter of the Society, felt that he had to give up as Visitor, and advised Fr. Paul to make his choice between the Episcopalian Church and Roman Catholicism.[28] In the spring of 1909, both Fr. Paul and Mother Lurana began to make enquiries about the possibility of the Society of the Atonement

23. Gannon, op. cit., pp. 128–32.
24. ibid., p. 104.
25. Spencer John Jones was a graduate of Worcester College, Oxford. He became Rector of Moreton-in-Marsh in 1887. He was a Proctor in Convocation 1898–1900.
26. Gannon, op. cit., p. 132.
27. ibid., p. 151.
28. ibid., pp. 123, 153. Bishop Kinsman himself went over to Rome in 1919.

making a corporate submission to the Holy See. Cardinal Gibbons of Boston advised Fr. Paul to 'Be patient and follow the leading and guiding of the Holy Spirit.'[29] Corporate submission was an unusual, almost an unprecedented step. Nevertheless, Fr. Paul received an encouraging reply when he approached the Apostolic Delegate, Monsignor Diomede Falconio. On Mgr. Falconio's advice, Fr. Paul made a formal request that he and those who felt with him should be corporately received into the Roman Catholic Church and accepted as members of the Franciscan Third Order.[30] By mutual agreement, Mgr. O'Keeffe, priest of the nearby Roman Catholic parish, was appointed to instruct the Community. On 30 October 1909, Fr. Paul, Brother Jacob, Mother Lurana, four Sisters and ten tertiaries were received into the Roman Catholic Church and affiliated to the Franciscan Third Order.[31]

Mother Lurana died on 15 April 1935, Fr. Paul on 8 February 1940. When their lives are considered as a whole, 30 October 1909 was a beginning rather than an end. When Fr. Paul died, the Society of the Atonement had grown to number 170 friars, 230 sisters and 1,000 tertiaries,[32] very different from the little band who had followed him in making his submission. It could hardly be said otherwise than that he achieved his life's work only after he left the Episcopalian Church. The story of his life after 1909 has been related by David Gannon in *Father Paul of Graymoor*, that of Mother Lurana by Sister Mary Celine in *A Woman of Unity*. It is of note that, after their submission, the members became Franciscan Tertiaries Regular rather than Friars Minor and Poor Clares. The Society has remained American-based and its members now work in many Roman Catholic dioceses in the U.S.A. But their work is not confined to America. In 1938, the Sisters of the Atonement opened a house in Southwark, and later one also at Pontllanfraith, Monmouthshire and at Rossinver, County Leitrim.[33] Only the one in Leitrim is currently open. Two of the Friars worked for a time in Kent before the Second World War. In 1959, the Friars returned on a more permanent basis when they took over the work of the Catholic Central Library. It was then at 33 Wilfred Street SW1, but a year later the Toc H premises in Francis Street, behind Westminster Cathedral, were purchased and converted into a Friary and Library. The Brothers moved in 1961.

The Society of the Atonement by its history has shown how the modern devotion to St. Francis cuts across church frontiers and its

29. Gannon, op. cit., p. 153.
30. ibid., p. 156.
31. ibid., p. 161.
32. ibid., pp. 344–45.
33. Anson, ROC, p. 275.

work for church unity is particularly appropriate as well as being a tribute to the Founder. The Way of St. Francis has never been easy, and the pioneers in the American Episcopalian Church encountered unusual difficulties. But even there, Father Paul left his legacy. His Community supplied a need in the American Church, and its secession to Rome, so far from discouraging others, only stimulated them to make a second attempt.

22

The Order of St. Francis

The second American Franciscan foundation, the Order of St. Francis, was made up of a First Order, the Poor Brethren of St. Francis, a Second Order, the Poor Clares of Reparation and Adoration, and a Third Order, which included Tertiaries Regular. It is convenient to treat the First and Second Orders together; the whole Order of St. Francis was the vision of one priest, Father Joseph, who for many years was Superior of the whole Order, and had the right of appointing the Reverend Mother of the Clares. The Third Order is treated separately; its membership extended to England, where some of its most interesting work was done.

At the beginning of the Third Order Manual, it was remarked that 'Those who are now of the Papal Obedience sometimes resent the ascription of the title Franciscan to anyone or anything outside that obedience.'[1] It goes on to explain that in the time of St. Francis, almost the whole of Western Christendom was under the Bishop of Rome – or, though it does not say so, were heretics. As remarkable a development as having Franciscans who were not Roman Catholics was having tertiaries who were not seculars, and the Norwich Tertiaries Regular (see following chapter) are mentioned in this connection. This preface is one reminder of how, by prayer and perseverance, the Order of St. Francis arose after the corporate conversion to Rome of the Society of the Atonement. Fr. Joseph was a staunch Anglo-Catholic. Some of his practices, such as his use of Benediction, were regarded by some as 'Romanistic' or 'Papalistic'.[2] In fact, Fr. Joseph discouraged individual conversions. His vision for the Order was that it should bring renewal and greater holiness to the Episcopalian Church. This vocation was shared by all the religious orders. There were already communities both of men and women in the American Church, but the Franciscan Way had a special part to play, both because of its antiquity, and because it was an antidote to the 'self-satisfied moralism' and the 'poisonous germs of secularity' in their Church.[3]

1. Third Order Manual (Little Portion, 1962), pp. 5–6.
2. One early postulant who left the Community described it as 'spiky'.
3. Fr. Joseph to Fr. David 24.12.60 and in *Adventure for God* (AFG) (Merrill, 1926), p. 8.

Prayer for a new Franciscan Order began in 1908 when the secession of the Society of the Atonement was already imminent. Fr. Joseph, who emerged as the leading spirit among those praying, was born Claude Jansen Crookston. His second Christian name reflects his Calvinist family background, against which he consciously reacted.[4] He was ordained in the Diocese of Fond du Lac (Wisconsin) in 1913.[5] He visited England in 1914, making contact with the Society of the Divine Compassion and meeting Brother Giles.[6] In *Adventure for God*, Fr. Joseph wrote that 'The Californian missions were centres of commercial, social, artistic, intellectual and religious life which should delight the heart of the modern Socialist – at least the Socialist, if there are any such, who knows the things of the soul to be more important than those of the body.'[7] Whether he could be described as a 'Christian Socialist' therefore begs the definition of the term. But it is of note that Eva Mack, who became Sister Mary Ursula, was drawn to the Franciscan life by reading Adderley's *Third Order of St. Francis*.[8]

Fr. Crookston (as he still was) became Rector of a church in Cincinnati, Ohio. Here he had a brush with his Bishop over the reservation of the Sacrament.[9] It was at Cincinnati in the summer of 1917 that the meeting took place at which twenty of those who had been praying for a Franciscan Order adopted a Rule of Life and so became a Third Order. This was the foundation of the Order of St. Francis. Membership of the First Order and Second Order was to be drawn from these tertiaries.

Fr. Joseph clearly felt the call to the religious life. In 1915 before he came to Cincinnati, Reginald Weller, his Bishop in Fond du Lac, had suggested his joining the Order of the Holy Cross.[10] Bishop Weller did not himself see the need for a new community of men, and thought it would be better for Fr. Joseph to join either of the well established communities, the Order of the Holy Cross or the Society of St. John the Evangelist.[11] Nevertheless, when Fr. Joseph persisted in his plan for a Franciscan community, and in the Diocese of Fond du Lac, Bishop Weller proved to be a good friend and protector. He believed that 'he will do a blessed work among our people in a poor mission field where the Catholic religion can only be propagated through

---

4. See AFG.
5. Letters of Orders.
6. Fr. Joseph to Fr. David 24.12.60.
7. op. cit., p. 12.
8. Letter to Fr. Joseph 8.8.21. She only mentions Adderley, though in fact the book was written in co-operation with Charles Marson.
9. Letters of Bishop of Southern Ohio to Fr. Joseph 1916.
10. Letter to Fr. Powell, S.S.J.E., 25.4.18.
11. ibid.

devotion and self-sacrifice on the part of some earnest priest.'[12] The Bishop was doubtful about Fr. Joseph founding a new community, partly because of his weak health, and these doubts were shared by the Order of the Holy Cross and the Society of St. John the Evangelist.[13] In 1918, Fr. Joseph suffered a heart attack, which seemed to confirm their fears.[14] Fr. Joseph endured physical privations, particularly in the early days at Merrill and again at Little Portion, and he was an indefatigable traveller in his missionary zeal. In spite of this, he lived to old age, though in his latter years he had to take account of climate.[15]

After the meeting in 1917, preparation for a First and Second Order went ahead. Fr. Joseph received a training in the novitiate from the Society of St. John the Evangelist. Three women tertiaries were likewise trained as novices by the Sisters of St. Anne. In 1919, Fr. Joseph was invited to take charge of building up a community for men at Chattanooga, Tennessee.[16] However, he felt his call to return to the Diocese of Fond du Lac, where he became Rector of the missionary parish of Merrill, a recently developed town in northern Wisconsin. One attraction was that the Rectory was big enough for a community to occupy. Another was that by taking on the mission station at Tomahawk in addition, there was sufficient income to support a community. Fr. Joseph reckoned the First Order to have begun on the Feast of the Exaltation of the Holy Cross (14 September) 1919, though the priest and the layman who with him were to found the first community were not ready to join him for another two years.

The first attempt to found a women's community foundered. Not until 1922 was it possible to try again, this time with success. Again, the Sisters of St. Anne trained the recruits in the novitiate, and Fr. Joseph asked one of them, Sister Mary Christine, to guide the infant community. Fr. Joseph's aim was that his Second Order should be like the traditional Poor Clares, enclosed, who by their prayers would play a vital role in supporting the active work of the First Order.[17] Until the move to Little Portion in 1929, it was not possible to attain full enclosure. Both the First and Second Orders wore a grey habit recalling the traditional dress of the Conventuals, and this they retained until their union with the Society of St. Francis.

In the 1920s, women Tertiaries Regular were engaged in the parish of St. James', Cleveland (Ohio) where they were under the joint

12. ibid.
13. Fr. Powell to Fr. Joseph 29.4.18.
14. ibid.
15. Fr. Joseph, Pastoral Letter 11.9.65.
16. Letters between Fr. Robertson and Fr. Joseph 27.1.19 and 12.2.19.
17. AFG, p. 36.

supervision of the Rector, Fr. Peterson, and Mother Mary Christine of the Poor Clares.[18] The Sisters did devoted work in the parish, although Mother Mary Christine had trouble with her health, and two of the Sisters would have preferred the contemplative life, but gladly accepted their work under obedience.[19] Another early recruit, Sister Mary Elizabeth, left the Poor Clares to engage in other active work, being engaged in prison visiting.[20] With Sister Sybelle, she tried to found a new community dedicated to this work. In the 1930s, women Tertiaries Regular were working at Pontiac, Illinois.[21]

During the 1920s, both the First and Second Orders grew in numbers, though slowly, and became established in their work. As the Sisters of St. Anne guided the Second Order, so the Order of the Holy Cross and the Society of St. John the Evangelist helped the First Order through its early days.[22] Despite this growing stability and maturity, by 1927 Fr. Joseph was looking for a move. The strain of looking after both Merrill and Tomahawk was considerable. He was, in addition, a great missionary preacher, and was much in demand to preach parish missions, conduct Lent courses, give Holy Week addresses, Quiet Days and retreats. It was difficult to answer such calls while in charge of a parish and a mission station, for that might be to leave them without a priest, and it was only after the move to Little Portion that Fr. Joseph was able to devote more of his time to such work. His considerable journeys were made by train. Bishop Weller was understandably reluctant to see them go, knowing that it would be very difficult to find anyone to take on their work; but he did not oppose their going. Several possibilities were considered between 1927 and 1929 – New York City; Bridgeport (Connecticut); or rather vaguely 'nearer Chicago'. Fr. Joseph's dream at one stage was to take over a farm and establish a virtually self-supporting community. One thing he desired was to be near water – lake, great river or sea.[23] The matter was settled by the bequest to the Order of a site of nearly thirty acres at Mount Sinai, near Port Jefferson on Long Island. Here the Brothers moved in 1928, followed some months later by the Sisters.[24] A member of the family who gave the property joined the First Order soon after.

The property was entrusted to Fr. Joseph and two senior Brothers until the Order was constituted a legal corporation under New York

18. ibid.
19. Sister Mary Anthony Trinity VI 1927.
20. Report to the Bishop Protector 1929.
21. Third Order Acta Book.
22. Letter of Bishop Weller 1927.
23. AFG.
24. Fr. Huntingdon to Fr. Joseph 22.2.28.

State law.[25] It was situated about sixty miles from New York City, but had the peaceful seclusion conducive to prayer and the training of novices. The house was surrounded by extensive woodland, but when the Brothers first moved in, it was without many modern amenities. During the Order's first winter there (1928–29) the weather was so severe as to make it virtually uninhabitable, and the Society of St. John the Evangelist offered to take the Brothers in at their house in Brooklyn, but they stayed and made the best of it.[26] In due course, the building was made more suitable. The Brothers gave their house the Franciscan name, Little Portion, and kept the name when they moved to their present, smaller house a short distance away. When the Sisters followed them to Long Island, they took over a separate but adjacent house to the Brothers' which had formerly been used by the caretaker of the property. But although the site was made comfortable, and the location was in many ways more suitable than at Merrill, Fr. Joseph's health was seldom at its best on Long Island with its severe winters and humid summers. By the time of the move, there were six members in both Orders. In the First Order there were three professed Brothers and three novices. Three Sisters were at Little Portion and three at Cleveland. The income of the Order was adequate[27] but in the early days, money needed to be spent on the buildings; a new kitchen for the monastery; a new chapel for the Sisters.[28]

Contacts existed over a number of years between the Order of St. Francis and various English Franciscan communities. Mother Mary Elizabeth of the Community of St. Giles asked Fr. Joseph for copies of the Office Book used by the Order of St. Francis. Fr. Joseph was a liturgiologist of no mean distinction and worked for many years on a Breviary for the American communities. As this was not ready, he advised Mother Mary Elizabeth to use the Day Office. Unfortunately, by the time Fr. Joseph had completed his work, modern liturgical reform had outdated it. An approach was made to link the Order of St. Francis with the Fellowship of the Way, but Fr. Andrew (of Plaistow) thought that it would not be possible unless the Order of St. Francis had a house in England.[29] Fr. Algy sounded out Fr. Joseph with a view to linking the Order of St. Francis and the Society of St. Francis. According to Fr. Joseph, 'obvious difficulties made a formal union impossible.'[30] Nevertheless, he was prepared to place the English

25. Report to Bishop Protector 19.1.29. (For year 1928).
26. Letter 11.12.28.
27. Reckoned at about 15,000 dollars per annum. Reports to Bishop Protector 1929.
28. ibid. Until the union with S.S.F., the Brothers' house was known as a monastery not a friary.
29. Sister Mary Francesca to Fr. Joseph 28.6.33(?).
30. Fr. Joseph to Fr. David 11.10.61.

tertiaries under the Society of St. Francis, but Brother Douglas thought it better for one of their own tertiary priests to take charge (see next chapter). Fr. Joseph's vision for the Order of St. Francis was still clear. Its role was to revitalise the Church; to make priests better priests; to encourage vocations to the priesthood. He hoped the Order could establish a home for retired priests which would also be a temporary refuge for the overworked.[31]

By the 1960s, Fr. Joseph was himself feeling the strain of age and ill-health. He made way for Fr. Paul to succeed him as Superior who had been a service chaplain in the Second World War before joining the Order. Fr. Joseph moved to Florida, where the Order had taken over an old rectory at Orlando from which they did parish work, as later at Orange City. For a time they ran a Conference Centre at Avon Park, and they worked among the poor in Miami. But they did not find a permanent base for their work in Florida. When an invitation came from Bishop Myers of California to work in a mission district of San Francisco, they had to choose (because of manpower) between that and continuing in Florida; they chose San Francisco.

Since the Second World War, the Order has become more directly involved in work among the poor and deprived. In the early days at Little Portion, they ran a Sunday school for coloured people, mostly farm labourers. As well as the work in Miami, Fr. Stephen, who had joined the Order in 1929, felt moved to work for four years in Harlem in the 1960s. This was under his own auspices, but since then members of the Order have been working for several years in Manhattan. As recently in England, the American Franciscans have sought to identify themselves with the life of the 'inner city'.

Following the work at Avon Park, the Order has taken charge of the Bishop's Ranch at Healdsburgh, California. The Diocese of California acquired the property after the Second World War and made use of it, chiefly in the summer months, as a Conference Centre. The Franciscans took it over in 1973. As a resident religious community, they have been able to extend its use. It also meets something of Fr. Joseph's plan for a home in convalescence and old age.

The Order shared the problems general to religious communities in the 1960s when traditional roles had to be re-examined. Many men came forward to test their vocation, though few of them stayed to profession; there was, nevertheless, a slight increase in numbers. In 1967, they decided to seek union with the English Society of St. Francis. The decision meant a determination to overcome the difficulties which had previously stood in the way of merger. Brother Michael attended the American Chapter at Michaelmas 1967, and the English Chapter

31. Little Chronicle, April 1961.

in October agreed to the proposed plan for union. The Order of St. Francis was to become the American Province of the Society of St. Francis, retaining the name 'Order of Poor Brethren of St. Francis'. The constitutional provisions of the Society of St. Francis were accepted in general, recognising that their revision was under discussion.[32] The American Province joined before completion of the new Constitution in 1969. The Minister-General (Br. David) spent a year in America before the union was completed, and an exchange of Brothers between the two provinces took place.[33] At the union, the American Brothers adopted the English brown habit.

The Poor Clares of Reparation also became members of the Society of St. Francis, but did not amalgamate with the Englsh Second Order. However, the Mother from Maryhill visited Freeland, and two English Clares were sent to Long Island. The American Clares adopted the Franciscan Office Book and the English Sister's Constitution and brown habit.

It was only some years after moving to Long Island that the American Sisters fulfilled Father Joseph's vision of becoming an enclosed community. The enclosure was strict, and in the years following the move, it was difficult to maintain numbers, so that there were only three or four Clares professed at any one time. But in time, extern sisters were also recruited who protected the enclosure by maintaining the necessary contact the outside world. At one point, Mother Mary Catherine was the only professed Clare remaining, but she persevered, and new recruits came – an extern sister and a tertiary were professed. In the 1940s, the Sisters moved from their original site, literally having their wooden house removed down the hill. The more convenient position which they took up they named Maryhill in honour of the Blessed Virgin.

The union has produced wider opportunities for both provinces. The English-based Community of St. Francis have opened a house in San Francisco. The American Brothers now have one in Trinidad. An American Brother was among the first members of the Community in Auckland, New Zealand. The Bishop's Ranch was the site for the first inter-provincial Chapter of the Third Order, who also had been brought together in the union of 1967. A comment on that event showed how the Anglican Franciscan movement had developed: 'Thus for the first time are we able to talk together face to face as one family.'[34]

32. S.S.F. Chapter Minutes 27.6.67 and 2.10.67.
33. ibid. 2.10.67.
34. Br. Geoffrey: Memoir on Pacific Province (Hilfield Archives).

23

The American Third Order and the Mission Sisters of the Charity of St. Francis

The American Third Order evolved out of the group who had prayed from 1908 for the formation of a new Franciscan Order in the Episcopalian Church.[1] It came into being at the meeting in Cincinnati on the Feast of the Sacred Heart, 1917.[2] At this meeting, twenty men and women adopted a Franciscan Rule of Life, and so became the nucleus of the Order of St. Francis. As has been seen, it was from this group that the First and Second Orders were to grow, many of them being former tertiaries. The original group grew slowly in numbers, particularly after the First Order was established in its work under Father Joseph at Merrill. By the time of the move to Little Portion, they numbered about 150.[3]

Their numbers might have grown more rapidly still, for a great number of men and women were attracted to the Franciscan ideal through Father Joseph's missionary preaching. But though many joined, many only stayed a year or two.[4] One problem in establishing a Third Order in the American Episcopalian Church is that members are likely to be scattered and therefore isolated. The problems of keeping contact between tertiaries tend to be much greater than in England. Much depended on the contact, largely by letter, which members of the First Order, particularly Fr. Joseph, were able to maintain, and he recognised that they were scarcely enough Brothers to maintain the necessary contact.[5] The members of the Second Order helped to maintain vital links, particularly with women tertiaries. As well as the Third Order, there were two confraternities, those of St. Saviour and St. Francis. The members did not formally adopt a Rule of Life, but pledged themselves to the ideals of the Order. A third, the Confraternity of the Living Rosary, was made up of those who in

1. Fr. Joseph, *Adventure for God* (Merrill, Wisconsin, 1926), p. 8.
2. The Friday after the Octave of Corpus Cristi (i.e. the second Friday after Trinity Sunday).
3. Reports 1929.
4. ibid.
5. ibid.

addition pledged themselves to share the intercessory prayer of the Poor Clares.

The first Manual for the Third Order was published at Merrill in 1924 with the title *A Bunch of Myrrh*. A second edition came out from Little Portion in 1929 called the *Little Book of the Rule*. Father Joseph, who was largely responsible for these Manuals, wrote:

It is obvious that a Religious Order needs unity; and one great means of this is coherence in the faith.[6]

The Manual included a *Credenda* – the seven Sacraments of the Church, the Sacrifice of the Mass, and an intermediate state between Heaven and Hell. The Immaculate Conception and the Assumption were named as pious beliefs. The teaching of the first Seven Ecumenical Councils was affirmed 'in so far as [it was] accepted by the Undivided Church.' The distinctive Franciscan theology was affirmed that God created the visible world with the intention of becoming Incarnate.[7] This reflected the Anglo-Catholic outlook of the Order. The tertiaries were under the careful guidance of the First Order and remained so until the revision of the Constitution (1969). But both this close guidance and the *Credenda* were needed to keep the tertiaries together in the early days. The tertiaries also had a distinctive dress which was called a habit. The greater habit – for men, a cassock with scapular and cord of three knots, for women, a white veil – was worn only for gatherings of the Third Order and for burial. The lesser habit – a cord and scapular – was worn at all times except for bathing and sleeping.

Fr. Joseph visited England at least once more after 1914, in 1919,[8] and attended one of the Anglo-Catholic Congresses. He made a number of contacts with English Anglo-Catholics, and from these built up a small but devoted band of tertiaries in England.[9] The Society of the Divine Compassion, the Brotherhood of the Holy Cross and later the Brotherhood of the Love of Christ all had tertiary groups, though it was not until the formation of the Society of St. Francis in 1937 that there was a Third Order which met the general need in England. Fr. Joseph had been at work long before this, but he was far from being an 'Empire-builder'. After 1937, he himself felt that the English tertiaries should be attached to the Society of St. Francis. He evidently discussed this with Brother Douglas, who nevertheless telephoned Fr. Joseph from London to tell him that he had entrusted their care to

6. Third Order Manual (privately printed 1962).
7. ibid., p. 27. The teaching is particularly associated with the great Franciscan theologian Duns Scotus (c. 1264–1308).
8. CC p. 527.
9. In 1964 they were twenty strong.

one of their own number, the Rev. George Hall of Norwich.[10] The English tertiaries like the Americans wore the habit and also took a name in religion.

One of the best known of the English tertiaries was Fr. Desmond Morse-Boycott. He worked in the parish of St. Mary, Somers Town (North London) from 1919 to 1935. His concern for the poor boys of the parish led him in 1932 to found the Choir School of St. Mary-of-the-Angels. He aimed not only to educate the boys and train them for the service of God, but to inspire them with Franciscan ideals and foster vocations to the priesthood among them. To this end he formed a band of 'junior tertiaries'.[11] When the tertiaries were constituted as the 'English custody' they were placed under Fr. Morse–Boycott's spiritual direction at a ceremony at St. Mary's, Somers Town. As a tertiary, he took the name Father Anthony.

Among the women tertiaries, one of the most remarkable was Mabel Julia Mary Pinco, known as a tertiary as Sister Mary Francesca. She first came into contact with Fr. Joseph in 1925. She was then living at Verwood, Dorset. She was a nurse by profession but felt a strong call to the religious life. Fr. Baverstock[12] of the nearby parish of Hinton Martell had allowed her to take an exterior life vow of religion.[13] An interregnum at Verwood brought an American priest to the parish who advised her to contact Fr. Joseph. They corresponded, and in 1926 she planned to join Fr. Joseph at Merrill and test her vocation with the Sisters. Unfortunately, she had difficulty obtaining permission from the immigration authorities.[14] However, it appears that she did subsequently test her vocation in America, but had to give up through ill-health. She returned to England and laboured hard to build up the Franciscan group, though it was long her dream to found a house of Tertiaries Regular in England. Fr. Morse-Boycott said that she 'undoubtedly kindled the little Franciscan flame among us', but because of her ill-health he had doubts as to her suitability for the religious life.[15] He persuaded Fr. Joseph to allow her to wear the religious habit. She was in contact with Fr. Harding of St. Stephen's, Devonport,

10. Fr. Joseph to Fr. David 24.12.60. Fr. Hall was ordained in the Diocese of Montreal. He became Curate of Thorpe Episcopi (Norfolk) in 1938 and Rector of St. George's, Tombland, Norwich in 1941. As a tertiary he was known as Father Agnellus.
11. See his letters to Fr. Joseph (undated) 1926 and 21.2.30.
12. Alban Henry Baverstock was Rector of Hinton Martell near Wimborne Minster 1899–1930. He became Chaplain to the Lady Henry Somerset Homes at Duxhurst near Reigate (see Chapter 18) 1930–32. He was one of the original Guardians of the Shrine of Our Lady of Walsingham.
13. Sister Mary Francesca to Fr. Joseph 1.9.25.
14. Fr. Joseph to the General Commissioner of Immigration 27.4.26.
15. Letter to Fr. Joseph 21.2.30.

where at one time she had hopes of establishing a house.[16] Then she worked for a time in Bristol, and subsequently with Fr. Morse-Boycott at Somers Town.

Sister Mary Francesca will be chiefly remembered for the work of her later years when she at last realised her dream of a community of Tertiaries Regular. She was joined by another tertiary, Sister Mary Magdalene, who in fact became senior, and together in 1952 they began the religious life in a small house in Rose Lane, Norwich, being known as the Mission Sisters of the Charity of St. Francis. Fr. Hall acted as their chaplain and spiritual director.[17] The Sisters received training in the novitiate from Mother Kathleen Mary of the Community of Jesus the Good Shepherd.[18] They worked chiefly among women and girls, providing beds for the destitute and looking for 'lost' girls.[19] They worked a long day from 5.30 in the morning until 10.30 in the evening, and both Fr. Hall and Mother Kathleen Mary persuaded them to allow themselves slight mitigations.[20] Their work won them praise on all sides. The Bishop of Norwich licensed them as Diocesan Women Workers. The County Authorities asked them to extend their work, but they felt that without more Sisters, this was impossible – a novice who had begun with them did not persevere, though they were later joined by Sister Mary Colette.[21] Fr. David, then Minister General of the Society of St. Francis, expressed himself 'immensely impressed' by their work.[22]

The Minister-General's visit was a step in the union of the English and American Franciscans. Brother Michael became Warden of the Norwich Sisters in 1968.[23] It was unfortunate that the two Sisters had begun their life in community too late for it to achieve permanence, though it was hoped for a time after the union that Sisters of the Community of St. Francis might be able to carry on their work.[24] Interchanges of Sisters took place between the two Communities, but a merger did not prove to be possible. When the Norwich Sisters were no longer able to continue their work, through old age, they retired to join the Sisters of the Good Shepherd at West Ogwell, Devon.

The union and the new Constitution were not acceptable to all the

16. Letter of William Ellis to Fr. Joseph 17.10.28; Letter of Sister Mary Francesca 19.12.28. Frederick Howard Harding was Vicar of St. Stephen's, Devonport 1922–32.
17. Letters of Sister Mary Magdalene to Fr. Joseph 29.11.57, 31.12.57.
18. ibid., 15.9.57.
19. ibid., undated, c. 1960.
20. ibid., 29.11.57.
21. ibid., undated, c. 1960; 16.12.63.
22. S.S.F. Chapter Minute 2.10.67.
23. ibid., 6.2.68.
24. ibid.

English tertiaries of Fr. Joseph's foundation. On the world scale, it was a momentous step bringing together a much wider family, quite as great a leap forward as the establishment of a single English Third Order had been in 1937. As has been seen, the American tertiaries were the hosts for the first inter-provincial Third Order Chapter. Numbers of tertiaries in the American Province have continued to grow steadily. Distance has continued a problem since these include tertiaries in Canada, and more recently Trinidad, as well as in all parts of the United States. But modern speed of communication must work to reduce distance and isolation.

Later developments are described in appendix II.

PART IV

THE SOCIETY OF ST. FRANCIS

24

The Coming Together of the English Communities, 1937

In 1936, the Brotherhood of St. Francis of Assisi and the Brotherhood of the Love of Christ agreed to merge to form the First Order of the Society of St. Francis. The Brotherhood of the Holy Cross was originally to have been a third partner, but later drew back. The Community of St. Francis became affiliated in 1964 and the Community of St. Clare was founded as an enclosed Second Order. The Third Order fostered by Christa Seva Sangha and the Brotherhood of the Love of Christ became the basis for a Third Order for the Society. The Anglican Franciscan movement had shown a tendency common among religious orders of individuals or small groups breaking away to found fresh communities, as Brother Giles and Father William had broken away from the Society of the Divine Compassion. But a centripetal movement had been at work for several years before the Society of St. Francis was formed.

It began as early as March 1927 when some fifty young men of different schools of thought within the Church of England met in the Jerusalem Chamber at Westminster Abbey.[1] From this meeting was founded the Brotherhood of the Expectancy. The members were drawn together first, by a common expectation of some new movement of the Holy Spirit in their own time; secondly by loyalty to the Church of England and a longing for her unity; and thirdly by a desire for a deepening of prayer life both for the Church and for individuals as a necessary preparation for revival.[2] With this in mind, the Brotherhood resolved first, to spend time in prayer daily with love and self-sacrifice; secondly to give their lives to God in the Church and go where the Spirit sent them; and thirdly to pray for the Brotherhood at Holy Communion, remembering the common expectation of the coming of the Lord into men's hearts.[3]

The members met again on 4–5 January 1928 at Church House, Westminster. A definite programme was agreed upon, and the mem-

1. Hilfield Archives C. 600.
2. ibid.
3. ibid.

166

bers found themselves to be a federation of groups rather than an organic unity. But they felt that their spiritual bond was sufficient for them to continue in prayer. There were five groups within the Brotherhood. The Nigeria Group was directed towards witness among the Hausa-speaking Muslims in Northern Nigeria. The Tokyo Group was concerned with establishing a students' hostel in the Japanese capital, supported by the Society for the Propagation of the Gospel and the Church Missionary Society. The Cambridge Brotherhood in Peking aimed to establish a monastic community in the Chinese capital. For the Franciscan movement, the other two groups were particularly significant. One was Christa Seva Sangha, to which two members, Algy Robertson and William Lash already felt drawn. The other was the English Group based on Salisbury, seeking prayer and the direction of the Spirit. W. F. Tyndale-Biscoe who later joined the Brotherhood of the Love of Christ at St. Ives as Father Francis belonged to this group; so did Derwas Chitty, well known for his work in the Fellowship of St. Alban and Sergius. St. Clair Donaldson, Bishop of Salisbury, Visitor of Brother Douglas' Community at Hilfield, was also a member.

An impulse towards unity among the Franciscans came in a more definite form through the Fellowship of the Way. This was also formed in 1927, but it sprang initially from the sorrow engendered by the Great War. One of its early members has written that it stemmed from reaction to the extreme poverty and distress of the 1920s and 1930s – an emotional response to the poor and slum-dwellers of the northern cities.[4] The aim of the Fellowship was Christendom – Christ reigning in all human life through love. One of their leaflets stated:

> We believe that as the Divine Love shone forth through the life of Our Lord, so it should continue to shine forth through the Church which is His Body. All His members, living and working in the world, consecrated to His will in a fellowship of love, joy and peace, are called to live the corporate life in which God reigns. We believe this corporate life is to be realised in every sphere of human life – in field and factory, mine and dockyard, school and sanctuary, hospital and home.[5]

The Fellowship was to have three orders, not exactly those traditional in the Franciscan Order. First there were the Tramp Preachers. These took vows of extreme poverty, forswearing property of any kind and eschewing violence in any form. They were to be the spearhead of the movement, spreading the Gospel among the working classes and meeting Marxist secularists face to face. Brother Donald, Brother

4. Letter 1.5.71. Hilfield Archives C. 600.
5. Hilfield Archives C. 600.

Edward Bulstrode's former companion, became one, but his health
soon broke down under the rigours of the life. Their work continued
the 'wayfaring' that James Adderley, Giles, Douglas and Edward
Bulstrode had all pioneered. In their privations they were to be supported by a second order of men and women living in communities,
self-supporting and sharing what they earned, and a third order of
sympathisers living in the world and giving moral and financial support. The ethos of the Fellowship was said to be very much influenced
by Tolstoy and his views on the Sermon on the Mount.[6]

The Fellowship was active for about five or six years (1927–33)
which coincided with the worst period of the Depression, and it continued until the outbreak of war in 1939. It had a permanent influence
in drawing closer together the four communities with a common outlook who formed the 'Second Order' of the Fellowship: the Brotherhood of St. Francis of Assisi, Christa Seva Sangha, the Brotherhood
of the Holy Cross, and the Sisters of the Community of St. Giles at
East Hanningfield. The Chapter was made up of men who all played
some significant part in the Franciscan movement: Fr. Barnabas of the
Society of the Divine Compassion; Brother Douglas; Frank Dyson; Fr.
Peter Hardy, Chaplain to the Community of St. Giles; William Lash;
Fr. J. R. H. Moorman (later Bishop of Ripon); George Potter; Fr. J.
A. Ramsbotham, Missionary Secretary to the Student Christian Move-
ment (later Bishop of Jarrow) and Algy Robertson.[7]

Another body, less directly connected with the Franciscan movement, was the League of Our Father. This began in 1902, and the
President for many years was Cordelia Jane Hawksley. The League
established 'Church Ramblers' Rests' – like Brother Douglas, they
eschewed the word 'tramp'. At these Rests, 'At Homes' were held,
beginning at 3.0 p.m. and lasting two or three hours. Two or more
invitations were given to ramblers to pass on to any men they met on
the road. Those who came were given tea and scones, then they played
dominoes or draughts or did jig-saw puzzles. Dice and cards were not
allowed. A paper called 'To men on the road' was read. The main
event of the meeting was always the corporate saying of the Our
Father, and the League aimed to make the Lord's Prayer familiar to
men unaccustomed to use it. Baptised men over twenty could join the
League, membership being renewed annually. Details were kept of
members' name, age, place and date of baptism and status, married
or single. Smoking was not allowed at the 'At Home', but guests were
given tobacco or cigarettes when they left.[8] Alice Bulstrode, sister of
Brother Edward, was a prominent member of the League, and close

6. Letter quoted supra.
7. Hilfield Archives C. 600.
8. League of Our Father booklet.

contacts were kept with the Hilfield Community. The League flourished until the Second World War, and its witness was particularly valuable in the years of the Depression.

The Brotherhood of St. Francis of Assisi developed in an important way after 1933. In that year, Bishop Donaldson approved the appointment of Brother Douglas as Prior. Chapter Meetings were held on a regular basis three times a year. At such a meeting held at St. Francis House, Brecon, it was resolved: 'The Brotherhood considers that the time is now ripe for the release of Friars for their special vocation, and for the finding of specialists for the management of Homes and Industries.'[9] The maturity of the Brotherhood as a religious community and its detachment from pre-occupation with a specific work made it possible for it to enter relations with other communities. The Brecon meeting also looked forward to the formation of a Third Order in cooperation with Christa Seva Sangha and the Brotherhood of the Holy Cross.[10]

In May 1934, a meeting took place at the Friary at Peckham attended by representatives of the Brotherhood of St. Francis, the Brotherhood of the Holy Cross, and Fr. Algy's community at St. Ives. They inserted a statement in their respective manuals looking forward to the establishment of a single Society of St. Francis.[11] Members of the communities met again at Nunhead in July for a short retreat. From the beginning it was hoped, not least by Fr. Algy, that some women religious could be included under the 'umbrella', as their association came to be called. The Community of St. Giles had been part of the Fellowship of the Way, but their numbers were declining, and in 1936 their care for leprosy patients at East Hanningfield was taken over by the Community of the Sacred Passion, into which they were absorbed (see Chapter 9). The Society of the Divine Compassion, despite its many links, was not drawn under the 'umbrella'. Fr. Barnabas, who was then Superior, had reservations about the communities at Hilfield and Peckham (see Chapter 6). In 1933–34, it seemed possible that Mother Teresa's Servants of Jesus and Mary would become the Second Order of a Society of St. Francis,[12] but in the long run they chose to remain independent.

Representatives of the Hilfield, Peckham and St. Ives Brotherhoods met again at St. John's, Waterloo Road (SE1) in June 1935. So that they might become a single First Order, they discussed a common Rule, a common habit, and a common novitiate.[13] Fr. Northcott of

9. B.S.F.A. Chapter Minute Book pp. 101, 103.
10. ibid., p. 108.
11. Fr. Denis, op. cit., p. 112.
12. ibid.
13. ibid., pp. 1113–14. B.S.F.A. Chapter Minute 4.6.35.

Mirfield accepted an invitation to become Spiritual Director to all three communities, to be Novice Master for a time, and to train Brother Charles to take over from him, though in the event it was Algy who became Novice Master. Hilfield was to be the site for the common novitiate. In September 1935, Fr. Algy conducted a retreat for the Brotherhood at Hilfield, and stayed on to discuss items of mutual interest with them.[14]

In January 1936, Fr. Algy and Fr. Francis of St. Ives produced a Rule comprising those of the three communities.[15] In August, it was decided to issue an annual newsletter with news of these communities, and also Christa Prema Seva Sangha and the Third Order.[16] In October, the Brotherhood of the Love of Christ agreed to adopt the brown habit worn by the Brotherhood of St. Francis. Each community was to keep its own name, but the whole took the name the Society of St. Francis.

The name particularly recalled that of the Hilfield Community which now became the common training ground for novices and whose Prior was now Minister of the larger Society. But the new Rule, and the new spirit of the Society, were those of Fr. Algy.[17] In order to take up his duties as Novice Master, Algy obtained leave of absence for a year (October 1936–37) from St. Ives. Brother Douglas was willing to stop the work for wayfarers at Hilfield if it stood in the way of training novices – a remarkable gesture of humility over his life's work. Fortunately, this did not prove necessary, but it was the kind of attitude which made it possible to bring his community and Algy's together. At the end of his year's leave, Fr. Algy resigned the living of St. Ives and moved to Hilfield permanently as Fr. Guardian. Fr. Potter took the same title as head of the house at Peckham. In October 1937, Douglas, Algy, George Potter and Brothers Kenneth, John and Charles took their life vows before Bishop Parsons of Southwark, the Visitor of the Society.[18] Brother Arthur also took his life vows but *in absentia* – he was much occupied with the home for wayfarers at Brecon.

In the years of coming together, the house of George Potter's community at Peckham provided a useful meeting place, being of easier access than either Hilfield or St. Ives. Not only did representatives of the Brotherhoods meet there, but at St. Francis' tide 1935, a meeting of tertiaries took place there and a council of representatives of the communities and tertiaries. Over fifty tertiaries met there again on 6 June 1936. The Brotherhood of the Holy Cross continued at Peckham

14. B.S.F.A. Chapter Minute 29.8.35.
15. Fr. Denis, op. cit., p. 115.
16. B.S.F.A. Chapter Minute 5.8.36.
17. Fr. Denis, op. cit., p. 115.
18. B.S.F.A. Chapter Minute 14.10.37.

until shortly after George Potter's death in 1960. Those of Fr. Algy's community who came in with him left St. Ives in 1937. The Brotherhood of the Holy Cross Quarterly in 1936 announced that the Society of St. Francis had come into being as the fruit of prayer and conference between the three Brotherhoods. It noted that the Third Order was already well established. 'We hope soon', it added, 'that a Second Order, for women, will come into being.'

25

The Society of St. Francis 1937–69

Between 1937 and the outbreak of the Second World War, the Society
of St. Francis developed from its new beginnings. Its old work was
re-appraised, new enterprises were launched. The Brothers from St.
Ives who took up residence at Hilfield adopted the brown habit of the
Brotherhood of St. Francis of Assisi.[1] The Franciscan newsletter went
ahead (see Chapter 24), price 6d. (2½p).[2] Douglas was elected
Father-Minister of the Society of St. Francis by the joint Chapter in
London.[3] Fr. Potter's health necessitated a Friar being sent to Peckham
so that he could take time off to recover; in the event, he handed over
charge of St. Chrysostom's to Fr. Francis from the Brotherhood of the
Love of Christ.[4] The work of the Friars was helped by setting up a
central fund. It was then reckoned that the keep of a Friar was £1 a
week or £50 a year. Friars travelling on behalf of the Homes were to
receive their expenses from this central fund.[5] A crucial meeting of the
joint Chapter took place in London in October 1938. The members of
the Brotherhood of the Love of Christ agreed to become part of the
Brotherhood of St. Francis of Assisi. The Brotherhood of the Holy
Cross preserved its independence at least for the time being. The two
Brotherhoods which merged took their place within the Society of St.
Francis under a common Rule, with a common novitiate at Hilfield.[6]
A paper was drawn up, almost certainly by Algy, which envisaged a
novitiate of two years, followed by three years in simple vows. The
Rule of St. Francis of 1223 was accepted. The Rules of the Brotherhood
of St. Francis and the Brotherhood of the Holy Cross were combined,
with a commentary taken largely from the Brotherhood of the Love of
Christ.[7] A novitiate had been continued at St. Ives in 1937, but Algy's
resignation as Vicar heralded the withdrawal of the Friars.[8]

1. Chapter Minutes 22.7.36, 14.10.36.
2. ibid., 5.8.36.
3. ibid., 14.10.36.
4. ibid., 24.2.38, 12.7.38.
5. ibid., 24.2.38.
6. ibid., 26.10.38.
7. ibid., insert 1939.
8. ibid., 28.4.37.

Road missions in the old style were sent out in October 1936.[9] The Home at Lockeridge was closed.[10] Tyn-y-Cae caused some anxiety: its finances were precarious, and Brother Arthur, who had largely created the Home, was failing in health. It was closed for six months in 1937–38, but there was feeling that it was a good base for evangelism and relief work, and John Morgan, Bishop of Swansea and Brecon, urged that it should be retained.[11] Dyffryn, in North Wales, was thought a suitable base for a new 'cell' of the Society of St. Francis.[12]

An important development, which took place on the very eve of war, was to take over the work of the Oratory of the Good Shepherd at Cambridge. The Society of St. Francis took over Lady Margaret House and the Sunday Eucharist at St. Edward's Church. In 1946, they transferred to the adjacent parish, St. Bene't's, where Fr. Denis was made Vicar; he was succeeded by Fr. Lothian in 1949.[13] Fr. Denis was the first to take charge of the Cambridge house. Although war broke out in September 1939, the plans for Cambridge went ahead. In October, the Friars moved in, and their housewarming party was attended, among others, by the Earl of Sandwich, the Superior of the Oratory of the Good Shepherd,[14] and Brother Douglas. The Bishop of Ely, Bernard Heywood, preached in Chapel.[15]

The Society observed the Church Unity Octave in January 1939 with a daily Eucharist. They invited the Abbé Couturier, who had done so much to promote the observance, to visit the Friary at Hilfield when he was in England,[16] but the outbreak of war prevented this.

George Lansbury visited Hilfield in August 1939. In the afternoon he talked to the 'whole family' and to individuals, and the evening was spent in prayer for peace.[17] When war came, its first impact was the arrival of sixty evacuated children with two schoolmasters. 'A certain amount of readjustment had had to be made,' the Minute Book records, 'but the regular Community life had not been seriously interrupted.' Four children were also received at the Sherborne Home, and it was considered whether some mothers and babies could stay there.[18] Twelve boys were transferred from Hilfield to Sherborne where on arrival they were found to be suffering from lice-infested heads – not uncommon among evacuees. Another twelve were moved to Bradford

9. ibid., 10.9.36, 1.10.36.
10. ibid., 16.12.36.
11. ibid., 16.12.36, 20.10.37, 10.11.37.
12. ibid., 12.7.38.
13. ibid., 12.7.38, 15.9.38, 2.2.49.
14. Edward Wynn, who succeeded Bernard Heywood as Bishop of Ely (1941–57).
15. Chapter Minute 26.10.39.
16. ibid., 5.1.39.
17. ibid., 24.8.39.
18. ibid., 7.9.39.

Abbas. About thirty stayed on at Hilfield, and a school was started for them.[19]

An ambulance unit was set up at the Friary, and all the Brothers who went in for the ambulance examination passed.[20] Juniper House was closed to save expense, but was opened later in the war as a remand home for boys – the beginning of an important new work for the Brothers.[21] The first Christmas of the war was described as 'very happy', though two wayfarers stole the safe during the Midnight Mass.[22] Three new postulants came to the Friary in the first six months of the war. There were departures, too, and Brother Maurice Serres, serving with the Royal Army Medical Corps, was taken prisoner in 1941.[23]

Despite the depletion of manpower, new work was taken on during the war-years. Fr. Denis directed his first fruit-picking mission at Wisbech in the summer of 1940,[24] a work taken over from the Oratory of the Good Shepherd. In 1944, two Friars visited the hop-picking mission in Kent with a view to the Society of St. Francis taking it over from Brother Edward Bulstrode (q.v.).[25] The sands mission at Weston-super-Mare still carried on.[26] Fr. Algy's greatness of vision during the Second World War is shown not only in the way that the Third Order (q.v.) was built up, but he also made plans for an enclosed Second Order. Two Sisters of Jesus of Nazareth worked at Peckham during the war, and there seems to have been an idea of making them the nucleus of a Second Order, but as they were engaged in active work, this was not possible.[27] In 1943, however, the meeting took place at which the Oblates of St. Clare were established, and at the end of the war some of these began to live in community, and from this the Second Order evolved (see next chapter).

In 1944, the Society took over No. 84, Cable Street, El, a property which had formerly been a brothel, in a 'rough' dockland district of London's East End. St. Francis Hospice, as it became, was the base from which devoted work was carried on, notably by Brother Neville (Palmer). Neville was a pacifist by conviction who joined in the protest marches to Aldermaston. But on his home patch, he was a true peacemaker, quietly separating men in street fights. He also won the confidence of African, Asiatic and West Indian seamen and settlers in

19. ibid., 14.9.39, 1.11.39.
20. ibid., 14.9.39, 28.9.39.
21. ibid., 16.11.39, 26.6.40.
22. ibid., 4.1.40.
23. ibid., 1941.
24. ibid., 18.6.40.
25. ibid., 26.1.44.
26. ibid., 20.10.44.
27. ibid., 26.1.42.

the district. Fr. Kenneth Leech, who worked with him between 1958 and 1963 when he left for Ceylon (Sri Lanka) paid warm tribute to him on his death, in *The Franciscan* (June 1976).

In May 1945, at a Chapter Meeting attended by Fr. Bill Lash and Deaconess Graham, Christa Prema Seva Sangha was affiliated to the Society of St. Francis.[28] The Chapter also decided that, although the war had ended, the work for boys on remand at Juniper House should continue.[29] Brother Owen had shown great talent for this work. 'He was one of a handful of pioneers in the field who tried to understand and relate creatively to [delinquent] children.'[30] In October 1945, the Society took over Hooke Court at Beaminster (Dorset) and opened it as a Special School.[31]

The Society of St. Francis had close links with Brother Edward Bulstrode's Village Evangelists, formed in 1947. Bishop Carey, their Co-Warden, became a member of the Third Order. The Society took over the Kent hop-picking mission from Brother Edward in 1947.[32] The same year, the Society took over Glasshampton, where Fr. William Sirr (q.v.) had laboured to establish the contemplative life. Although the Society's tradition had been the active life, they recognised that the time he had spent in the *carceri* had been an important part of the life of St. Francis and that contemplation was therefore part of the Franciscan tradition.[33]

Although the Brotherhood of the Holy Cross remained independent, it had closer co-operation with the Society of St. Francis from 1947. It was agreed that there should be a joint Council Meeting each year, and that they should co-operate on missions; a joint novitiate was envisaged.[34] The growth of the Third Order during and after the war made it possible for a group of women tertiaries to share their life and work as the Company of St. Francis (q.v.).

In the early 1950s, a number of missions were undertaken – six in 1950, fourteen in 1951, and these included familiar ground at Weston-super-Mare and Wooler Camp.[35] In 1952, the Society took over the work of the Society of the Divine Compassion at Plaistow at Fr. Barnabas' request, an undertaking which Fr. Algy accepted as a 'debt of honour'.[36] Co-operation with the Brotherhood of the Holy

28. ibid., 22/23.5.45.
29. ibid., 24.5.45.
30. Obituary, SPAN Easter 1981.
31. Chapter Minute 5.10.45.
32. ibid., 23.10.46, 20/21.1.47.
33. ibid.., 28/29.5.47. *Carceri* = cells; a site near Assisi where St. Francis lived for a time as a hermit.
34. Chapter Minute 6/8.10.47.
35. ibid., 30.5.50, 8/10.2.51, 9/11.10.51.
36. ibid., 27.1.53.

Cross went ahead; they were to send representatives to the Chapter and their novices were to be trained at Hilfield. But they retained their identity, their house, and their distinctive grey habit.[37]

Something of an epoch came to an end with the passing first of Father Algy (November 1955) and then of Brother Douglas (September 1957). Less than a year before he died, in December 1954, Algy received the 'accolade' of a canonry in Salisbury Cathedral. Douglas was seriously ill for some time before his death, but found love and care from many who owed it to him, and his last days were spent at the Hostel of God, Clapham Common, very peacefully.[38] But a generation had grown up in the Society of St. Francis ready to carry on when the founders had passed. It fell to Fr. Denis first to assume the leadership after Algy's passing. It was a sign that a generation had passed that these years saw the first biographies written of some of the founders – Fr. Adderley's had been written in 1943, Fr. Andrew's life and letters in 1948, Brother Douglas' in 1959, Fr. Algy's in 1964. A different 'coming of age' came when the Friary and Flowers Farm at Hilfield were purchased from Lord Hinchinbrooke in 1957 for the use of the Friars.[39]

Although the Society was growing in numbers, requests for several new ventures at home and abroad had had to be turned down in the 1940s and 1950s. But in July 1958, the Society was requested to send Friars to New Guinea. This was given careful consideration and prayer, and in 1959, Fr. Geoffrey was sent out, with others to follow.[40] This was the beginning of work which was to lead to the creation of a whole new province of the Society, the story of which is traced in the concluding chapter. Franciscans had worked in Africa since the days when the Society of the Divine Compassion were at Thlotse Heights. But a new beginning was made in 1961, when Fr. Peter was sent to work in schools in Northern Rhodesia (Zambia).[41] Nearer home, the Society were able to encourage the Franciscan Movement in the Church of Sweden. Swedish Brothers of the Holy Cross came to Hilfield to stay and work as guests, and novices were sent out to Sweden.[42] But other work from earlier times came to an end at Poona when Christa Prema Seva Sangha was dissolved in 1963.[43]

In England, a new Friary was opened at Alnmouth. This reduced pressure on accommodation at Hilfield which was becoming over-

37. ibid., 25/27.1.54.
38. ibid., 6.10.57.
39. ibid., 7.10.57.
40. ibid., 2.7.58, 14.8.58.
41. ibid., 10.10.61.
42. ibid., 10.10.61, 2.10.62.
43. ibid., 4.6.63.

crowded and also gave the Society a firm base in the North. The Sisters of the Community of St. Francis moved from Dalston to their new home at Compton Durville where they could keep closer contact with Hilfield. As the Society was firmly established at Glasshampton, they were confirmed in the use of that site.[44] Desire to live the contemplative life led Father Aelred and two companions to make a new venture. They lived for a time in a cottage at Freeland, but Aelred later went on, alone, to settle at a house in the grounds of the Benedictine nunnery at West Malling (Kent) where two other recruits, not from the Society of St. Francis, joined him. As their way of life developed, they came to see themselves in the Cistercian tradition rather than the Franciscan, but the initial stages of their experiment were taken under the auspices of the Society of St. Francis.[45]

Between 1966 and 1969, a number of significant changes took place which taken together mark a turning point in the history of the Society. It was a critical period for the religious life, not only in the Anglican Communion but in the whole of Western Christendom. The validity and meaning of the religious life were questioned. Loss of vocation was common, even among those who had spent many years in the religious life.[46] Older established communities in the Church of England, both of men and women, found it difficult to attract recruits, and there was a danger of their becoming aging societies – a fate which had already overtaken the Society of the Divine Compassion. In 1966, the Cowley Fathers took the opportunity of their centenary to rethink their work and bring up to date aspects of their life. The Society of the Sacred Mission ended their work of theological training at Kelham and renewed their life in a number of smaller houses with more varied work. The Society of St. Francis was subject to the same pressures and made a comparable response.

The Society had three main problems which were met by the revision of the Constitution. One was to adjust the religious life to the circumstances of the time. In the summer of 1966, a four-fold Daily Office was adopted (Morning Prayer, Midday Prayer, Evening Prayer and Night Prayer or Compline) a pattern which has become common among religious communities, particularly those engaged in active work. The new experimental services (Series II and later Series III, both Eucharist and Office) were used, and Hilfield Friary became an important centre of liturgical experiment for the Diocese of Salisbury. But it was agreed that these new forms should be dropped if the Church decided against them.[47] The Chapter of Faults became a

44. ibid., 23.1.62.
45. ibid., 8.6.65, 1.2.66.
46. ibid., 1.2.66, 4.10.66.
47. ibid., 31.5.66, 8.6.66.

'gathering of the family for mutual explanations and apologies'.[48] At
the same time, the religious character of their life received safeguards.
Houses were, wherever possible, to have a common room for the
exclusive use of the Friars. Postulants were to stay at Hilfield until
they were clothed, and then were to spend their first year under the
Novice Master at Glasshampton.[49]

The second problem concerned the relationship of the ordained and
lay members of the First Order. This was no new problem, and had
been felt, perhaps, most keenly in those Franciscan communities which
were closely linked with parishes, as at Plaistow and Peckham. One
step taken was that all members of the First Order, both priests and
laymen, were to be known as Brother, or else simply called by their
Christian name.[50] This was a return to the custom of Brother Douglas
in the days of the Brotherhood of St. Francis. A more serious step was
the decision to open all offices to both priests and laymen. This move
was not made without some heart-searching and even opposition by
some Friars of long-standing.[51] It was a bold move, but in principle at
least it brought the Society of St. Francis into line with monastic
communities in the Age of the Fathers, and with the Franciscan Order
in the days of St. Francis himself.

The third problem was organisation. The Society had expanded
almost out of recognition from its beginnings in small communities in
a single house. In 1967, the American Order of St. Francis requested
union with the Society. This union, together with the work which had
expanded in the Pacific in the 1960s, made the Society of St. Francis
a world-wide organisation. The problem was to devise a form of
government which would allow local self-government and initiative,
while maintaining the unity of the Society. The solution was the
creation of the office of Minister General, to whom Ministers Provincial
were to be subordinate while being the vital links between authority
above and below. The First Order Chapter also played a key role.
Each province was represented by its Minister Provincial and two
elected representatives, and the annual meeting was to be held suc-
cessively in each province. But such matters as the admission of novices, professions and the opening of new houses (provided that they
could be supported by the province) were to be dealt with on a
provincial level.[52] Relations between communities within the Society
were strengthened by Brother Michael becoming Warden of both the

48. ibid., 8.6.66.
49. ibid.
50. ibid.
51. Hilfield Archives A. 120.
52. ibid.

Community of St. Francis and the Mission Sisters at Norwich.[53] The Constitution has been subsequently revised, and the duties of the officers and organs of government and their relationship to one another carefully defined. One change has been that the First Order Chapter meets only every three years in the normal way, but it deals only with matters affecting the Brothers in all the provinces. Provincial Chapters now have responsibility for much of the Society's affairs within their areas. In the years when the First Order Chapter does not meet, there is usually a meeting of Ministers.[54] Changes to the Constitution can only be made with the consent of each of the constituent parts of the First Order.[55] Each province now has a Deputy Minister who is one of the representatives *ex officio* on the Chapter. Recent revisions of the Constitution have provided for the admission to the First Order of Persons not in Communion with the See of Canterbury. This is possible with the consent of the Bishop Protector of the province. From the Bishops Protector, one is chosen to be Protector General.[56]

Meanwhile, the work of the First Order has continued to expand. The size of the Order and the need for a complex machinery of government has been balanced by the opening of several new houses, often small in size and therefore intimate and personal in their community life. The work at long-established centres, Hilfield, Cambridge, Hooke Court, Glasshampton, Plaistow and Alnmouth continues. The Friars have a house now at Canterbury, one of the earliest cities in England where the Franciscans settled. A trend since Second World War has been to establish a Franciscan presence in industrial cities – Birmingham, Ashton-under-Lyne, Liverpool and with the First Order Sisters at Newcastle-under-Lyme. If the old saying is true that 'Francis loved the towns'[57] there is a parallel with the Saint's own life – before the great ministry to the towns, he had first to find his spiritual strength in quieter, more remote places, to which perforce he often returned. Special mention should be made of the house in Belfast – both because of the need of 'instruments of peace' in that city, and as the first religious house of men in the Church of Ireland.[58] The house in Edinburgh means a Franciscan presence in Scotland; that at Llanrhos, Llandudno, continues the presence in Wales begun with the

53. ibid. Letter 9.2.68.
54. First Order Constitution.
55. ibid.
56. ibid.
57. Bernardus valles, colles Benedictus amabat, Oppida Franciscus, magnas Ignatius urbes – Bernard loved the valleys and Benedict the hills, Francis the towns and Ignatius the great cities.
58. It was the first Anglican religious house of all in Northern Ireland. South of the border there have been two houses for women – the Community of St. Mary the Virgin (1887) and the Community of St. John the Evangelist (1912), both in Dublin.

hostel at Tyn-y-Cae in wayfaring days. The houses in the British Isles have been divided into a Southern Region and a Northern Region. The latter includes Wales, Scotland and Ireland.

In 1967, Brother Peter was allowed to go to Italy for the winter for his health's sake. He acted as Assistant Anglican Chaplain in Florence.[59] He died suddenly on the Feast of the Stigmata (17 September) 1969. The Abbot of the Benedictine Monastery of San Miniato al Monte had welcomed him as part of their religious family, and when he died, he was buried in the vault reserved for monks. The basilica was placed at the disposal of the Society for the Requiem and Funeral Service from the Book of Common Prayer. The Abbot gave the address.[60] It was an illustration of the warm ecumenical links which have been forged in recent years between Anglican Franciscans and Roman Catholic religious. Later, a Friar was sent to act in Assisi itself as Anglican Chaplain.

In recent years, one Anglican Franciscan Friar has become a suffragan bishop, another a university professor. We conclude this survey of recent years by noting these 'firsts'. So rapid has been the development since 1969 that any history must have difficulty keeping up with events. But as the remaining chapters will show, the pace of development has not been confined to the First Order.

59. Chapter Minute 27.6.67.
60. *The Franciscan*, December 1969.

26

The Community of St. Clare

It was Fr. Algy who conceived the idea of an enclosed Second Order within the Society of St. Francis, and the inspiration is said to have come when he was on pilgrimage with Brother Kenneth at Assisi in 1937.[1] He was not the first to think of it. Ever since the prospect opened of restoring the Franciscan Life in the Anglican Communion, there had been hopes for a women's community on the lines of the Poor Clares. This had been part of the vision of both Fr. Paul and Fr. Joseph in the United States. In England, there had been hopes that one or other of the women's Franciscan communities would fill the role of a Second Order, but those founded down to 1937 had been active rather than contemplative. Algy's dream was fulfilled through his labours and those of First Order Brothers who felt with him and the response of the women who answered his call. The Community of St. Clare is the most recent of the Franciscan foundations. This only reflects that in the Anglican Communion, the place of the active religious communities was recognised much earlier than that of the contemplative.

The Community of St. Mary the Virgin at Wantage played an important part in fostering the new Community, particularly Sister Evelyn Angela. She was the sister of Phyllis Bettell, a Franciscan tertiary who Algy hoped would seek the life of the Clares, but who developed tuberculosis. Algy sought his potential recruits among those to whom he was spiritual director, women who were seeking a life of prayer. A meeting took place on 15 March 1943 at the Wantage Mission House in Camberwell. Fr. Algy and Brother Michael were present, Sister Evelyn Angela and four ladies who became Oblates of St. Clare. One of these was later professed in the Community of St. Clare (Sister Kathleen).

The Oblates grew in number to nine or ten, but because of family commitments or reasons of health, not all were free to test their vocation to the religious life. In August 1944, Algy arranged with the Mother General at Wantage for two of the Oblates, Elizabeth and

1. CC p. 525.

Joan, to live at St. Agnes' House at Wantage as religious postulants
with Sister Evelyn Angela. They said the day Hours together and
joined the Wantage Sisters for the Eucharist in the Convent chapel.
In March 1945, they moved to Cassington in Oxfordshire, very near
to where the Community was finally to settle. Four attic rooms in the
Vicarage were placed at their disposal by the Vicar, Father Brancker.[2]
Sister Evelyn Angela stayed until July 1945 when she returned to
Wantage, and Elizabeth and Joan were on their own for a year until
two other Oblates joined them. The Sisters lived simply on about 10/-
(50p) a week, rising at 5.30 a.m. and retiring at 9.30 p.m. Their daily
life revolved around the Office and the Eucharist in the parish church.
About two hours each morning were spent in housework at the Vicarage and about an hour each afternoon working in the Vicarage
garden. They were not fully enclosed at Cassington, but their only
visitors were other Oblates.

In January 1947, they moved to Ty Mawr near Monmouth. Fr.
Algy had arranged with the Society of the Sacred Cross, an enclosed
Community with some Cistercian features,[3] for the Sisters to live with
them to be trained in the religious life and to experience full enclosure.
On 19 January, they visited the Friary at Hilfield and stayed the night
with an old friend of the Brothers, Mrs. St. John Hornby. This break
in their journey helped to underline the family link between the two
Communities.

They lived at first in part of the guest wing of the Convent. They
joined the Sisters of the Sacred Cross for the Liturgy, and on special
occasions such as Christmas 1947 shared recreation with them. Mother
Guenvrede, S.S.C. trained them in the religious life, visiting them for
an informal class daily. Otherwise they lived apart from the home
Community. In July 1947 they could be more completely separate
when Brother Stephen from Hilfield put up a Nissen hut for them
which they named *Little Portion*. This was their enclosure, where only
Mother Guenvrede was allowed to join them. Fr. Algy continued to
foster the growth of the Community, but even he was not allowed into
Little Portion. The Sisters' life was austere, more so because their first
year at Ty Mawr coincided with the severe winter of 1946–47 and the
drought in the autumn following the very warm summer.

Of the four Oblate Sisters who had come from Cassington, one
decided not to continue in the religious life. The other three became
religious novices in September 1947. Two more recent recruits were
then made postulants and proceeded to the novitiate in April 1948.

2. Thomas Brancker was Vicar of Cassington from 1939 to 1948 when he retired. He
   was a friend of James Adderley in his latter years (Stevens, op. cit., p. 76).
3. CC p. 508. The Society of the Sacred Cross was also a war-time foundation, dating
   from December 1914. They settled at Ty Mawr in 1923.

Another recruit later joined them, and six was the maximum who could be accommodated at *Little Portion*. The Community began to look for a permanent home, but at Ty Mawr they had not only received the necessary training in the religious life but gained experience of outdoor manual work.

Brother Charles, one of the Hilfield Brothers who had worked closely with Algy for the young Community, discovered a suitable site at Freeland near Oxford. St. Mary's House, as it was called, was the property of a Miss Shipman, who had bought it in the 1920s and ran it as a retreat house with the help of two other ladies, Miss Jebb as housekeeper and Miss Victor as gardener. During the Second World War it was used by the Choir School of All Saints', Margaret Street. After the war, Miss Shipman handed it over to the Fidelity Trust with the wish that it should be used by a religious community, preferably an enclosed order. Miss Jebb and Miss Victor continued meanwhile to keep it in excellent condition. Mother Guenvrede came over to inspect it with the Sisters and to give it her approval. On Christmas Day 1949, the Community of St. Clare became the legal tenants. It kept its name as St. Mary's Convent. Mother Guenvrede took three of the Sisters by car on 23 January 1950. Brother Stephen brought the other three the next day, with the Community's possessions in the Friday van from Hilfield. The chapel was re-arranged choir-wise, and an enclosure screen and door were fitted to divide the guest wing from the Community's quarters. Mother Guenvrede stayed a few days until the Community had settled in and then returned to Ty Mawr. Though she remained interested in the Community, she did not wish to influence its subsequent development.

On 6 February 1950, the two senior novice Clares took their first vows, and the Community of St. Clare really dates from this event.[4] Algy, Charles and Denis were all present, also Mother Guenvrede. The Diocesan Bishop, Kenneth Kirk of Oxford, insisted that a religious Sister in life vows should live with the Community to advise and guide them. By arrangement with Mother Elfreda of the Community of the Holy Name, Malvern Link, Sister Audrey Mary was sent who as well being a good organiser continued the teaching in doctrine and the religious life. Both Mother Elfreda and Bishop Kirk visited the Community in its early days at Freeland. By the autumn of 1952, the Community was sufficiently of age to have its first Reverend Mother. The choice fell on Sister Elizabeth, who had been one of the earliest Oblates, and she was installed by Bishop Kirk on 2 October 1952. Algy and Charles were again present. Sister Audrey Mary returned to

---

4. Peter Anson in CC dates the Community from '1940–50' (p. 525) but the years before 1950 were properly years of preparation.

Malvern. Dr. Robert Mortimer, Bishop of Exeter, became the first
Bishop Protector of the Community, which he visited for the first time
in October 1950. In 1955, he decided that the Community was ready
to hold an election for Mother Superior. The then Assistant Superior
was chosen and was installed in September 1955. Sadly, Fr. Algy was
not present, being too seriously ill. He had done much to inspire and
guide the Community without over-influencing it. By the time of his
death (23 November 1955), it was firmly on its feet.

As soon as they settled at Freeland, it was possible for the Sisters
to begin building up the life of worship and intercession which is their
special vocation. Not till they moved to Freeland did they have their
own chapel. Brother Stephen celebrated their first Community Mass
the day after they moved in – 25 January (the Conversion of St. Paul)
1950. The Blessed Sacrament was reserved and Benediction given for
the first time in May.[5] With their training at Ty Mawr behind them,
the Sisters at once began to sing the Divine Office.

It was some time before the Community found a resident Chaplain
to stay any length of time. An Oblate priest and some Friars from
Hilfield came for a time, and a number of priests came and went,
though one stayed as long as four years. It became easier when a
cottage adjoining St. Mary's became available where a married Chaplain could live with his family. The Friars at Hilfield had always
helped out with turns of duty. From 1969, when their numbers had
sufficiently increased, it became possible for them to take the responsibility of providing a Chaplain. As the Community grew, a new chapel
was built which was dedicated by Bishop Mortimer in April 1961.

The Old Parsonage at Freeland, adjacent to St. Mary's Convent,
was owned by an Oblate, Miss Margaret Hill, and her sister Blanche.
This they sold to the Community and it was converted into a new
guest house. Here it was possible for retreats and quiet holidays to
take place near to the Community without being under the same roof.
The Oblates had played a vital role in fostering the Community since
its beginnings in 1943, but in the 1970s, new Oblates were no longer
recruited, though existing Oblates continued in that status. Some had
joined the Community of St. Clare; one joined the Community of St.
Francis at Dalston. The rest continued, like other Oblates, to lead a
life of prayer in the world.

The Clares have followed a tradition almost universal in monastic
communities in offering hospitality to guests who are welcomed to join
in worship in the chapel but otherwise are set apart from the Community. It was a work which grew rapidly, from about 25 guests in

5. This has perhaps more significance for a community of Clares than for other
communities. St. Clare's devotion to the Blessed Sacrament is well known, and her
traditional symbol is the monstrance.

the first year at Freeland to over 100 by 1955 and over 500 by 1980. The Sisters call themselves Clares, as following St. Clare's way of life, rather than Poor Clares. The Franciscan ideal of poverty is an important part of their life. This ideal they see as promoting a reverence for all creation, and a flexibility that welcomes change in the direction of simplicity of life. Work and leisure are both parts of prayer, and in this vision, nothing is trivial and even hardship and suffering, to which the Community have been no strangers, are shot through with joy.

Like other Franciscan communities, the Clares aim to be as nearly self-supporting as possible. Crafts have been built up according to the skills of the Sisters – Christmas and Easter cards, printing, sculpture, painting, making vestments. From the Convent of St. Thomas, Oxford, the Sisters took over the baking of Communion wafers. Gardening, keeping hens and looking after the guests are other activities. Manual work of some sort is part of the pattern of daily life.

But prayer is the main purpose of any enclosed Community. The ideal of enclosure has never been readily understood in the Anglican Communion. Living within the confines of the convent and its grounds, the Clares seek God in little things and in the commonplace matters of everyday life. The silence, the enclosure, the solitude which are an important part of their life, are not intended as restrictions, but as necessary tools in the life of prayer. So far from being self-centred – probably the commonest misconception regarding the enclosed life – the Franciscan ideals of poverty and penance are intended to turn the heart and indeed the whole of life away from the self and to promote a reverence and care for the whole of creation. The need to earn a living, the problems simply of living in community, and concern for the whole work of the Society of St. Francis, keep the Sisters in close touch with what is commonly called 'reality'. Prayer for the unity of the Church is an important part of their intercession. Links have been established with convents of Poor Clares in the Roman Catholic Church, and there are of course particularly close ties with the Episcopalian Clares in the United States (see Chapter 22). An important recent development has been the establishment of a Community of Clares in Australia which is described in the concluding chapter.

At home, the Community has continued to develop and to draw a steady stream of recruits. As a young community, much of its history must lie in the future, but at least the immediate future seems assured. Its past already includes the fulfilment of the hopes for an Anglican Second Order on the traditional lines of the Clares. Part of its vocation in future may be to make the enclosed life better understood and appreciated in the Anglican Church.

27

The Third Order and the Companions

The present Third Order of the Society of St. Francis has brought together men and women who became tertiaries under the auspices of the Society of the Divine Compassion, the Brotherhood of the Holy Cross, and the American Order of St. Francis. But its real origins stem from India and the Christa Prema Seva Sangha. It has already been related how a Third Order began in India, and likewise how Fr. Algy left India to gather the Brotherhood of the Love of Christ around him at St. Ives (Chapters 16 and 17). The present Third Order largely came into being through Algy's contact with an English laywoman outstanding in her Franciscan zeal – Dorothy Swayne.

Dorothy was born in 1887. Her father, William Shuckburgh Swayne, rose to be Bishop of Lincoln (1920–33). Dorothy went to Oxford, but left to nurse her sick mother.[1] Both mother and daughter suffered from a disease of the circulation,[2] and Dorothy described herself later in life as suffering from 'ill-health of a crippling nature'[3] which made it difficult for her to stand or even to be seated. It was impossible for her to have considered entering the religious life, but from early years her energy for church work seemed limitless. It began when she started a branch of the King's Messengers in the parish of St. Peter, Cranley Gardens, when her father was Vicar.[4] In the 1920s, she began work in the Diocese of Southwark under Bishop Garbett, social work in Bermondsey, and then parish work on the St. Helier Estate at Morden. It was thus that she came into contact with Frank Dyson.

Frank Dyson was a parson's son, educated at Clifton College and Trinity College, Oxford. After training at Westcott House, Cambridge, he was ordained to a curacy at St. Mary's, Lewisham, in 1923. He felt a call to some kind of religious life, and with another priest, Norman Faull, began a community on Dartmoor where they built a chapel and

1. Fr. Denis, *Father Algy*, Biographical Index.
2. *Third Order Chronicle*, October 1971.
3. Dorothy Swayne, *Simplicity of Life*.
4. *Third Order Chronicle*, October 1971. William Swayne was Vicar of St. Peter's, Cranley Gardens 1901–18. He was Dean of Manchester 1918–20 before becoming Bishop of Lincoln.

two huts. Fr. Faull, however, felt called rather to the mission field.[5] Dyson then returned to London, and when Dorothy Swayne met him, he had become Diocesan Missioner for Southwark. He became a prominent member of the Fellowship of the Way (Chapter 24). He chose to live in great poverty in the Elephant and Castle district (SE1) subsisting for a time on about 18/- (90p) a week and sleeping in common lodging houses with the 'down-and-outs'.

In 1928, when he became Master of the College of St. Saviour, Carshalton, he, Dorothy Swayne and a small group of other priests and lay-people pledged themselves to live on £5 a week, giving away anything they had above that to the service of God and their neighbour.[6] Dorothy Swayne was to reproach herself with 'infirmity of moral stamina and purpose',[7] but those who knew her say that she 'clearly exercised a most effective ministry in Bermondsey through her actual poverty'.[8]

In 1930, Frank Dyson's mind suffered a tragic breakdown, and he spent the last thirty years of his life in mental care.[9] Dorothy Swayne thus found herself without her spiritual mentor. She turned for advice to her friend Deaconess Carol Graham. Deaconess Graham was a tertiary of Christa Seva Sangha in India, and she lent Dorothy her Manual. She also arranged for her to meet Jack Winslow, who was then on his way to England. He met Dorothy Swayne at her flat in Bermondsey. They arranged a further meeting for 4 October (St. Francis' Day) at Church House, Westminster. Others interested were invited, and these included Fr. Algy who had recently returned to England. Jack Winslow suggested him as a Franciscan religious obviously suited to guide the formation of a Third Order in England.

Fr. Algy and Dorothy Swayne met again, the most convenient venue for which, despite its elegance, was a London club.[10] At this meeting, they prepared a Manual for the Third Order which was soon ready and published. From the Rule of the Christa Seva Sangha they adopted the Principles – The Object, the Aims (To make our Lord known and loved everywhere; to spread the Spirit of Brotherhood; to live simply), the Three Ways of Service (Prayer; Study; Work) and the Three Notes of the Order (Humility; Love; Joy).[11] Fr. Algy soon became established at St. Ives with the Brotherhood of the Love of Christ, and it became

5. Arthur Norman Faull was at Westcott House, Cambridge 1921–22. He was Curate of Frindsbury near Rochester 1922–27 when he became Chaplain to the South African Church Railway Mission in Northern Rhodesia.
6. Fr. Denis, op. cit., pp. 105–6.
7. Dorothy Swayne, *Simplicity of Life*.
8. *Third Order Chronicle*, October 1971.
9. Fr. Denis, op. cit., Biographical Index.
10. ibid., p. 106.
11. Third Order Manual.

possible to admit aspiring tertiaries to a novitiate.[12] Among the earliest were the Rev. Henry Lovell and his wife Lilian. Fr. Lovell joined Algy as his curate at St. Ives, looking after two small villages in the parish and living in great simplicity in a cottage at Woodhurst. He later became Rector of Lolworth near Cambridge. He was at one time Secretary of the Guild of Prayer for the Return of Our Lord, but one of his outstanding achievements was to draw up the Tertiary Office for the Manual.[13] This remained in use until the current revision of the Manual (1979) and still forms the basis of the Office. Tertiaries normally served six months as a postulant and two years as a novice before being professed.

Dorothy Swayne remained an outstanding personality in the Third Order until her death in 1971. She became Assistant Guardian of the Third Order and Senior Novice Mistress, and many have paid tribute to her wisdom as a spiritual guide, particularly of women aspirants to the Third Order.[14] In guiding men to become tertiaries, Fr. Algy himself originally played the leading role. Fr. Potter's house at Peckham in South London was a convenient meeting-place for tertiaries, and those particularly from the London area held a number of meetings there. The first meetings outside London were organised by Dorothy Swayne and took place at St. Thomas's Convent, Oxford.[15]

With the formation of the Society of St. Francis in 1937, what had hitherto been the Third Order of the Brotherhood of the Love of Christ became that of the whole Society of St. Francis. It also opened the possibility of its becoming the Third Order for all the Franciscan societies in England. Neither the Brotherhood of the Holy Cross nor the Society of the Divine Compassion joined the Society of St. Francis, but when these societies were wound up, some oblates of the former and tertiaries of the latter were admitted into the Third Order of the Society of St. Francis. The Franciscan Sisters of Jesus and Mary at Posbury also did not join the Society of St. Francis, nor have their tertiaries become part of the Third Order. On Fr. Algy's advice, the Posbury tertiaries have the distinctive name, externs. In recent times, they have shared meetings with tertiaries of the Society of St. Francis, showing how the two Societies have drawn closer together.

The Third Order was in its early days closely dependent on the First. The Guardian and Chaplain-General of the Third Order were priest-friars appointed by the First Order Chapter, and other friars served as pastoral officers to the Third Order. The Novice Master and

12. Fr. Denis, op. cit., p. 106.
13. *Third Order Chronicle*, April 1971.
14. ibid., October 1971.
15. ibid.

Mistress were also appointed by the First Order.[16] This accorded with Dorothy Swayne's own wishes. The view held among tertiaries at the time was that the Third Order received its inspiration from the First, and it was right and logical that the Third Order should be under obedience to a Guardian of the First Order. Fr. Algy was elected as Priest-Guardian in 1941. Nevertheless, the Third Order had a large measure of control over its own affairs from the start.[17] The Constitution of the Third Order was worked out by Fr. Algy, Fr. Charles (the Chaplain-General) and Dorothy Swayne during the Second World War.[18] On the Council of the Third Order, there was equal representation between the First Order and the Third, with the Father Minister as Chairman.[19]

Numbers in the Third Order grew slowly but steadily during the war. Discipline was built up by tertiaries sending in a quarterly report to the Chaplain. A successful conference of tertiary priests was held in 1946.[20] This was followed by a week for tertiaries, priests and lay, at Darley Dale in 1948, and a Third Order Congress at Bristol in 1949.[21] Numbers continued to grow after the war, and in 1951 had reached 361, including postulants, though women were more numerous than men. It was found necessary to sub-divide the tertiaries into priests, laymen and women. Fr. Crank[22] took charge of the priest tertiaries, Richard Paynter[23] of the laymen and Dorothy Swayne of the women, though ill-health compelled her to give up in 1949.[24] Ordinands came forward for the Third Order, but the numbers of laymen continued to be few. In the early 1950s, attendance at Third Order retreats was said to be disappointing; the cost of fares and accommodation was partly to blame.[25]

With the increase in numbers, it became desirable to hold area meetings in order to foster a sense of fellowship. Barnabastide (11 June) was a favourite time for these and in most areas meetings took place three or four times a year, though not all tertiaries wished to take part.[26] A corporate sense was also fostered by observing the Friday

16. *Third Order Chronicle*, October 1968.
17. Society of St. Francis Chapter Minute 17/18.9.41.
18. ibid., 15.6.43.
19. ibid., 14.10.42.
20. ibid., 23.10.46.
21. ibid., 7/8.10.48.
22. James William Crank, Vicar of St. Alban's, Stoke Heath, Coventry, 1940–49, then of St. John the Baptist, Leamington Spa.
23. Later Lower Master at King's School, Canterbury.
24. S.S.F. Chapter Minute 8/10.6.49.
25. ibid., 30.5.40, 4.10.50, 8/10.2.51.
26. ibid., 23.10.46.

before Palm Sunday as a 'Day of Humiliation and Penitence'.[27] In 1952, tertiaries from a wide area met at rallies held on 21 June at Birmingham and Peckham.[28] In 1956, there was a Third Order pilgrimage to St. David's.[29] Every year there was a day Chapter for all professed tertiaries.

A number of tertiaries, both priests and laity, found their way to special vocations in the Church,[30] and this was welcomed, though it was not the prime purpose of the Third Order. Other tertiaries continued to feel the sense of isolation, and it was recognised that the friars had an important role to play in encouraging them.[31] An important part was played by Fr. Lothian, the friar-vicar of St. Bene't's, Cambridge, who was Chaplain-General and then Guardian of the Third Order. In time, tertiary priests came to play a fuller part, as for instance in conducting retreats.[32]

An important development in the 1950s and 1960s was the growth of the Third Order outside Britain. Where there was no friary, as in South Africa and New Zealand, the tertiaries were the real pioneers, and it was important for friars from England to foster fellowship among them. In 1954, Fr. Joseph met South African tertiaries at Cape Town on his way to Fiwila (Northern Rhodesia – Zambia).[33] Among the South African tertiaries was Mollie Lockyer, formerly Fr. Potter's helper at Peckham (Chapter 15). In January 1964, the first Franciscan retreat in Africa was conducted at Lusaka by Fr. Francis.[34] Fr. Peter, who was visiting Church schools in Southern Rhodesia (Zimbabwe) was also able to encourage the tertiaries in Central Africa.[35] In 1966, the Father Minister visited the tertiaries in New Zealand while touring the Pacific and Australasia.[36] The opening of houses in Brisbane, Auckland and New Guinea has brought tertiaries in the Pacific area into regular contact with the First Order. The union with the American Franciscans constituted the tertiaries there as a separate Third Order province, and there are separate provinces now for tertiaries in the Pacific and in Africa.

Mention has already been made in Chapter 22 of the first official inter-provincial Chapter which was held at Bishop's Ranch, California, in 1976. Three representatives attended from each of the four provinces

27. ibid., 9/11.10.51.
28. ibid., 4.1.52.
29. ibid., 22.5.56.
30. ibid., 1.10.56.
31. ibid., 26.5.58.
32. ibid., 23.1.62.
33. ibid., 25/27.1.54.
34. Hilfield Archives C. 525.
35. ibid.
36. S.S.F. Chapter Minute 4.10.66.

(European, American, Pacific and African). The Way of St. Francis, together with the Constitution, the Rule of Life and the Form of Profession were accepted as the Manual for all provinces. Such matters as the Third Order Office and other devotional material might vary according to local need. It was agreed that the original Principles developed from the rule of Christa Prema Seva Sangha should be included in the Source Documents (commonly known as the Book of Roots). The Profession Cross produced in the Pacific province was accepted for use generally. The African representatives made an important contribution at this Chapter with their understanding of the Third Order life. New ideas were generated about vocation and training.

Horizons have also been widened through contact with Roman Catholic tertiaries. In 1965, the latter for the first time invited Anglican tertiaries to attend their meeting.[37] In the 1970s, links were developed with the International Council of the Roman Catholic Third Order of the Friars Minor, now known as the Secular Franciscan Order. Representatives of the Third Order of the Society of St. Francis have been honoured guests at their gatherings, and have made their contribution to discussions about the Rule.

In the 1960s, a Third Order Regular was established. A novitiate was opened at Hilfield in 1962. It was laid down that there were not to be more than two novices in training at any one time, and the total of tertiaries regular was not to exceed a fifth of the professed members of the Third Order.[38] However, recruits were few, and in 1968 it was decided not to admit any new novices, though those already professed were to continue. The experiment had met the need, if a limited one, for those unable to share the full religious life, but seeking to participate in community life. Other experiments in living in community are discussed below.

The revision of the Constitution in the 1960s brought important changes to the Third Order, and representatives of the tertiaries were invited to attend part of the First Order General Chapter in May 1966 to discuss the relationship of the First and Third Orders.[39] The opening of offices in the First Order to all friars had its counterpart in the Third, and in 1973 a tertiary became Guardian of the Third Order for the first time. This was the Rev. John Betton. The Chaplain has continued to be a friar.

The Chapter of the Third Order became the executive body, with members elected by the professed tertiaries. General Chapters for all professed tertiaries were held for a week-end at Whitelands (SW

37. ibid., 8.6.65.
38. ibid., 12.6.42.
39. ibid., 20.5.64.

London) in 1972 and York in 1975. Since then, General Chapters have been held on a regional basis at irregular intervals. Area meetings remain an important feature, and in addition encouragement has been given to small groups to meet in the homes of tertiaries wherever possible. Particular sections from time to time hold conferences, family camps, study weeks and holiday groups. The annual retreat has always been a top priority for tertiaries, and over thirty Third Order retreats are now organised.

The distinctive witness of tertiaries as Franciscans living in the world was recognised by St. Francis himself and by Anglican pioneers like Josa and Adderley. The Society of St. Francis has always recognised this importance: 'Although the Third Order is not a community in the strict sense of a group of persons with a common aim living under one roof, there is yet a sense in which the Third Order *is* a community' – and one way in which that is expressed is that its policy is decided by its own Chapter.[40] The Third Order is recognised by the Religious Advisory Council of the Church of England as a religious order because its members make profession with a life-long intention, though this now has to be renewed annually. All tertiaries must have a personal spiritual director or guide. Among other things he advises the tertiary about his own Rule of Life which is drawn up in the light of the Third Order Rule. The Third Order has been described as a religious order in the world, and the members, married and single, who live in their own homes, are engaged in a wide range of work and interests. Their participation in the life of the local church is of great importance as well as their sharing of life with other tertiaries. Part of the witness of the Third Order has been seen as the reflection of Our Lord's life at Nazareth – the 'hidden years' before the beginning of His public ministry.[41] For long, reticence was the mark of the tertiary, and recruitment came largely through personal contact and recommendation. In recent years, more open witness has been encouraged.

One result has been a more rapid increase in membership. Developments in the training of novices have followed from this increase. In the European province, responsibility has been shared widely among professed members, and much has been done to help these Assistant Novice Counsellors in their task. A set of 'Letters to Novices' has been drawn up covering the basic points of training. The role of the personal spiritual director remains of great importance. The Third Order has been organised on a regional basis. There are (1980–81) twelve regions in the British Isles – Eastern, North East, North West, Severn, South-

40. *Third Order Chronicle*, October 1968.
41. ibid., April 1967.

ern, South East, South West, Thames, West Midlands, Yorkshire and East Midlands, Scotland and Ireland. Most of these are sub-divided into areas. There are also a few tertiaries in Sweden, India and South-East Asia who will be referred to at greater length in the concluding chapter. In countries where there is no house of the First Order, the witness of tertiaries to the Way of St. Francis has especial importance and may call for particular strength and courage.

The Company of St. Francis

The Company of St. Francis was not, in the strict sense, a religious community, but a group of Franciscan women most of whom were tertiaries sharing life and work together under a rule of obedience.[42] They lived in 'comparative poverty,'[43] under annual vows. A friar acted as chaplain, and the Company was thought of by the First Order as being tertiaries regular. It was at least an approximation in Anglican experience to what that term would mean in the Roman Catholic Church. A daily Eucharist and the Divine Office formed the basis for worship, and the Rule provided for prayer, study and intercession.

The Company has been called Fr. Algy's 'brain-child'. The enterprise began in 1950 when five tertiaries undertook to run the Durham Diocesan Retreat House at Low Fell, Gateshead. The group was led by Mrs. Weller-Pooley who took the name Sister Ursula. Fr. Joseph acted as their first chaplain.[44] They wore a habit and came to be called the Company of Brown Ladies. Their pattern was not to renounce individual possessions but to share them. Those who had means to contribute to their 'keep' did so; two Sisters who owned cars shared them for use by the others; they all lived a simple life. There was a short postulancy at the end of which the Sisters were 'cloaked'[45] in Chapel with the brown dress and brown cloak and hood. The Sisters ran the retreat house, assisted the Friars on missions and undertook parish work – visiting, teaching in Sunday schools and speaking to groups like the Mothers' Union.

Worship was an important part of their lives. The old stables were converted into a chapel and vestry. The coke-shed and wash-house were made into an oratory where the Blessed Sacrament was reserved and watch was kept on several major festivals during the year. The Sisters had a regular choir practice in order to sing the Eucharist on Sundays and Feast Days with full ceremonial. They made vestments,

42. CC p. 527.
43. ibid.
44. S.S.F. Chapter Minutes, 11.10.49 7/10.2.50.
45. A less formal term than 'clothed'.

and the Stations of the Cross were erected in the garden. When no priest was available to celebrate the Eucharist in the house, the Sisters would cycle to a nearby parish church or go by train to Newcastle Cathedral. As well as the Sisters who lived in company, two other tertiaries lived at the Lodge and helped in Chapel.

The Company made a special work of helping people with mental problems such as depression. Several of those they helped were able to make a new start in life – one became a nurse, another a teacher, several entered the religious life, others went into missionary work. But the main work of running the retreat house went on, and an annual holiday week at the house to which children were welcomed as well as their parents. An outhouse was converted into a resting-place for wayfarers. Peter Anson has described the spirit of the Company as one of 'definitely Franciscan joyousness'.[46]

As the Sisters only took annual vows, it was possible for them to leave the Company after a period of years, and some did so. The Company itself came to an end after about eight years, and the members dispersed.[47] It has been the most important, but not the only attempt by Anglican tertiaries to share a common life. A mixed group of tertiaries shared a common life in a Somerset vicarage for a few years, and three tertiaries, two sisters and a friend, together ran a retreat house in Hampshire. As in the days of St. Francis, a spontaneous desire seems to have moved some of his disciples to share their lives, though this has not as yet produced permanent communities of tertiaries regular.

The Guild of St. Francis and 'Juniper'

The members of the Guild are neither tertiaries, companions nor a religious community, but an association inspired by Franciscan ideals. The Guild began among younger members of the congregation at St. Catherine's, Leytonstone (E11) who began their association in April 1938. Membership was open to communicant Anglicans, associate membership to those seeking confirmation. Their purpose has been described as quite simply 'the extension of the Kingdom of God in the world'. Their Rule of Life was to use daily the prayer of St. Ignatius of Loyola ('Teach us, good Lord, to serve Thee as Thou deservest'), to read the Bible daily, to worship in Church every Sunday, to receive Holy Communion at least once a month, to be regular in almsgiving and Christian service, and as a group 'so to present Christ Jesus in

46. CC p. 527.
47. S.S.F. Chapter Minute 27.1.59.

the power of the Holy Spirit that men may come to put their trust in God through Him, accept Him as their Saviour, and serve Him as their King in the fellowship of His Church.'

Most of the founding members of the Guild were young in years, but they included some older members whose experience helped to stabilise the whole group. They elected their own leader. They rented a railway arch and turned it into a meeting-room, and here the Guild met each week for prayer; once a month they invited a guest speaker. In 1940, fellowship was extended to members of other churches. The Guild published a magazine, *The Franciscan*, (not to be confused with the S.S.F. publication of that name), which helped to keep contact with members away from Leytonstone. During the war, they helped to settle a Quaker refugee family. Two members in due course went to serve in the mission field.

In 1951, their pattern changed. Members ceased to meet as a Guild. A house was rented in Wanstead which was later purchased for them by trustees. This was named Juniper, and it was run to offer hospitality to British and overseas students who were invited to regard the house as their home and its members as their family. Compline, as a corporate act of Christian prayer each evening, was an important part of the life of the house, though attendance was voluntary and not all residents were Christians.

The household came to number about seventeen, including the resident housekeepers. Student accommodation has usually been fully occupied, and through careful management, the house has been virtually self-supporting. Friends of Juniper, the successors of the original Guild, support the house by prayer and practical help. Arthur Cuff, the first Warden of Juniper, held the position long enough to establish the venture firmly (1951–78). Like others concerned with the Guild, he felt the challenge of St. Francis' acceptance of poverty and its witness to the modern world.

Neither the Guild nor Juniper has had any formal connection with the Society of St. Francis, but both have witnessed in their different ways to the Franciscan ideal. But the First Order has taken a close interest in it from the first, and frequent visits have been made by the Friars.

The Companions

The First, Second and Third Orders together constitute the Society of St. Francis. Like many Religious Orders, the Society has the support of priests and layfolk who are not members (as tertiaries are) but who share its aims and ideals. For the Society of St. Francis, this role is supplied by the Companions.

The Companions were first formed in the early days of the Brotherhood of St. Francis of Assisi.[48] Their prime duty has always been to support the Society by prayer. The Society issues a regular Intercession Paper, and using this Paper the Companions pledge themselves to pray, at least once a week, and if possible before the altar, for the sanctification of the Society. They also pledge themselves to aim at simplicity of dress, to avoid all waste and extravagance, to help those in distress, and to strive to bring others to the knowledge and love of Christ.[49] The way in which the last obligation is fulfilled has always depended upon the capacity of the Companion. Those able to devote the time have assisted members of the Society on evangelistic missions. In former days, particularly between the wars when the Society was responsible for a number of Homes and Hostels (see Chapter 13), some Companions worked full time in them, and had the status of Companion-Workers. Priest-Companions are asked to preach once a year on the aims of the Society. The Companions have always given alms to support the work of the Society. There is a form of service for admission as a Companion comparable to the forms used by other religious guilds and associations.

The Companions have for long been sufficiently numerous to be organised on a local basis, in England by county or area. Scotland and Ireland are separate areas, as are the overseas provinces. Each area has a Chaplain (usually a Priest-Companion) and a Secretary. These convene the meetings and other activities according to local need, and these may include Retreats and Quiet Days for Companions. One of the Friars is Warden of the Companions and for many years this office was held by Brother Kenneth.

The Companions have a special role to play and a special witness distinct from that of the three Orders of the Society. In order to fulfil their part, their own spiritual life is built up. They are recommended to have a personal Rule of Life and to review it annually; to pray daily and to receive Holy Communion weekly; to heed the Prayer Book counsel on the Sacrament of Penance; to undertake a serious and responsible approach to almsgiving and use of possessions; to undertake the service of others and to grow in knowledge of God.[50] If it is objected that these 'Guiding Principles' are only the obligations of all churchmen writ large, it may be replied that some of the best Fran-

48. They originate from about 1924–25.
49. Booklet: The Companions of the Society of St. Francis – The Rule (in a later version, Obligations).
50. ibid. (revised form).

ciscans have seen their Way as no more than the fulfilment of their baptismal promises.

As the Society of St. Francis has become a world-wide organisation, so have the Companions. The importance of their witness has been sufficiently demonstrated in New Zealand (see Chapter 28) where the Companions were the first on the ground, then the Tertiaries, then the First Order. Like the Tertiaries, the Companions can be pioneers as well as supporters. If the vocation of the Third Order finds inspiration in the 'hidden years' at Nazareth, the vocation of the Companions may perhaps be compared to that of the 'companions' of Our Lord who followed Him from Galilee and 'ministered to Him of their substance'.[51]

51. St. Mark 15 v. 41; St. Luke 8, vv. 1–3.

28

Wider Horizons

So rapid has been the expansion of the Society of St. Francis during the past ten or twenty years that any statement of events can only be interim. When the Society was divided into provinces, the term 'English Province' was still in use. The use of such terms as 'English Province', or later 'European Province', when these areas included places far distant from the geographical areas in question is a mark of this rapid expansion. Though their continued use might indicate origin rather than location, it may be compared to the way in which, in the Anglican Communion, missionary dioceses remain under the Archbishopric of Canterbury until the time comes for them to assume full provincial status.

Because of its ecumenical significance, one important development has been the growth of the Third Order in Sweden. As has been shown in Chapter 25, links were established in the early 1960s with the Lutheran Church of Sweden. The hope at that time was to establish a house of the First Order in Sweden. This did not come to fruition, but from the links which had been established, a small group of Swedish Lutherans were nurtured in the Third Order. The first group of tertiaries were professed in 1974. In 1980 there were seven professed members and two novices, who included three priests of the Church of Sweden and a member of the Swedish aristocracy. These constitute a region within the European province and are known as the Franciscan Third Order in the Church of Sweden. The Manual and the other basic documents have been translated into Swedish.

As has been seen (Chapter 16), Christa Seva Sangha played an important part in the development of the Franciscan movement. There is no house of the First Order in India now, but there are a few members of the Third Order. The Third Order also includes members in Singapore, Hong Kong, Sarawak and Malaysia. In 1980 there were nine professed tertiaries and eight novices in the Far East. These include four priests, and as in Sweden, it may be hoped that these will extend knowledge and acceptance of the Franciscan Way. The tertiaries in the Far East include members of both European and Asiatic descent.

But by far the most dramatic expansion has been in Africa. There are now tertiaries in South Africa, Lesotho, Tanzania, Zambia and Zimbabwe/Rhodesia. In 1980, these numbered forty-three professed members and twenty-seven novices, of both African and European descent, including ten priests. The Third Order in Africa has grown sufficiently in numbers and responsibility for it to become a separate province. The only house of the First Order in Africa is at Mtoni Shamba near Dar es Salaam, and this remains under the English Province. The recruitment of African members of the First Order has proceeded to the point where an African Province of the First Order also can be confidently looked for, and the indigenous African Franciscanism, hoped for ever since the Society of the Divine Compassion were at Thlotse Heights, at last achieved.

In the expansion of the Third Order, the greater measure of autonomy and responsibility enjoyed since the 1960s has undoubtedly played a part. This is particularly true of England and Africa. In the Far East, much has been owed to the dynamic role of the Minister General. That office is likely to remain of great importance for the Third Order until developments take place comparable to those in Africa. The establishment of the Pacific base in New Guinea was of great importance in building up the Third Order in Australia and New Zealand. The founding of First Order houses at Brisbane and Auckland has given an indigenous centre for the Franciscan life in those countries, and Australia now has a house of Clares as well.

The establishment and growth of the Pacific Province has been equally dramatic. In July 1958, the Diocese of New Guinea made a request for Friars to be sent out. Although the Society of St. Francis had had to turn down a number of such requests in the 1940s and 1950s, their numbers had increased to the point where this new work could be seriously considered. It was decided to send out Brother Geoffrey, with others to follow.[1] Geoffrey arrived at Port Moresby on 3 March 1959. His first base was at Koke, where there was a missionary school and chapel near to the poor and needy in the middle of the town. A new wing was built on to accommodate the next batch of Friars, Stephen, Mark and Andrew, who arrived in June. In the first year, two Papuans wished to test their vocation to the First Order. A more secluded and suitable site for a novitiate was found at Jegarata (now called Haruro). The house was dedicated by the Bishop (P. N. W. Strong) on the Stigmata Festival, 17 September, 1960. The first postulants arrived in January 1961, and the first Papuans, Russell and Philip, were noviced on 8 November 1961. The same year, the house at Jegarata was constituted a Friary with Brother Geoffrey as Guard-

1. S.S.F. Chapter Minutes 2.7.58, 14.8.58.

ian.[2] In 1964, St. Francis' College for training Evangelists was opened with Brother Brian in charge. This was built despite shortage of available money, as was a new church in Koke. The Companions of St. Francis in Australia and New Zealand raised £12,000 towards the cost of the church.[3]

In 1962, a postulant called Michael Davis arrived at Jegarata to test his vocation, the first of a 'steady stream' of recruits from the Solomon Islands. In 1967, the Bishop of Melanesia invited the Society of St. Francis to open a house there. The result was a joint venture at Honiara with the Sisters of the Church. A house was purpose-built with separate wings for the two communities but with a refectory and chapel where they could eat and worship together. The Brothers arrived in August 1970 and the Sisters in December, and both were still having to camp out when the Bishop dedicated the house on 17 January 1971. It was completed in March. The intention was that candidates from the Solomon Islands should serve a postulancy at Honiara before going on to the novitiate at Jegarata.[4] After a while, it was found convenient that the two communities should be quite separate. The building was divided, and the Sisters built themselves a new kitchen. Since separating, the two communities have found it easier to work together, and each has continued to develop, independently, on its own lines.

The work in the Pacific had grown to the point that in 1965, Brother Geoffrey was appointed Deputy Minister. It was envisaged that this appointment would be for six years, but before then the Pacific had become a full Province with Geoffrey as Minister. From 1966, elections to profession were entrusted to the Brothers in New Guinea. The same year, the first Evangelists trained at St. Francis' College were commissioned by the Bishop. Prince Charles visited Jegarata and Koke on his tour of the Pacific in 1966.[5]

As early as 1961, Brother Geoffrey saw the need of a First Order house in Australia, 'a base where we could train people for the ultimate staffing of all our work in the Pacific'.[6] Brother Charles had visited New Zealand in 1956, and this led to the enrolment of the first Companions there. The advantage of a permanent base over the occasional visit was obvious. Bishop Strong, who had invited the Friars to New Guinea, was translated as Archbishop of Brisbane in 1963. He offered the Brothers St. Christopher's, Brookfield, eight miles from the centre of the city. Five brothers were sent out from England and took up

2. ibid., 23.5.61.
3. Br. Geoffrey, Memoir. Hilfield Archives.
4. ibid.
5. S.S.F. Chapter Minutes 8.6.65, 1.2.66, 31.5.66, 8.6.66.
6. Br. Geoffrey, Memoir.

residence at St. Christopher's in 1964. This, however, proved a temporary arrangement, and they soon moved to St. Clare's when a new diocesan house was completed for the old ladies who were still looked after there. The move was made shortly before a disastrous fire at St. Clare's in which, fortunately, no lives were lost.[7] After the fire, the Brothers moved back to St. Christopher's where they remain. At St. Christopher's and St. Clare's, the Society stepped into territory where the indigenous Australian Daughters of St. Clare had worked (see Chapter 19). Although founded from Hilfield, it was hoped from the first that the house at Brisbane would become a genuine Australian community.[8] This was helped by placing it early on under the jurisdiction of Brother Geoffrey in New Guinea rather than under the Mother House at Hilfield.[9]

In 1975, the Community of St. Clare took over what had at one time been a Rectory, at Stroud in the Diocese of Newcastle, New South Wales. The numbers at Freeland had grown sufficiently for them to send out four Sisters to begin the Community. In 1979, the Sisters began work on a new house built of mud bricks which they call their 'monastery' (thus reviving the ancient meaning of the term). This is set in about thirty acres of land outside Stroud. The Sisters have now vacated the old rectory and moved into the monastery. A hermitage was also built nearby where a priest-brother could live while acting as chaplain, and where he and another Brother could follow a life of prayer. The new building was a financial venture, but the Community has become settled and numbers have grown. It is the first time that an Anglican enclosed contemplative community has been established in the Pacific area, and it is significant that this venture should have been made by one of the youngest religious orders.[10]

Developments in New Zealand have followed closely behind those in Australia. Brother Geoffrey made a visit in 1962 to keep contact with the Companions and establish links with the Church in New Zealand. In 1962, the first novices in New Zealand were admitted to the Third Order. From 1963, it became the custom for one of the Franciscan Brothers to visit New Zealand every year. Not surprisingly, there was a desire for a First Order house – indeed, there had never been a religious house for men in New Zealand, though the Sisters of the Church settled at Dunedin in 1896, and the Sisters of the Order of the Good Shepherd, an indigenous community, had begun even

7. ibid.
8. S.S.F. Chapter Minutes 20.5.64, 8.6.65.
9. Br. Geoffrey, Memoir.
10. *Church Times* 11.7.80 (Article by Br. John Charles, S.S.F.)

earlier at Auckland in 1893, concluding their work in January 1958.[11] It was St. Francis' House, Auckland, where the Order of the Good Shepherd had worked, which the Society of St. Francis took over. To staff the new house, and to express the unity between the Franciscan provinces, a Brother was sent out from each of England, America and Australia. When they became established, the Brothers took part for a time in the Auckland City Mission.[12] In 1973, they moved to take charge of an Anglican–Methodist parish at Glen Innes, and in 1979 moved to a new house in Parnell, Auckland.

The rapid developments in the Pacific led the Provincial Chapter in September 1976 to divide the Province into two regions. The northern region takes in the Solomon Islands and Papua/New Guinea, the southern region Australia and New Zealand.[13] These have now (1981) become separate provinces. The tertiaries of the Pacific Province are divided into an Australian Province and a New Zealand Province.[14] The work of Brother Geoffrey in the Pacific largely mapped out the role of Minister General even before that office was created. It was entirely fitting that he should be its first holder, and his work continues at the time of writing.

Looking over Blackmore Vale, Brother Douglas is said to have had the vision of 'a great army of men in brown habits' going out two by two from Hilfield 'bringing the hope of a new life of common brotherhood and interior peace to a distracted generation pursuing pleasure in the midst of economic distress'.[15] The hunger for such a message is no less in the 1980s than in the 1920s. The vision now must be not for all roads to lead from the Mother House, but for there to be houses in every land from which not only Brothers but Sisters and tertiaries as well go out with the message of hope. Nothing else would be true to St. Francis' dream of making the Lord known and loved everywhere.

11. CC pp. 441, 589. The remaining Sisters of the Order of the Good Shepherd were absorbed into the Community of the Holy Name at Cheltenham, Victoria, Australia.
12. Br. Geoffrey, Memoir.
13. SPAN December 1976.
14. S.S.F. Third Order Address List 1980–81.
15. Fr. Francis, op. cit., p. 5.

Appendix I

Mother Gertrude's letter to Fr. Henry Chappell

This letter quoted twice in chapter 8, is preserved in the S.D.C. Minute Book in the Bodleian Library at Oxford. Because it concerns three key figures – Mother Gertrude herself, Fr. Adderley and Fr. Chappell – and a critical stage for both the Society of the Divine Compassion and the Society of the Incarnation of the Eternal Son, it is reproduced here in full, retaining the original punctuation.

10 S. Bruton Mews.

Friday 17 Sept. 1897.

Dear Fr. Chappell,

I feel I ought at this crisis to write and tell you that I must withdraw my sisters from working at St. Philip's.

Please do not take this as a personal matter, it is not so, I will explain myself.

I know that you and Fr. Andrew are acting sincerely, so though withdrawing, I can still pray God to bless you in your life and work. At the same time I cannot see the religious life as you see it.

First I believe most firmly that the Superior's office is a most sacred one, and that God directs him, though mistakes may be made into paths He knows best for the community.

Therefore it seems to me to disobey the Superior in the spirit, even though not in the letter, is to disobey the voice of God.

If this is not true I fail to see how any community is called of God to the R.[eligious] life.

I believe with other orders that members of a Community should go in faith where the Superior may direct, and mistrust their own judgment rather than his.

Such trust and faith in the voice of God through the Superior is the groundwork of the Religious life.

Forgive me for saying that such faith and trust has not been yours & Fr. Andrew's during the last 3 years.

I have found this out, not from what Fr. Adderley has said, for he has been most careful not to judge or speak about private matters of the Community, but simply from what I have been obliged to realise as I worked among you at St. Philip's.

I started my life among you all trusting in you *all* equally and believing fully in Fr. Adderley's powers to guide us as a society and in his gt. holiness of life.

All that I have known since of him has only strengthened this belief.

But a Superior of a new order especially, is indeed handicapped, when his novices' want of faith and trust, prevent his carrying out a conceived plan for his order, which he believes God has set before him.

Secondly I feel we have all been in too great a hurry, for this I blame myself. One of the reasons I left Plaistow was that I and the Sisters God has lent to me, may more slowly and yet I hope surely lay the foundation of a life which has to do with Eternity.

I hope you will not think I am dictating, I do not want to, but I feel I must be honest in stating my reason for withdrawing. I am sure we can trust ourselves to God and that He will give to Father Adderley sometime in the future those He knows will support and help him. For God's successes are often what the world calls failures.

Please believe that I write in no unkind spirit, for you and Fr. Andrew will always have a warm place in my heart. And also believe that my Sisters unanimously agree with what I have written.

We will work if it please God and you at Plaistow until Christmas, unless you find others sooner to fill our place. I am asked to go to a guild meeting on Monday please write and tell me if you do *not* wish me to be there, under the circumstances.

Yours very sincerely,
Gertrude +

Appendix II

Brother Giles' last Letter to the Brethren at Hilfield

The letter is reproduced here as it conveys something of his character and his sadness at parting. It is dated 'Saturday Oct. 7th 1922'. It has no address.

Dear Brothers,

I have not been told what has been planned for the future of Flowers Farm so I cannot myself throw any light on the matter. Until matters have been settled your obedience passes to the Warden pro. tem.[1] Major Lloyd will direct secular matters & Fr. Hall will still act as Confessor until the Warden, should he do so, makes a change. You will of course have the opportunity of telling the Warden and whatever Priest Religious is appointed to act with him, each one of you your views and wishes as regards your future. You will all of you make this a very special subject of prayer, otherwise God's will may be missed. I have no doubt as to the need of the life we have been aiming at, but experience has shown it must be conducted on different lines – it must be free from secularities & given to much more prayer. I see no reason why the work at Flowers Farm should cease. May God help you to forgive me & please pray that I may grow daily in the spirit of penitence & prayer & devote my remaining days, D.V., to these works. May God guide, bless & strengthen you in the Spirit of Jesus & his little brother Francis.

Yours unworthily in X$^{t.}$ Jesus,
Giles.

---

1. Rev. G. Popham, Rector of Tatsfield, Surrey, from 1914. Charles Frank Hall was Rector of Stock Gaylard (Dorset) 1923–25 when he became Priest-in-Charge of Cerne Abbas (about eight miles by road from Hilfield).

Appendix III

The American Third Order Today

I am indebted to the Rev. John Scott, Guardian of the Third Order, American Province, for supplying this further information:

From the time of the consolidation of the American Franciscans (Order of St. Francis) with the Society of St. Francis in 1967, virtually ninety per cent of the present 400 Third Order members (professed, novices and postulants) of the American Province of the Third Order have entered its ranks. The extraordinary growth pattern has accompanied the assumption of responsibility for training, guidance and governance of the Third Order by its own members. The sense of belonging to the whole S.S.F. has been strengthened, not diminished by less dependence upon the First Order direction of Third Order affairs.

In 1967 there were approximately 100 tertiaries, all of whom had entered the Third Order under the guidance and charismatic leadership of Father Joseph, and had accepted the post-Trent *Credenda*. The transition to the Principles derived from the Christa Seva Sangha was not easy for many and some members withdrew, the *Credenda* and the wearing of habits seeming to be so very basic to their beliefs and practices in the Order of St. Francis. English tertiaries had not had the same experience except for the two dozen or so English tertiaries who followed Father Joseph. The English and American tertiaries of the Order of St. Francis had no contact, and the English group does seem to have been strongly called to community life in the manner of the numerous Roman Catholic Third Order Franciscan communities.

However, of the minority of present members of the American Province who antedate 1967, significant leadership was provided by Peter Funk in the development of a series of thirty letters on Franciscan spirituality which became the basis of postulant and novice training administered by the novice directors and counsellors within the Third Order in the last dozen years. The first Guardian of the American Province was the Rector of St. Mary's Church, Hamilton Village on the University of Pennsylvania campus: John M. Scott (1973–80). In addition to several others who were among the first elected members of the Chapter, outstanding Franciscan witness in their lives and

206

ministries (from the pre-1967 group) has been provided by priests such as H. Baxter Liebler, Hendrik B. Koning and James G. Jones, and lay members such as Marie Webner, Mona Hull, and Anna and Alvah Hoffman.

Father Liebler, now 92 years old, is also the American Province's longest professed tertiary (1926), founder of a mission among the Navajo Indians of Utah and Arizona, and still active there. Henk Koning, an electrical engineer by profession, has pioneered creative educational alternatives jointly sponsored by the Philadelphia School District, major businesses, and the teachers' union. Jim Jones is the dynamic and charismatic founder of Concept House in Miami, a residence and treatment centre for former prisoners and addicts of all sorts. Marie Webner, an editor, has pioneered creative fellowship programmes and inspired many to Franciscan vocations; Mona Hull, a scholar, has edited the papers of Sabatier which are in the custody of the Boston Public Library; the Hoffmans (before Alvah's early death) were planning a Franciscan-oriented Retirement and Nursing Community.

The witness in many varied ways can be multiplied many times by the Third Order members who have entered since 1967 and presently are the members of the Chapter, Novice Directors (Kenneth Cox and Glen-Ann Jicha, both laypersons), and the Guardian (Dee Dobson) and Chaplain (the Rev. Robert Goode). There are sixteen active fellowships meeting regularly in the United States, Canada, Trinidad, and Colombia. In addition the fast growing membership in 1981 has been among Amerindians in the remote country of Guiana, and the most promising Third Order community development is in the Yukon! In the latter wilderness, novices Llewellyn and Carol Johnson have built a retreat centre on the Pelly River. In 1981, three convocations or conferences of Third Order members and their friends were held, the largest involving some sixty people near New York in September. Intense sharing of people's spiritual journeys and witness to the Franciscan life characterized all these events. Finally, the 800th anniversary year has spawned a drama written by Kenneth Arnold (an O'Neill fellow and editor of Temple University Press) entitled 'Buckskin and Burlap: the Life of Christ as performed by Francis of Assisi for Buffalo Bill Cody's "Wild West Show"!' which has now had five performances in Philadephia and the text is available and adaptable to all who wish to have it. The other 800th anniversary event is the formation of numerous Franciscan Councils in the United States, bringing together Anglicans and Roman Catholics.

Bibliography

(Except where otherwise indicated, place of publication is London)

The archives of the Society of the Divine Compassion and the Brotherhood of the Holy Cross are in the Bodleian Library, Oxford. Those of the Brotherhood of St. Francis of Assisi and the Society of St. Francis are at the Friary, Hilfield where there is also a collection of private publications, papers and memoirs of the various Franciscan societies. The archives of the Order of St. Francis are at Little Portion Friary, Long Island.

Adderley, James, *Francis, The Little Poor Man of Assisi*, 1908
—, *In Slums and Society*, 1916.
—, *Monsieur Vincent*, 1902.
—, *Stephen Remarx*, 1893.
Adderley, James, C. L. Marson, *Third Orders*, 1902.
Andrews, C. F., *John White of Mashonaland*, 1935.
Anson, Peter, *The Call of the Cloister*, 1964.
—, *The Hermit of Cat Island*, 1958.
—, *The Religious Orders and Congregations of Great Britain and Ireland*, Stanbrook Abbey, Worcs, 1949.
Burne, Kathleen E., *The Life and Letters of Father Andrew*, S.D.C., 1948.
Carpenter, S. C., *Winnington-Ingram*, 1949.
Chadwick, Owen, *The Victorian Church*, 1966.
Clifton Kelway, A., ed., *A Franciscan Revival: The Story of the Society of the Divine Compassion*, Plaistow, 1908.
Curtis, Geoffrey, *William of Glasshampton*, 1947.
Denis, Father, *Father Algy*, 1964.
Elizabeth, Mother, *Corn of Wheat*, Oxford, 1981.
—, *Into the Deep*, 1917; revised 1967.
—, *Letting Down the Nets*, 1923.
—, *We Would See Jesus*, 1932.
Francis, Father, *Brother Douglas*, 1974.
Franciscan Servants of Jesus and Mary, *Mother Teresa and the Franciscan Servants of Jesus and Mary*, Posbury St. Francis, 1980.

Gannon, David, *Father Paul of Graymoor*, New York, 1959.

Hutton, Edward, *Cities of Umbria*, 1905.

Josa, Luigi, *St. Francis of Assisi and the Third Order in the Anglo-Catholic Church*, London and Oxford, 1903.

—, *The Tale of a Roaming Catholic*, 1920.

Joseph, Father, *Adventure for God*, Merrill, Wisconsin, 1926.

Mary Celine, Sister, *A Woman of Unity*, New York, 1956.

Moorman, J. R. H., *The Franciscans in England*, London and Oxford, 1974.

Norman, Edward, *Church and Society in England 1770–1970*, Oxford 1976.

Packard, Kenneth, *Brother Edward*, 1955.

Potter, George, *Father Potter of Peckham*, 1955.

—, *More Father Potter*, 1958.

Prestige, G. L., *The Life of Charles Gore*, 1935.

Putterell, Jack, *Thaxted Quest for Social Justice*, Marlow, 1977.

Steere, Douglas V., *God's Irregular: Arthur Shearley Cripps*, 1973.

Stevens, T. P., *Father Adderley*, 1943.

Williams, T. J., *Priscilla Lydia Sellon*, 1950.

Winslow, Jack, *Christa Seva Sangha*, 1930.

—, *The Eyelids of the Dawn*, 1954.

Newspapers and Periodicals
B.H.C. Quarterly
The Church Times
The Franciscan
Isis
The Little Chronicle
SPAN
Stratford Express
Third Order Chronicle.

Lives of St. Francis of Assisi
Englebert, Omer, *Saint Francis of Assisi*, tr. and ed. Edward Hutton, 1950.

Holl, Adolf, *The Last Christian*, New York, 1980.

Jorgensen, Johannes, *St Francis of Assisi*, 1912.

Moorman, J. R. H., *Sources for the Life of St. Francis*, Manchester, 1940.

Okey, T., ed., *The Little Flowers of St. Francis*, 1923.

Oliphant, Margaret, *Francis of Assisi*, 1879.

Sabatier, Paul, *Life of St Francis of Assisi*, Louise Seymour Houghton, 1894.

Index of Names and Subjects

210

Index of Anglican Religious Communities, Guilds and Societies

213

Roman Catholic Communities

For Roman Catholic communities, see Chapter 1 chronologically; also under Elizabeth Lockhart and Mother Francis Basil p. 14; for the Society of the Atonement see supra; for the Society of St. Paul, pp. 146, 149; for San Miniato al Monte, Florence, see p. 180.